"There is simply no better book for anyone in the job search market than the one Carl has written. It gives you the step-by-step tools to be successful in your search in a direct and easy to understand manner. His expertise provides a 360-degree view of the process from the employer's, job seeker's, and recruiter's perspectives, which prevents you from making poor choices and wasting hours in unproductive activities."

—Kristin Walle, VP, Finance, ADP, PhD,
Organizational Leadership and Executive Coach

"Carl Wellenstein has an amazing talent. He is able to effortlessly walk a mile in YOUR shoes. When he coached me for the interview for the position I hold today, I was ready. I knew where my head and my *heart* were, and I was confident I could articulate that to my company. We *think* we know ourselves and our strengths; Carl helps you look under the rocks to find the (sometimes) hidden, unique talents that make us all special people."

—John Scott, Chief Evangelist,
Green 960 Online and Radio, San Francisco

"Wow! *12 Steps to a New Career* is the most thorough job search/career change advice book for executives and managers that I have come across in my 37 years as a career counselor and coach. Following the advice in this book is the next best thing to having a favorite uncle who is an experienced executive recruiter."

—Richard Knowdell, NCCC, CCMF,
Executive Director of Career Development Network,
President, Career Research & Testing, Inc.

12 STEPS
to a
NEW CAREER

WHAT TO DO
WHEN YOU WANT
TO MAKE A
CHANGE NOW!

CARL J. WELLENSTEIN

CAREER
PRESS

Franklin Lakes, NJ

12 STEPS TO A NEW CAREER
EDITED BY JODI BRANDON
TYPESET BY EILEEN MUNSON
Cover design by Lucia Rossman/Digi Dog Design
Printed in the U.S.A. by Courier

Cartoons on pages 15, 124, 135, 160, 179, 214, and 248 by Steven Lait.

To order this title, please call toll-free 1-800-CAREER-1 (NJ and Canada: 201-848-0310) to order using VISA or MasterCard, or for further information on books from Career Press.

CAREER
PRESS

The Career Press, Inc., 3 Tice Road, PO Box 687,
Franklin Lakes, NJ 07417
www.careerpress.com

Library of Congress Cataloging-in-Publication Data

Wellenstein, Carl J.
   12 steps to a new career : what to do when you want to make a change now! / by Carl J. Wellenstein.
      p. cm.
   Includes index.
   ISBN 978-1-60163-062-9
      1. Career changes. 2. Career development. I. Title.

HF5384.W47 2009
650.14--dc22

2008054048

To Mark

You are forever in our hearts.

Acknowledgments

I thank the following people. Without their wisdom, knowledge, and perspective, this book would have remained an unfulfilled dream:

Richard Nelson Bolles for starting it all with his classic book, *What Color is Your Parachute?* (Ten Speed Press), and for encouraging others to adapt his material for specific audiences. I've attempted to give specific attribution where I felt it was appropriate.

Jane Bartlett for her energy and enthusiasm in putting her heart and soul into helping clients make decisions that literally changed their lives. My apologies to Jane, though, for my inability to learn the "proper English" she tried in vain to teach me.

My wife, Chris, for reviewing and re-reviewing each chapter and being able to concentrate on the message to make sure it flowed and made sense to someone who's not an expert on the subject.

My daughter, Kristin, for reminding me that the concepts and principles in this book are just as important and applicable to younger, lower-level but experienced staffers who are seeking new jobs or need to change careers.

My early editor, David Cunningham, for his ability to turn what is clear to me into sentences that are also clear to others, and his persistent efforts to help improve my writing style.

The reviewers I selected who looked at early drafts and contributed ideas from a different perspective that kept my thinking fresh and the content orderly. Special thanks to two reviewers, Terry Crowther and Kristin Walle, who are colleagues in a mastermind group.

Contents

Section IV:
Mastering the Different Ways You Communicate With Others

Section V:
Keeping Yourself Focused and on Track

Preface

You're a manager, an executive, or a professional on a management track, and now it's time to take that next big step. What's your best approach?

The process for searching for a new job or exploring a career change for you will be quite different from other employees. Surprisingly, you'll find very little current, reliable, and accurate information on the subject directed at your level.

Most of the books in this genre, though well-intentioned, are written by academics, psychologists, journalists, or recruiters and convey *theories* about what they think you should do, or give narrow, one-sided views, or cover the subject with a generalized, one-size-fits-all approach.

One size doesn't fit all. This I know because of my own experience from:

» My own job and career changes at the executive level.

» Being on the other side of the table as a recruiter participating in countless interviews by the recruiters who worked with me.

» Participating in candidate interviews with our employer clients.

» Coaching and working with other executives, managers, and senior staff to help them make job or career changes.

Too many people change jobs to get away from the ones they have or to move to "just another job" for some short-term reason. They usually do so without a long-term career plan that is based on understanding their strengths and preferences.

The purpose of *12 Steps to a New Career: What to Do When You Want to Make a Change Now!* is to help you make a life-changing leap from thinking of changing jobs as "a job change" to thinking in terms of a career path that will lead you to finding a job you can say you are eager to get up every morning to do, love what you do, and believe you are blessed with being able to get paid to do what you do.

This book will help you make your job or career change match your goals and desires regardless of whether you're a 30-year-old new manager or a 50-year-old seasoned executive. It is divided into five conceptual sections and 12 chapters. The five sections will help you to quickly grasp the overall process. The chapters will help you to achieve the objectives in each section by covering what you need to do, why you need to do it, when you need to do it and, finally, how to do it. Your journey will reflect a sequential process, each step building on the last, eventually taking you through a linear approach to Chapter 12, where you'll roll it all together into a strategic action plan.

I'll be your career coach in this book. I'll explain how each step in the process works and why it's important. I'll give examples of how to do each step, and then I'll guide you through a few exercises that will help you learn by getting you actively involved. I'll then share real-life experiences showing how others have been successful, and how recruiters and employers make their decisions.

To help you understand my vantage point, here's a bit about my journey. I left as partner at Arthur Young & Co. (now Ernst & Young), a Big 8 accounting firm at the time, after 15 years, including five years in charge of the firm's Saudi Arabian practice.

When I left the firm, I didn't think I'd have any trouble finding a new job. Unfortunately, I left during recessionary times. Outplacement was in its early stages of development and I hadn't even heard of it yet, so I started doing the usual things you think you need to do when you look for a new job. I called people I knew to tell them I was looking, and I started sending letters to recruiters and employers.

I found that most of the books and advice about conducting a job search were more appropriate for younger and much less experienced people. The advice directed at senior levels was contradictory, one-sided, and based more on theory than actual experience.

During this exercise, I found that my logical career progression—a senior financial executive—wasn't right for me. I moved to the UK and started an executive search firm with an international focus. I concentrated on learning the executive search business and creating processes that would consistently result in our being able to evaluate and recommend top candidates for our clients.

Shortly thereafter, I co-founded a career consultancy with a colleague, Jane Bartlett. Although I enjoyed the search business, I soon realized we were competing with other search firms that didn't share my ideals of integrity and professionalism. Jane took the lead role in developing the career consultancy, and we worked together to create a career search program specifically for executives and managers, which we fine-tuned over six years. During the seven years that I headed our UK search business, I found myself most energized when I was giving career advice to executives who didn't make it to our shortlists. In the process, I found my true passion: coaching senior-level people going through their own job transitions and career changes, just as I had done.

When I returned to the United States, I restructured our program and expanded it to reflect the 12 steps that job seekers and career changers should go through, based on my real-life experiences. I found that, if they followed these steps in sequence, they accelerated the process of finding a new job or making a career change.

I've attempted to take the mystique out of how the job market works for senior-level people and debunk the often-heard myth about "hidden" jobs. I've heard recruiters give great advice to executives, but, as a recruiter and a career coach, I know much of that advice can be self-serving.

In this book, I explain what works and what doesn't. I strip away the jargon and mystique. I share with you insights about decisions you'll never hear from others. This information will positively impact your search for a new job or a new, rewarding career.

One note on my use of pronouns: Rather than write "they" or "he/she" when referring to a single person of unidentified gender, I use the common practice of randomly choosing either "he" or "she." It's simpler.

Introduction:
How to Get the Most From Using This Book

Who Should Use This Book?

This book is aimed at executives, managers, professionals, and senior staff who have several years of work experience and wish to search for a new job or explore a new career. Many of the examples relate to my own job and career search, and the executives and managers I encountered during the seven years I owned and managed an international executive search business or worked with as a career coach.

Although the concepts and recommendations are geared toward executives, they apply equally well to most experienced workers from 30 years of age and on. I've organized the text so you can use it as a workbook. Chapter 1 starts with how to initiate a job search or make a career change. Each successive chapter takes you through a process that builds on the information you learned and the exercises you completed in the preceding chapters.

How Should You Use This Book?

Scan the book first to get an overview of the entire process, so you know what to expect as you progress through the five sections and each chapter. Then go back and start with Section 1 Chapter 1, reading it and completing the exercises. I don't recommend moving on to Chapter 2 or successive chapters until you've read and understood the material and completed the exercises in each chapter. The Milestones section at the end of each chapter provides a checklist of what you need to accomplish before moving on to the next chapter.

To get the most from this book, you will need to complete some tasks. When I believe you can complete a task with limited guidance from me, I call it an **Exercise**. When I believe a task would be more involved and you would benefit from using a pre-defined format, I've developed a **Worksheet** that you can use. These Worksheets are available on my Website. In a few sections, I'll refer you to **Reference** material that provides more extensive information you will find useful in your search, and is also available on my Website where I can keep the content current.

You can easily download all of the following Worksheets and References at *www.ExecGlobalNet.com* in the **Career Center**:

Worksheets
    1.1: Identifying Your Values
    2.1: 8 Categories of Achievements

Section 1

Finding Who You Are
and
What You Bring to the Table

Take Stock

You cannot get there from here without knowing where here is.

Chapter Overview

In Chapter 1, you'll take stock of yourself by gaining a better understanding of your values, beliefs, personality preferences, and goals. Taking stock is vital to helping you make better decisions about where to spend your effort and how to become better prepared when you target potential opportunities. Specifically, you will:

» Take an inventory of your values and learn how they affect your decisions about potential opportunities.

» Recognize how your personality type influences your success in a job.

» Identify realistic goals and create a way to help you achieve them.

» Learn the personal characteristics you should embrace to increase your success at finding what you want.

» Understand how a support network can decrease the time it will take to find what you really want to do.

The main sections in this chapter include:

» How you make decisions.

» Personal characteristics you must exhibit.

» Create a support network.

» Milestones.

If you ask for directions on how to get somewhere, you first need to know the starting point of the journey. Suppose I asked you to sell a new product or service but couldn't tell you very much about it. How could you possibly tell anyone about its features and benefits in any meaningful or convincing way?

The beginning is the most important part of the work.

—Plato

By the same token, when making a job or a career change, you need to take stock of yourself to fully understand your own beliefs, personal characteristics,

14

and preferences. Being aware of these will give you clarity and a sharper focus. It will save you time, help you to make better decisions more quickly, and lead others to take you seriously. They'll be willing to provide assistance when you need it most.

Attempting to start a job or a career search without knowing your starting point may result in you getting somewhere you don't really want to be. Take stock at the beginning, and you'll be able to talk about your strengths confidently and convince others of your passion and the resoluteness of your career path.

Illustration by Steven Lait.

If you can't convince others of your passion and show that you're in charge of your career, they'll be hesitant about considering you. They might want to interview other candidates or, even worse, just eliminate you right away.

This chapter can bring clarity to your job or career search by helping you understand what's important to you, what filters to use to assess whether a potential opportunity is right for you, and how to focus your efforts without wasting precious time exploring dead ends.

How You Make Decisions

You make choices every day—whether you're deciding on movies, clothes, friends, or articles in the newspaper to read. You're making these decisions based on an internal set of attitudes, both preconceived and learned.

When I ran my executive search business, I knew I always had to keep my fingers crossed as soon as a client offered a position to a candidate. Sound crazy? Not really. Even though we put candidates through extensive interviews before presenting them to our clients, and even though they survived multiple sets of interviews with those clients, I knew it could still all go awry.

Why? Because that's when the realization hits the candidate that he has to make a decision whether to take the offer or not. This is often the time he begins to think seriously about the commute or whether he really wants to travel as much as the job requires. He also begins to think whether it would be preferable to make an industry change or whether this a good career move. Sometimes he even tries to renegotiate the salary or benefits or discuss his future career potential in more detail.

When you receive an offer, employers expect that you'll want to think about it and talk it over with others before making a decision. But too often, candidates come back with more questions.

Many clients withdraw their offer when a candidate seems to vacillate or take too long before deciding. Employers believe candidates should be prepared and know the answers to many of their questions before starting their job search, or certainly before completing the interviewing process. They fear that, if a candidate has difficulty making a decision about his career when he has had plenty of time to think about it, he won't be able to make business decisions when he only has limited information and time in a business environment.

Employers also feel executive-level candidates should be clear on the basics about their career. They feel an executive who isn't clear probably wouldn't be effective at anticipating problems at the corporate level.

Let's start with the basics you need to bring into focus before you even begin to consider making a job or a career change: values, preferences, and goals.

Values

When you make a choice about anything, you do it by evaluating each option against your values. Sometimes this process is very conscious and takes time. More often, however, you probably do it instinctively and without much thought.

The example I just used is based on an actual situation: A candidate hadn't thought about his options in advance and suddenly needed time to evaluate them. It was time he really didn't have, because, when you're under pressure to make a life-changing decision, you tend not to do it rationally.

Think of an instance when you were in a checkout line at the grocery store and bought something that was conveniently located to you—an impulse item. If you had more time to think about it, you probably wouldn't have bought it.

People sometimes have difficulty thinking about their values, dismissing them as intangible feelings that are hard to describe or to put in writing.

Your values evolve as you grow older. Your life changes and you take on more responsibilities, such as a spouse and children. For example, pursuing a healthy lifestyle doesn't usually rank very high when you're a teenager interested only in lying on the beach to get a sexy tan. It often becomes more important when your chest begins to fall, your waistline starts to bulge, and—oh, by the way—all that tanning you did as a teenager has led to melanoma.

You should reassess your values any time you're considering or facing a life-changing event, and a job or a career change certainly fits that description.

The table in Worksheet 1.1 lists some keywords that indicate values you can use to start thinking about your own. Add additional keywords at the end if you don't see one of your values listed.

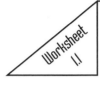

Identifying Your Values

Review the following list and check a box to the right of the value to indicate how strong that value is to you. Add values you feel strongly about even if you don't think they're important to a job search or a career change.

Identifying Your Values					
Value	1 Very important	2 Important	3 Somewhat important	4 Not very important	5 Not at all important
Advancement	❑	❑	☑	❑	❑
Autonomy	❑	❑	☑	❑	❑
Belonging to a team	❑	☑	❑	❑	❑
Challenges	❑	☑	❑	❑	❑
Collegial/Friendly environment	☑	❑	❑	❑	❑
Company stability	☑	❑	❑	❑	❑
Contributing to society	❑	☑	❑	❑	❑
Family needs	☑	❑	☑	❑	❑
Financial independence	☑	❑	❑	❑	❑
Fun	❑	☑	❑	❑	❑
Helping others to succeed	☑	☑	❑	❑	❑
Independence	☑	❑	❑	❑	❑
Intellectual stimulation	❑	☑	☑	❑	❑
Job satisfaction	☑	❑	❑	❑	❑
Job security	☑	❑	❑	❑	❑
Job stimulation	☑	☑	❑	❑	❑
Learning new skills	❑	☑	❑	❑	❑
Personal growth	❑	☑	❑	❑	❑
Power	❑	☑	☑	❑	❑
Recognition/Rewards	❑	☑	❑	❑	❑
Status	☑	❑	❑	❑	❑
	❑	❑	❑	❑	❑
	❑	❑	❑	❑	❑
	❑	❑	❑	❑	❑
	❑	❑	❑	❑	❑
	❑	❑	❑	❑	❑

Next, highlight or put a mark by each of the values that you consider Very Important. On a separate sheet of paper, list each of the Very Important values and then describe what that value means to you. For example:

> Belonging to a team—I want to work in a collaborative
> environment where there's a positive team spirit and people
> are willing to share their knowledge and expertise and offer
> help to others for the benefit of the team and the
> organization.

List your remaining values, using as few words as possible, and then describe what each means to you. When you complete your list of values, number them in order, starting with the one you feel strongest about, down to the one you feel least strong about. Prepare a new list with your values in the order of your preference.

You now have a list of the values most important to you, against which you can now compare any opportunity. More importantly, you now have a list you can use when searching for opportunities and when discussing with others the types of opportunities you want. You're already on your way to being prepared to convince others that you're the one in charge of your career.

When you're exploring potential career opportunities and sitting in interviews, you'll know what to look for and what questions to ask to determine if your top values would be met.

Even if an opportunity doesn't match your prioritized list of values, don't completely discard it without further consideration. Reassess your values against the opportunity. Is the opportunity worth considering as a stepping-stone to another job? Or will it facilitate your making a career change to something that matches your values more closely?

Knowing your values isn't all you need to know in order to accept or decline an opportunity, but it does enable you to compare each of your strongly held values with each opportunity. If you choose to accept an opportunity that doesn't match your values, at least you'll have had the criteria to know which value(s) you would have to compromise and the basis on which you're willing to make that compromise.

Your values will change as circumstances change, and you'll need to reprioritize them periodically. As you find out more about yourself during your job or career search and as you consider other opportunities, modify, add, and delete values. When you finish this book and complete the worksheets, review your list of values to see if there have been any changes.

Known Likes and Dislikes

You've already built up a history of what you like doing versus what you don't like doing. You probably also have some personal characteristics others know about and take for granted.

Understanding these will help you know yourself better and make more informed decisions about where you need to target your efforts and where you need to rely on others for support or assistance.

You can't be all things to all people, and you can't be skilled in everything, no matter how successful you've been in your career so far. A simple exercise will help you see what you like to do versus what you don't like to do.

Exercise 1.1: Known Likes and Dislikes

Using two sheets of paper, label one "Tasks, Responsibilities, Situations, or Activities I Like Doing" and label the other one "Tasks, Responsibilities, Situations, or Activities I Dislike Doing." Drawing on your experience (include work and non-work situations), list those things you either liked or disliked doing. Start with your current job and work backward. You should have at least 10 on each list.

Be objective when you prepare your two lists. Don't list something you really don't like doing on the "like doing" list just because you think it's a natural part of the job or you think the job requires it.

Personality Type

Whereas your values and work preferences change often, you have some fundamental preferences that make up your personality type. Your personality type probably hasn't changed significantly since you were a child, even though you may have adapted your style to fit certain situations.

Personality type evaluations began in the early forties under a U.S. government contract for the military during World War II by Isabel Myers and Kathleen Briggs as a measure of Carl Jung's theory of psychological types. The result was a questionnaire called the Myers-Briggs Type Indicator (MBTI), which measures four dimensions of your personality by looking at the opposites for each dimension. These are illustrated on page 20 with a brief description of the characteristics of people for that dimension.

The MBTI is the gold standard of personality type questionnaires. It has been validated by millions for more than 65 years and is the most widely used measurement of this kind throughout the world.

Where You Get Your Energy

	Extroverts	Introverts	
E	You look forward to attending events because they stimulate and energize you. You are one of the last to leave. The night is always still young.	You need time alone to recharge your batteries. You are one of the first to leave events because they tire you. You like quiet time to organize your thoughts.	**I**

How You Gather Information

	Sensing	Intuition	
S	You look, feel, see, and decide on what your senses tell you is there.	You focus on possibilities and patterns, what-ifs, and rely more on gut feel.	**N**

How You Make Decisions

	Thinking	Feeling	
T	You decide from your head using objective criteria.	You decide from your heart using subjective criteria.	**F**

How You Live Your Life

	Judging	Perceiving	
J	You prefer to plan, organize, and take very logical actions.	You're flexible and spontaneous, and prefer to keep your options open.	**P**

As a tool for considering career options, the MBTI can often help you make better career decisions, and it is a common tool used by companies when they need to assemble teams that work together. Unfortunately, people often try to use the MBTI in situations where it's not appropriate, such as to help decide whether to employ someone.

Some personality types might be more suitable to some occupations and not others. Knowing yours will help you understand why you like doing some things that others don't, why you tire easily from some activities and others seem to gain energy from the same activities, and why you see things so easily while others don't.

As an illustration, let's assume that you took the MBTI questionnaire and your results showed you were an ISTJ, a very common type. You shouldn't be too surprised if you're in accounting, IT, law enforcement, banking, or other occupations requiring someone who prefers to work alone; you see what's there (just the facts), you make decisions more with your head (not your heart), and you like to plan and organize your activities.

On the other hand, if you were in one of those occupations and your type is the opposite, ENFP, you'd be very uncomfortable and frustrated because you prefer to work in groups, you look at possibilities rather than what's there, you make decisions more with your heart rather than your head, and you like to do things on whim and not in a structured environment. An ENFP, you might now see, would be more comfortable in roles needing creativity and the imagination of possibilities.

Being a particular type doesn't necessarily force you into a particular field. Many people work in a field that's different from their natural type by consciously adapting themselves to work in a different way. You've probably seen this in people you work with, because it can sometimes cause stress, frustration, and misunderstanding of others.

Knowing your type can be very useful if you're unhappy in a job and aren't sure why, or you want to make a career change and aren't sure what you want to do. ("Reference 1.1: Myers-Briggs Type Characteristics," available at *www.ExecGlobalNet.com* in the **Career Center,** includes a brief description of the 16 various types.) If you want to read more on your own about the different types, including examples of typical careers for each, I suggest *Do What You Are* by Paul Tieger and Barbara Barron-Tieger (Little, Brown & Company, 2001).

If you're considering a career change or are unhappy in your job, start with *Do What You Are* or seek out a certified MBTI professional who can give you appropriate feedback. They'll help to open your thinking to other possibilities you may not be considering. People sometimes see themselves as slightly different from what the questionnaire seems to indicate, and the results often do border between different dimensions. You'll need someone skilled with the MBTI to help interpret your results if you fall into either of these situations.

Others have taken a different approach to interpreting our personalities. *Please Understand Me II* by Dr. David Keirsey (Prometheus Nemesis Book Company, 1998) developed the Keirsey Temperament Sorter to identify one's basic temperament. You can take the Keirsey Temperament Sorter test online at *www.keirsey.com* and print an instant report. (You can find reviews of the books mentioned here and others at *www.ExecGlobalNet.com* in the **Career Center.** Select "Reference 1.2: Career-Related Reading List.")

Goals

When I start talking about setting goals with my clients, I often see their eyes begin to roll back as they think in the context of preparing a budget or a business plan. They picture success being measured in terms of plan (the goal) versus accomplishments. Some people also think setting goals is a waste of time because they say they never achieve them anyway.

This often occurs when we attempt to define dreams or desires as goals or use generalized statements that are difficult to monitor. You will be far more effective at achieving goals if you use the acronym **S.M.A.R.T.** when setting your goals. Although the origin of S.M.A.R.T. has been lost to history and different versions of S.M.A.R.T. exist, the following is a framework that is consistent with how many others have used the concept:

Specific—What you want to achieve must be clear, focused, and easily understood. If it is too general and you can't meet all the criteria listed here, you'll need to re-define the goal.

Measurable—You must be able to benchmark progress and recognize the ultimate achievement of the goal. If progress toward an achievement can't be measured, you'll need to re-define the goal.

> *Things won are done;*
> *The joy's soul lies in the doing.*

> —William Shakespeare, *Troilus and Cressida*

Attainable—You need to have a reasonable expectation of achieving the goal. If it is too short-term and simple, it's probably a task (tactical) and not a goal (strategic). What you need to do to achieve your goal must be measurable so you can assess progress or completion.

Realistic or **Relevant**—The goal must be relevant to your overall career objectives and it must be realistic to believe that you will be able to achieve the goal.

Time-Sensitive—Your goal must have starting and ending points, and you need to be able to measure progress toward its completion within a reasonable timeline.

Setting personal goals is a fluid and flexible exercise because your goals change as events affect your life. Setting goals is important whether you're considering a career change or preparing for interviews.

In interviews, you'll inevitably be asked a question such as, "What goals have you set for yourself in the next 12 months (or three years or five years)?" You'll need to respond with a well-thought-out and reasoned response. If you don't, the interviewer will make assumptions about your lack of focus and may probe your response to find out why you haven't given it careful thought.

Exercise 1.2: Goals Summary

Using a notepad and referring to the S.M.A.R.T. characteristics, list your goals in six different time frames on separate sheets of paper:

▶   Within one month.

▶   Within two to three months.

▶   Within four to six months.

▶   Within one year.

▶   Within five years.

▶   Before you die.

When you finish your lists, review them with your spouse or a close friend who knows you well to get his perspective on the appropriateness, importance, and priority of your list. When you've completed your review, re-number your list if you've made any changes, and put each short-term goal (using your own definition of short-term) on a separate sheet of paper.

On each sheet, list and then prioritize what actions you must take to achieve that goal. Next, add the date that you expect to complete each action step and the ultimate goal.

You may not meet every goal. If you don't, analyze what you did or didn't do that prevented you from achieving that particular goal. Was the goal overly ambitious? Did you fail to define it clearly? Did the goal become less important as others became more important? If necessary, redefine or reprioritize your goals or set a new goal, addressing whatever prevented you from achieving the original goal.

Personal Characteristics You Must Exhibit

I've noted that executives who are most successful in their job search display eight personal characteristics. If you lack ANY of them, there's a good chance your search will take longer than it should, you will face more obstacles than you would otherwise, and you may even fail to find what you want. These eight personal characteristics are:

1.   Complete honesty with yourself.
2.   Enthusiasm.
3.   Personal organization.
4.   Attention to detail.
5.   High activity level.
6.   Personal standards.
7.   Perseverance.
8.   Positive attitude.

Complete Honesty With Yourself

You must look at yourself honestly and accept who you are. Be open and receptive to criticism and accept that you're not strong in all areas. Focus on your strengths, not weaknesses. Your strengths are what others need to see.

Enthusiasm

Skills and brilliant qualifications are not enough. You must exhibit that magical ingredient: enthusiasm. It makes a huge difference in how you approach your search, whether others decide to help you, and whether you get the job.

Personal Organization

If you take the time to be well organized, your effectiveness will increase, your network will support and help you, and interviewers will view you as an effective leader.

Attention to Detail

Details make an impression. Confirm appointments in writing, send thank-you notes to those who help you, and show respect to administrative people. These actions are more important than you might think.

High Activity Level

People who are out of work often act like it. If you're in transition toward another chapter in your life, you need to maintain a working lifestyle. Exercise regularly. Get involved in activities where you interact with others. Keep your schedule full with job searching, volunteer activities, and personal health.

Personal Standards

You never know whom you will meet and when. Dress professionally even if you're involved in non-work activities. Others need to see you as an executive looking for the next opportunity, not as unemployed and casually enjoying it.

Perseverance

The more effort you put into your search, the more you'll make your own luck. The more people you meet, the greater your chances of making a valuable connection. But be observant. Persevering is not the same as pestering. If you don't succeed with one approach, try another. You *will* hear an overabundance of no's before you will hear a yes. Get through the no's as quickly as possible.

Positive Attitude

Do you quickly recognize when someone else doesn't have a positive attitude? What judgments do you make about that person? You'll encounter setbacks yourself, and you'll hear a lot of rejection. You're far less likely to let these bother you if you maintain a positive attitude.

Create a Support Network

In your last job, you didn't achieve things without the participation of others. Your employers most likely encouraged a team spirit because they knew the benefits of people working together. A mistake many executives make is not taking advantage of their own positive experiences with group support. Instead, they try to change jobs or careers without involving others.

Now is *not* the time to work independently or in isolation. You'll need the support and assistance of others if you want to make your job or career change as quickly as possible. Developing multiple contacts enables you to connect with others and build relationships in which the support goes both ways: You help them; they help you.

Working with others also motivates you by making you accountable to someone else for completing your weekly objectives. By putting several minds together, you'll also be more energized and not feel so alone. Create a two-tier arrangement for your support network similar to the following:

1. Mentor

Having a mentor is a well-documented and effective way to guarantee success during your job search, as well as on the job. When choosing a mentor, consider the people closest to you—those you know well. Concentrate on the ones who will tell you what you need to know, not what you want to hear.

When you ask a person to be your mentor, explain that you need an objective viewpoint on what you're thinking and planning from someone whose opinion and judgment you value.

Use your mentor to review your background, comment on your resume, evaluate the reasonableness of your plan in relation to your goals, and act as a sounding board to confirm or question your own thoughts.

2. Mastermind Group

Working with a group is another effective way to get objective feedback, brainstorm new ideas, and stay motivated. Try to identify two or more executives who are also looking for new opportunities.

Become familiar with each person's background and the position each is seeking. Get together on a regular basis, perhaps once a week, to discuss what you achieved the previous week and what you plan to achieve the following week. She might have a different viewpoint on some of your plans or might suggest different options.

Ask someone from your mastermind group or your mentor to serve as your accountability partner while you're pursuing your job search or exploring new career options. Use him to review your periodic activities and to be the person to whom you report your progress on a regular basis. You'll find that you stick to your plan much better if you have someone else involved in monitoring your progression.

In Chapter 8, we'll cover how your network will support your objective of making contact with others who can facilitate your search and connect you with potential employers.

☑ Milestones

Before moving to the next chapter, review the following milestones, which recap what you need to do to complete this chapter. If you aren't able to complete all the items in this chapter, start an "open items list" and set a target date to complete each open item.

❏ 1.   Complete **Worksheet 1.1: Identifying Your Values.** Prioritize the most important ones so that you can quickly assess whether new opportunities meet your values.

❏ 2.   Complete **Exercise 1.1: Known Likes and Dislikes.** If you have other strong feelings about previous jobs, use additional sheets for them and prepare a summary of your top five.

❏ 3.   Review your type in **Reference 1.1: Myers-Briggs Type Characteristics** and compare and contrast your preferences to the list you prepared in Exercise 1.1.

❏ 4.   Complete **Exercise 1.2: Goals Summary** so that you will have a good understanding of what you need to accomplish in the future. Bear in mind that your goals and values are not static, and you'll need to reexamine them again when you complete this book.

❏ 5.   Review and familiarize yourself with the personal characteristics that are common in executives who seem to be most successful in their search.

❏ 6.   Identify possible mentors. Discuss your current situation and your plans with them, and ask if they would be willing to serve as your mentor while you go through this process.

❏ 7.   Identify other executives in transition and put together a mastermind group where you can share ideas and exchange suggestions.

Achievements 2

Achievement stories are credible and memorable.
Skills and capabilities are subjective and forgettable.

Chapter Overview

In this chapter, you'll identify your own unique accomplishments. This discovery process will energize you and, if you don't already have one, help you develop a positive attitude about yourself and what you can do for others. Specifically, you will:

» Learn how to define an achievement so you can focus on how to write about it in detail.

» Gain experience at writing about how you accomplished your achievements.

» Learn how to describe your achievements in ways that help others understand their significance.

» Describe achievement stories in ways that leave a lasting, positive impression on others.

The main sections in this chapter include:

» How to identify an achievement.

» Why your achievements are important.

» Make your achievements credible and memorable.

» Milestones.

The degree and speed of your success at finding a new job or career will be in direct proportion to your ability to set yourself apart—in credible and memorable ways—from other executives who have similar skills and industry experience. You can't do justice to your career search until you gain a thorough understanding of where you are most successful with your skills, and how you prefer to use those skills. This chapter will focus on helping you write achievement stories. Chapter 3 will help you uncover your skills from your achievements.

How to Identify an Achievement

An achievement is something you accomplish by superior ability, special effort, or great courage. Achievements can demonstrate your uniqueness—what sets you apart from others.

Achievements or accomplishments (you can use the terms interchangeably) may result from personal quests, like climbing mountains or completing marathons. Sure, others may have done it before, but not everyone, so it's a mark of distinction for you to have scaled a peak or completed a grueling race.

Accomplishments may also be work-related. Maybe you sold X number of widgets in your first six months on the job. Others may have done it, but not everyone, so it's an achievement.

You want to accomplish three critical objectives when you describe your achievements. You want others to:

» Recognize it came from your unique talents and abilities.

» Understand its significance.

» Remember you for it, and repeat it clearly to others.

For the above to happen, the achievement must contain the following six components:

1. Be distinctive.
2. Be objective.
3. Demonstrate skills.
4. Show the significance of your role.
5. Demonstrate a clear result.
6. Be quantifiable.

Let me clarify and expand on each of these.

1. Be Distinctive

An achievement is usually a *clear* and *distinct* event that occurred within a relatively short period (for example, created a system, won an award, wrote a book), not a general activity over a long period (for example, progressed to CEO).

2. Be Objective

It must *objectively* and *accurately* portray what you personally achieved, so that others who know about the achievement would agree on its significance.

3. Demonstrate Skills

It must demonstrate *skills* you used to achieve what you did or skills you developed during the process of achieving what you did.

4. Show the Significance of Your Role

You must have played a *significant* role in the achievement. If you participated as part of a team, you need to describe your team role specifically and clearly.

5. Demonstrate a Clear Result

The *result* (that is, what you accomplished or achieved) must be easily recognizable.

6. Be Quantifiable

The listener or reader of your achievement must be able to put it into perspective so she can grasp the *significance of it* (for example, how did it help your company increase sales, cut costs, or lower risk?).

Why Your Achievements Are Important

Your education and technical knowledge played important roles in the decisions of others to hire you during the early stages of your career. Skills and experience eventually added to your value in the marketplace, but these alone aren't enough at the executive or manager level. Employers want to know what you've accomplished with all your skills, knowledge, and education. They also want to know about your ability to lead and manage others.

If you approach your search for a new job or career by simply listing your work history and skills, no one will be able to see what you've accomplished. Many others in the marketplace will be showing the same or similar skills. Your ability to describe the use of your unique skills will distinguish you from the crowd.

Here are just some of the benefits of clearly describing your achievements:

◆ You exhibit a passion for what you do that sets you apart.

◆ You demonstrate your skills dynamically, rather than simply listing them.

◆ You enable listeners to infer your positive personal traits and characteristics so you won't need to boast.

◆ You tell a story people will remember.

◆ Your memorable story helps others see you as achievement-oriented.

◆ Your memorable story and achievements are what people will tell others about you. They aren't likely to share a list of skills.

> **The power of achievement stories is that you don't have to get a listener to remember your skills and personal traits; the achievement story carries those thoughts with it.**

Let me illustrate the power of achievements with a simple example. Suppose you meet Kevin, and he tells you he's a great race car driver. He also tells you he's focused, goal-oriented, dedicated, and good at developing high-quality teams that work together harmoniously. Would you believe him? Maybe, but why should you? Where's the proof? Would you remember all his statements about his skills and traits?

Now, suppose you meet Kevin and he tells you he's a great race car driver *and* he drove in the 24 Hours of Le Mans (the world's most famous endurance race) last year. Now would you believe him? Perhaps more so, but he didn't say whether he finished. Maybe he crashed, taking out 20 other drivers in the process. You might still have doubts about whether he's a great driver. Good, certainly, but great?

Now, suppose Kevin only tells you that he *won* the Le Mans last year. Wouldn't you conclude he must be a great driver, even though he never said so? Wouldn't you remember him? When you talk to others about Kevin, you may forget about his skills and education, but you're very likely to remember his achievement story and repeat it to others.

When someone tells that kind of achievement story, listeners think of the skills it must take and the traits or characteristics someone would need to win the Le Mans. As people repeat the story, others also think of the skills and traits it must take to win.

Many people find writing about their achievements is enlightening because they're able to see how their skills and experience apply to new and different careers they may not have considered before. They quickly forget about bad experiences and focus on the characteristics that gave them the most pleasure—typically, where they had the most success.

Pain is short, and joy is eternal.

—Johann Schiller, *The Maid of Orleans*

Make Your Achievements Credible and Memorable

When you describe your achievements to others, focus on what skills you used or developed in the process. And when you describe your skill sets, focus on what you achieved by using them.

Don't limit your thoughts to the work environment. You may want to describe achievements from your involvement with a non-profit organization or when you volunteered on a community project or political activity. The skills you use in non-employment situations are usually the same or similar to ones you use at work.

Although the main objective of writing about achievements is to help you understand how you achieved what you did, another objective is to identify some of your skills. The following four-step process will help you write powerful stories that others will remember about you:

Step 1: Identify the achievement.

Step 2: Analyze the achievement.

Step 3:   Bring the achievement into perspective.

Step 4:   Tell the achievement story.

When you write your stories, follow this four-step process for each one. You'll find the process much easier to do, and you'll get more out of it, by taking it one step at a time. Let's look at these steps in more detail.

Step 1: Identify the Achievement

Start by describing an achievement as succinctly as possible, beginning with an action word. Don't expand on the statement by trying to quantify it or by explaining how you did it. Your objective at this stage is only to get the thought out in one sentence. Here are some examples:

» *I reorganized the accounts payable department and streamlined invoice processing, which eliminated our being assessed late-payment fees and enabled us to take advantage of payment discounts.*

» *I created a very successful promotional program for a new action-figure toy product line.*

» *For customers who made frequent small-dollar purchases, I developed an ordering system that increased the average order quantity per customer and reduced the frequency of orders.*

» *I initiated a new-hire training program that ensured all new production staff members had adequate safety training, which reduced on-the-job accidents.*

If you have difficulty getting started, think about things you might have achieved in each of the following eight basic categories relating to achievements:

1. **Created** or **Developed.** These relate to something that didn't previously exist. You created a new program, product, system, procedure, and so forth.

2. **Increased** or **Improved.** Something previously existed, but you made it better, perhaps by increasing sales or improving productivity.

3. **Decreased** or **Reduced.** These are the flip side of Increased or Improved. Maybe you reduced product spoilage, bad debts, employee accidents, and so on.

4. **Avoided** or **Bypassed.** These are usually tough ones, but think about things you did to avoid potential problems or bypass potential bottlenecks or roadblocks. What did you do differently to get around the issue?

5. **Suppressed** or **Prevented.** Similar to #4, but maybe you suppressed labor unrest by holding open forums, or you prevented a potential problem by making changes. What did you do that prevented adverse consequences?

6. **Repeated.** Perhaps you devised a process that became a regular activity, which not only saved time or money initially, but continued to do so over time.

7. **Maintained.** Consider activities you might have maintained in the face of adversity. Did you maintain a high level of customer support despite the loss of key employees? Perhaps you kept bad debts below normal during a time of high customer complaints about product functionality. Or maybe you maintained a high level of sales or sales support after a reduction in territory or the loss of a major customer.

8. **Distinctions** or **Awards.** Describe any awards, appointments to special committees, certificates, credentials, early promotions, recognition, and instances when you were quoted as an expert by others, interviewed by the press, and so forth.

In reviewing this list, you'll note that achievements aren't only linked to positive events. Achievements often occur as a response to business failures or areas of difficulty and challenge.

8 Categories of Achievements

Try to write at least one achievement for each of the following eight categories.

1. Describe something you **Created** or **Developed**:

_____

_____

2. Describe something you **Increased** or **Improved**:

_____

_____

3. Describe something you **Decreased** or **Reduced**:

_____

_____

4. Describe something you **Avoided** or **Bypassed**:

_____

_____

5. Describe something you **Suppressed** or **Prevented**:

_____

_____

6. Describe something you **Repeated** (repetition or consistency):

_____

_____

7. Describe something you **Maintained** (perhaps in the face of adversity):

_____

_____

8. Describe a **Distinction** or **Award** that you received:

_____

_____

Step 2: Analyze the Achievement

The next step is to take each achievement you wrote about in Worksheet 2.1 and analyze it by describing everything you did that resulted in the accomplishment. The purpose of this detailed analysis is to identify pertinent information about the *process* of the achievement, such as:

- » How you originally got involved.
- » What skills you used or developed.
- » What other resources you used.
- » Who else was involved (and what their role was).
- » What decisions were made.
- » What problems you encountered.
- » How you overcame obstacles.
- » Finally, what the result or outcome was.

Think of it as a story where you start at the beginning, then write the first sentence. Then ask yourself, "And then what did I do?" Write another sentence. Continue with the questioning until you get to the end—the result.

When you think you've finished the story, ask someone else to read it to see if he questions any part that isn't completely clear as to how you did something. Resist the temptation to cut the story short just to get to the end. The purpose of this process is to identify all the steps you went through, regardless of how much you think they might have been just second nature to you.

The example on page 34 illustrates an achievement statement, the details of how it happened, and the final achievement story. Notice that the story contains factual statements only, not opinions.

Detailed Description	
Achievement statement: Received an award for organizing an annual community event that was the most successful of its kind in 21 years.	(Leave a 2" margin)

Analysis: I was asked by the Great Falls Chamber of Commerce to organize the 21st Community Street Faire to raise funds for the handicapped, elderly and disadvantaged in the county. Although I had never produced anything like this before, I love the theatre, and it was an opportunity to widen my experience of project management while helping a good cause.

I started by interviewing those who had been involved before, reviewing previous efforts and preparing an outline plan of action. Then I identified potential scriptwriters from referrals and interviewed several.

I chose scriptwriters and helped them to create a story board for the program.

I wrote job descriptions for the production team and sent out a newsletter to the press and to people who had been involved in previous years or who had expressed an interest in getting involved.

I arranged and held auditions. The production director and I assigned roles. Approximately 30 volunteers were involved.

Using my computer and learning new software, I produced sponsorship brochures that attracted local businesses.

I came up with an idea to place a "price on the head" of each character, whom businesses could sponsor. They could then promote their sponsorship for each character. Businesses liked it so much that they began to bid against each other for the privilege of saying which character they sponsored. It created a lot of media attention and visibility for the sponsors, who contributed $16,000, which exceeded our budget by $4,000. We used the excess to fund more community programs as chosen by the sponsors.

I booked the school hall, negotiated charges with the school and persuaded a local accounting firm to keep financial records and write checks.

I managed the production team by holding weekly status meetings and kept detailed notes so I could report progress to the Chamber regularly.

I organized rehearsals, requiring detailed planning, and kept everyone informed. We began to fall behind in our preparations when work pressures for some of the key members took precedence. I convinced others to step up and cover for them, and we were able to get back on track with a minimum of disruption. I had to schedule my own time carefully because I was trying to wrap up a major project at work.

I took on cameo roles myself and had to "ghost sing" for one of the principals who took sick and couldn't sing.

I organized all the publicity and was interviewed by local press and radio.

We performed five superb shows to capacity audiences. Afterward, I arranged a debriefing meeting where I thanked everyone and evaluated what we had learned and what we could pass on for a future occasion.

I reported financial results to the Chamber. Our total costs were less than we had budgeted because some sponsors who originally declined to participate decided that they had to be involved after seeing how the other sponsors benefited. We ultimately netted over $16,000, and I received a "Good Citizen Achievement Award" for organizing the community's most successful event ever.

Achievement story: I received a "Good Citizen Achievement Award" for organizing the community's most financially successful fundraising event ever. I created highly entertaining programs, recruited talented people who donated their time, devised merchant sponsorship programs that increased revenue by 33% over estimates, effectively managed over 30 volunteers and delivered the most successful local program in over 20 years.

Whether you use a notepad or a word processing program to write your achievements, leave a 2-inch margin on the right side. I'll explain why in the next chapter.

If you have trouble getting started, try using a chronological sequence of events in a story format. "First I did..., then I did..., next, I...," and so on. Be very detailed at this stage because you're also trying to identify all the skills you used.

If you reach a point where you don't know what to write next, ask yourself, "And then what did I do?" If you can't answer that question, go back and look at your statement, because it's probably not specific enough.

Step 3: Bring the Achievement Into Perspective

You know how important your achievements are because you have the perspective of how much they impacted your job, your department, your career, your employer, or an activity outside of work. When you describe your achievements to others, they'll have difficulty understanding the significance of what you did unless you put it into perspective.

Suppose you told someone, "I was in the top of my group in increasing sales." This sounds good, but what does it really mean? You know the significance, but, unless you use numbers to quantify it, no one else will. What's worse, if you can't quantify it, the statement requires a subjective evaluation by others. When others have to make a subjective evaluation of your statements, it probably won't be favorable to you.

The following chart illustrates examples of the types of questions you can ask yourself when attempting to quantify your achievements with the resulting achievement statement.

Question	Answer
What was one of your achievements?	I served on the Strategic Alliance Investment Review Committee.
How did you get to serve on this committee?	I was asked by the CEO.
How many others served on this committee, and how many were asked by the CEO?	There were seven of us, and we were all asked by the CEO.
How many people work in the company who would have been considered for this committee?	All levels are represented, totaling 300 employees, so I presume at least 250 would have been considered.
How long did you serve on this committee?	Eighteen months.

(Continued on next page.)

Question	Answer
What did the Strategic Alliance Investment Review Committee do?	Our mission was to identify and review potential strategic alliance partners with synergistic products that could complement ours for possible investments.
How many companies did you investigate and consider for investments?	Fifty-five.
What was your role in the investigations and considerations?	I took the lead for investigating all the selected companies that had nano-technology products in development.
How many strategic alliance partners did the committee recommend investing in?	Eight, and three had nano-technology products in development.
How many strategic alliance partners did the company negotiate agreements with and invest in?	Five, and two had nano-technology products in development.
How much did the company invest in the strategic alliance partners?	We invested $34 million, including $15 million in the two nano-technology companies.
What were the results of the investments in the strategic alliance partners?	The company earned approximately $50 million, including $25 million relating to the nano-technology ventures, within two years of our investment.

Let's recap what we can now say is an achievement story:

> I was chosen by the CEO out of approximately 250 candidates to sit on a seven-person Strategic Alliance Review Committee. Our mission was to investigate and recommend potential investments in companies that had synergistic products. We recommended eight investments, from which five were selected as the most promising, and $34 million was invested. We earned approximately $50 million, of which half related to two companies I had recommended and which earned a 167% return on invested capital within two years.

TIP

When you're trying to ask the "How much?" question and it doesn't quite fit, consider these alternatives:

- ▶ How many?
- ▶ How often?
- ▶ How long?
- ▶ By what percentage?
- ▶ By what amount?

Review the stories you wrote and examine each sentence, asking yourself quantifying questions (such as "How much?" or "How many?") and add numbers or estimates.

Be mindful of the following caveats when you quantify your achievements:

❖ **Don't inflate the facts.** If they know you've inflated the facts, you're out of consideration. If they hire you and subsequently find out you inflated the facts, they'll likely terminate you.

❖ **Don't exaggerate.** What do you do if you increased or decreased a value by 1,000 percent or more because you were working at a new company that started a new product line? Don't use percentage increases. Instead, use a description that makes it understandable and believable (for example, "Increased sales from $5,000 to $500,000 in the first six months by...").

❖ **Be specific only when possible.** If you can't be specific, use such phrases as "in excess of..." or "decreased product delivery time by more than 12 days."

❖ **Acknowledge team accomplishments.** If you were part of a team, say so ("As part of a team that reduced workplace injuries, I..."). Another way of positively showing your team involvement is this type of statement: "Out of 250 employees, I was one of five selected by the CEO to be part of a team that...."

❖ **Turn negatives into positives.** You can always find achievements even in difficult situations. Some suggestions:

　➥ "I retained 95% customer satisfaction during...."

　➥ "I maintained current bank reconciliations for all 35 bank accounts by assigning the reconciliations of all minor accounts to the departmental administrative person."

　➥ "I kept product losses to within 20% of average compared to previous years."

　➥ "I recommended changes to the production process which reduced spoilage from 8% to 6%."

Step 4: Tell the Achievement Story

You've accomplished three things with your achievement analysis:

1. You've created a detailed account of an achievement you can use when you respond to an interviewer's pointed questions.

2. You've identified a number of skills you can demonstrate you possess. (I'll cover this in more detail in the following chapter.)

3. You've quantified your achievement and put it into perspective so others will understand its significance and see it as a verifiably objective statement.

Now you need to turn that achievement into a story for maximum impact, because stories are credible and more memorable than facts. You need a story that you can tell in a couple of minutes or less. If your achievement story is interesting to listeners, they'll ask you questions to learn more. You can then fill in the blanks and put some "meat on the bone."

Keep your achievement story to one short paragraph. Achievement stories are particularly important during a telephone interview when the interviewer is trying to determine whether she should invite you in for a face-to-face interview. Brief stories will help interviewers hear "success stories," and they will remember you by your stories and repeat them to others.

Write four or more stories to complete this chapter. You'll write three more in Chapter 3 and three more in Chapter 4.

☑ Milestones

The following milestones recap what you need to do to complete this chapter. Items you can't complete should be included in a summary-level open-items list.

❑ 1. Revise and complete your first achievement story.
   Title: _____

❑ 2. Complete a second achievement story.
   Title: _____

❑ 3. Complete a third achievement story.
   Title: _____

❑ 4. Complete a fourth achievement story.
   Title: _____

❑ 5. Quantify each achievement story where appropriate so others can put your story into perspective and understand its significance as well as you do.

❑ 6. Review your achievement stories with someone who was also involved in the achievements to make sure her understanding supports what you are saying. (You may need her as a reference to verify your achievement.)

❑ 7. Test some of your achievement stories with someone you know and get her response to see if she understands them the way you intended.

3 Skills

*You can't know what you want to do unless
you know what you're good at doing.*

Chapter Overview

Having a good grasp of your own skills and achievements is critical in the early stages of a job or career search. If you're seeking employment, employers hire you primarily for your skills. If you're seeking self-employment, you'll set yourself up for failure if you don't have a good understanding of your strengths and weaknesses. In this chapter, you'll:

- ❯❯ Learn the differences between skills, traits, and characteristics.
- ❯❯ Understand what your skills tell others about you.
- ❯❯ Learn and use techniques to identify your skills.
- ❯❯ Identify the skills you prefer to use most often.
- ❯❯ Understand the hidden (soft) skills that could be limiting your success.

The main sections in this chapter include:

- ❯❯ Skills and traits.
- ❯❯ What your skills tell others about you.
- ❯❯ Techniques to identify your skills.
- ❯❯ Job responsibilities.
- ❯❯ Strengths and weaknesses.
- ❯❯ Emotional intelligence.
- ❯❯ Milestones.

Why would any employer hire you if you didn't possess the skills they need? When considering you for employment, they may also want to feel comfortable they can work with you, and you with them. No matter how much they like you, however, they won't employ you if you don't have the skills and experience they need.

Southwest Airlines promotes its approach to hiring by saying they "hire for attitude, train for skills." Though that may be fine for ticket agents, cabin staff, baggage handlers, and possibly new maintenance technicians, I'd like to think they hire pilots based on their skills and experience first.

At lower levels, attitude may be more important than skills and experience. At the executive and manager levels, however, skills and experience are foremost in an employer's mind. Attitude certainly has value, but it follows skills and experience. You won't get the job, however, on skills and experience alone.

Skills and Traits

Skills stem from experience. You may have an inborn talent for something, but you can't become skilled at it without practice. Skills are objectively measurable. For example, if you say you're skilled at preparing marketing plans, an interviewer might ask: "How many plans have you prepared? How long were they? How effective were they?" These are all questions that could help someone else understand the significance of your skill.

Skills are objective;
traits and characteristics are subjective.

Traits and characteristics, on the other hand, aren't measurable. They are subjective statements describing how you do things. You may be a strategic thinker and proactive, but you can't describe these phrases objectively. When you make statements about your traits and characteristics, you may know exactly what they mean to you, but they may mean something completely different to someone else.

Employers and recruiters usually ignore statements about traits and characteristics. Some even look disdainfully at resumes and cover letters that contain glowing self-assessments of the writer's traits and characteristics.

During our candidate interviews, we always asked executives to describe their three strongest skills. Many would respond with a mix of traits and skills, such as strategic thinking, interpersonal skills, hardworking, proactive, and similarly hyperbolic statements. None of these terms meant anything to us, and usually resulted in our not considering the candidates further.

What Your Skills Tell Others About You

Although other executives may have many of the same or similar skills as you, only you possess your exact set of skills, experiences, and achievements. This unique combination sets you apart from everyone else.

You need to know ALL your skills. Here's why:

▶ Skills are the main *products* you're selling.

▶ Skills show what you can *do* for an employer.

▶ Skills show you're *qualified*.

▶ Skills set you *apart* from others.

▶ Skills show what *expertise* you bring to the table.

▶ Skills identify what kind of *resource* you are.

▶ Your *value* is higher if your skills are in demand and in short supply.

▶ Companies look for skills they don't have and those they think they *need*.

▶ Employers minimize their *risk* if you already have the skills they think they need.

▶ Employers know you can train others in your skills *only* if you already have them.

When you are describing your skills to others, don't think they really want to know all your skills. Pulling from your inventory of skills, describe only those that you believe would be relevant to them or their situation, keeping foremost in your mind they will be listening for answers to the following:

1. How current are your skills?
2. How transferable are your skills?

1. How Current Are Your Skills?

Employers either want someone with the same skills as the one who is leaving or they want new skills they don't already have within their organization. Companies don't employ people with old or "legacy" skills on a permanent basis. They can usually find those skills within their organization or can employ someone on a short-term contract.

You'll be competing against younger candidates who'll be promoting their current skills, and, if you emphasize skills not currently in demand, you'll date yourself.

If you're considering a career change instead of, or in addition to, a job search, then it's appropriate to identify all your skills so you can understand and consider more options.

> **TIP** Start by identifying the skills you currently use, and work backward through your career.

2. How Transferable Are Your Skills?

If you think you might want to work in a different industry and believe your skills are transferable, you'll need to describe them in ways that someone in the other industry understands. If you describe your skills as you used them within your current industry and assume those in other industries will see the transferability of your skills, you'll be sadly mistaken. Others will immediately stereotype you as skilled in *your* industry, not theirs.

When you hear about a position at your level that isn't in your industry, yet you know your skills are transferable, you'll probably say to yourself, "I can do that!" You probably can, but so can many other executives who already have that industry experience, AND so would thousands of others who also think their industry skills are transferable.

An employer or recruiter would have to reject every candidate who already has experience in their industry before they would even begin to consider you and the thousands of others who believe their skills are transferable.

> **T I P** *You* must connect the dots and translate your skills for the prospective employer and, most importantly, executive recruiters.

There's lots of confusion about describing skills. Whenever I see a resume with a list of skills as keywords, I feel sorry for the person whose name is at the top. This may be an effective technique when you're looking for work in sales, programming, account reconciliation, or a similar basic job. But it's ineffective when the keyword skills you list include such terms as: communication skills, interpersonal skills, M & A, SEC, or Channel Marketing.

The reader of your resume likely won't have any idea what you mean by "communication skills." For example, does that mean you're skilled at public speaking, preparing documents that must communicate complex technical language effectively, communicating one on one, making presentations, running training programs, and so forth?

> **T I P** Using a vague skill word doesn't mean much to your target audience. In my search practice, my recruiters and I ignored lists of skills.

Techniques to Identify Your Skills

Identifying your skills isn't as simple as it might seem. Sometimes you do things instinctively that others don't or can't do, but you just don't regard it as a skill. Other times, you've become adept at something you do so routinely that you never considered it a skill.

Just knowing a skill word is not enough. You also need to know the context in which you use the skill, so that, when you explain your skills to someone else, he'll understand what you mean.

For example, if you selected motivating as one of your skills, the listener might immediately wonder whom you motivate, how you do it, and what you motivate them to do. If you want others to understand your skills, you'll need to make "skill statements" that include two components:

1. An action word—a verb that indicates a skill.

2. The object of the skill—how and with whom, or with what, you use the skill.

Let's assume your list included the following action words:

» Driving.

» Writing.

» Organizing.

» Testing.

You then need to describe the object of each of the action words. The following chart illustrates this.

The Action (verb)	The Object of the Action (noun)
1. Driving	Formula One race cars
2. Writing	software programs
3. Writing	research reports
4. Organizing	project development teams
5. Testing	consumer electronic products

Sometimes it's easier to start with the action, other times it's easier to start with the object of the action. There may be times, however, when the action word and the object of the action sound similar, such as "I am skilled at sailing sailboats." Instead, you could say, "I am skilled at sailing," "I am skilled at sailing yachts (keelboats or schooners)," or "I am skilled at sailing 35-foot sailboats."

You may even find that a simple statement you make could hide one or more skills. For example, if you said you're good at getting projects back on schedule, it could include many skills, such as reviewing, analyzing, organizing, delegating, managing, and so on. Because we each learn in different ways, I'll suggest seven different approaches you can use to identify your skills. Some approaches will be easier for you to do than others. This is natural because you may not see a skill from one perspective, but it will become clear when you look at it from a different perspective.

Recognizing skills is itself a skill and will take some practice. Have a friend, colleague, spouse, mentor, or mastermind group member review the work you do in this chapter looking for skills you might have missed. Here are eight approaches that will help you identify your top skills:

1. Action words.
2. Achievement stories.
3. Skills with tangibles.
4. Skills with intangibles.
5. Skills with people.
6. Job profile.
7. Interviews.
8. Preferred skills.

Let's look at each of these in detail.

1. Action Words

Exercise 3.1: Action Words (Verbs)

Start with a list of words (verbs) that indicate a skill. These words can help you to identify activities you do or have done, whether on the job or beyond the scope of your work. Review the following list of verbs and mark each word you think corresponds to something you currently do or have done in the past that you think indicates a skill. Note them on a separate sheet of paper. Add other words (verbs) that come to mind that you don't see on the list.

Action Words (Verbs)				
Achieving	Assessing	Composing	Counseling	Determining
Acting	Attaining	Computing	Creating	Developing
Adapting	Auditing	Conducting	Deciding	Devising
Addressing	Balancing	Connecting	Decorating	Diagnosing
Administering	Budgeting	Conserving	Defending	Directing
Advising	Building	Consolidating	Defining	Discovering
Analyzing	Calculating	Constructing	Delegating	Dispensing
	sifying	Consulting	Delivering	Displaying
	ching	Contracting	Demonstrating	Distributing
	mmunicating	Controlling	Designing	Drafting
	npiling	Cooperating	Detailing	Dramatizing
	npleting	Coordinating	Detecting	Drawing

43

Action Words (Verbs)

Driving	Hypothesizing	Manufacturing	Processing	Revising
Eliminating	Identifying	Mastering	Producing	Reducing
Empathizing	Illustrating	Memorizing	Programming	Scheduling
Employing	Imagining	Mentoring	Projecting	Sculpting
Entertaining	Implementing	Mediating	Promoting	Securing
Establishing	Improving	Modeling	Purchasing	Selecting
Estimating	Influencing	Modifying	Questioning	Selling
Evaluating	Igniting	Monitoring	Quoting	Serving
Excavating	Initiating	Motivating	Raising	Setting up
Exhibiting	Inspecting	Navigating	Reading	Shaping
Expanding	Inspiring	Negotiating	Reasoning	Solving
Experimenting	Installing	Observing	Recommending	Studying
Exploring	Instructing	Obtaining	Recording	Summarizing
Expressing	Integrating	Operating	Recruiting	Supervising
Extracting	Interpreting	Ordering	Referring	Surveying
Facilitating	Interviewing	Organizing	Refining	Synthesizing
Filing	Inventing	Originating	Regulating	Teaching
Forming	Investigating	Overseeing	Relating	Testing
Formulating	Judging	Perceiving	Repairing	Trading
Founding	Launching	Performing	Reporting	Training
Fulfilling	Leading	Persuading	Representing	Transferring
Gathering	Learning	Piloting	Researching	Translating
Generating	Lecturing	Planning	Resolving	Undertaking
Guiding	Listening	Playing	Responding	Uniting
Heading	Logging	Presenting	Restoring	Valuing
Helping	Maintaining	Predicting	Retrieving	Weighing
Hosting	Managing	Preparing	Reviewing	Writing

2. Achievement Stories

In Chapter 2, you started writing about your achievements. You had to analyze everything you did that culminated in the achievement. You also completed Worksheet 2.1: 8 Categories of Achievements, where you used some of the action words listed here to look for achievements. Now, you'll see why you analyzed your achievements in detail.

Exercise 3.2: Skills From Achievements

Review each line of the achievement analyses you completed in Chapter 2 and underline or highlight action words (verbs) that indicate a skill or a statement that infers the use of a skill to achieve what you did. Next, list the skills in the right-hand column. Don't worry if you don't recognize many skills in your first attempt. People frequently assume that what they did was simply their job, or just part of the process, and not a skill.

Use both work and personal achievement analyses, because you'll find that you often use the same skills in both environments, and you may recognize different skills in the different environments.

The example that follows uses the achievement example in Chapter 2 to illustrate how you can do this.

Detailed Description	Skills Identified
Achievement statement: Received an award for organizing an annual community event that was the most successful of its kind in 21 years.	
Analysis: I was asked by the Great Falls Chamber of Commerce to organize the 21st Community Street Faire to raise funds for the handicapped, elderly, and disadvantaged in the county. Although I had never produced anything like this before, I love the theatre, and it was an opportunity to widen my experience of project management while helping a good cause.	
I started by interviewing those who had been involved before, reviewing previous efforts and preparing an outline plan of action. Then I identified potential scriptwriters from referrals and interviewed several.	interviewing, reviewing, analyzing, preparing plan of action; deciding, supporting, creating,
I chose scriptwriters and helped them to create a story board for the program.	
I wrote job descriptions for the production team and sent out a newsletter to the press and to people who had been involved in previous years or who had expressed an interest in getting involved.	creating job descriptions, convincing others to get involved,
I arranged and held auditions. The production director and I assigned roles. Approximately 30 volunteers were involved.	organizing and assigning responsibilities,
Using my computer and learning new software, I produced sponsorship brochures that attracted local businesses.	learning new software, producing brochures,
I came up with the idea to place a "price on the head" of each character, whom businesses could sponsor. They could then promote their sponsorship for each character. Businesses liked it so much that they began to bid against each other for the privilege of saying which character they sponsored. It created a lot of media attention and visibility for the sponsors, who contributed $16,000, which exceeded our budget by $4,000. We used the excess to fund more community programs as chosen by the sponsors.	developing innovative promotion, creating publicity, raising money, increasing revenue, budgeting and forecasting,
I booked the school hall, negotiated charges with the school and persuaded a local accounting firm to keep financial records and write checks.	negotiating, persuading

Detailed Description	Skills Identified
I managed the production team by holding weekly status meetings and kept detailed notes so I could report progress to the Chamber regularly. I organized rehearsals, requiring detailed planning, and kept everyone informed. We began to fall behind in our preparations when work pressures for some of the key members took precedence. I convinced others to step up and cover for them, and we were able to get back on track with a minimum of disruption. I had to schedule my own time carefully because I was trying to wrap up a major project at work. I took on cameo roles myself and also had to lip sync (ghost sing) for one of the principals who took sick and couldn't sing. I organized all the publicity and was interviewed by local press and radio. We performed five superb shows to capacity audiences. Afterward, I arranged a debriefing meeting where I thanked everyone and evaluated what we had learned and what we could pass on for a future occasion. I reported financial results to the Chamber. Our total costs were less than we had budgeted because some sponsors who originally declined to participate decided that they had to be involved after seeing how the other sponsors benefited. We ultimately netted over $16,000, and I received a "Good Citizen Achievement Award" for organizing the community's most successful event ever. **Achievement story:** I received a "Good Citizen Achievement Award" for organizing the community's most financially successful fundraising event ever. I created highly entertaining programs, recruited talented people who donated their time, devised merchant sponsorship programs that increased revenue by 33% over estimates, effectively managed over 30 volunteers and delivered the most successful local program in over 20 years. **Top Five Skills:** 1. Creating 2. Planning 3. Organizing 4. Managing 5. Communicating	managing, delegating, monitoring, preparing status reports, organizing, planning, informing, convincing, problem resolution, time management, scheduling, balancing, innovating, creating, risk-taking, organizing, PR, publicity, producing, networking, reviewing and debriefing, rewarding, reporting financial results, creative business development, achievement

Some skills will be easy to identify because you started the sentence with it or used its verb form. Other times, you'll have to look at the sentence and think about whether it reflects a skill or capability. If it does, choose your own words that describe the skill.

Reflect upon the achievement and the skills you id list the skills you think you used most often or you think in enabling you to achieve what you did.

As you write additional achievement stories in this chapter and the next, focus first on completing your analysis and then the story. When you complete each story, review the analyses, looking for skill words or skill statements, and complete your list of the top five.

3. Skills With Tangibles

When you look at your skills with tangibles, the object will be a physical and material thing.

Skills With Tangibles

Start by describing the tangible things you've worked on or with, or used in the past. Some of the following examples might help jog your memory.

animals	chemicals	electronics	machinery	musical instruments	plastics
antiques	clothing	food	medical products	office equipment	sports gear
automobiles	computers	furniture	metals	plants	wood

Next, think of an action word that best describes what you like doing with the physical things you chose. Use the action words from your list from Exercise 3.1.

For example, suppose you said "chemicals" as the tangible thing because you create non-hazardous chemical compounds for use in children's toys. However, if you hadn't thought of chemicals right away, when you went down the list of action words, you would have stopped at "creating" or "developing" and thought about the chemicals you created or developed in the past. You'll need to be more specific and describe the type of chemicals, so others will have a clear understanding of what you did.

TIP If you have difficulty thinking of tangible and physical things, try to visualize physical objects or things that surround you or that you enjoy using at work, at home (such as hobbies), or in organizations or associations in which you participate.

Enter in column 1 the types of tangible things you like working with. Next, enter in column 2 what you like doing with them. The first line here is an example. Alternatively, you can use a notepad to prepare your list.

What is the tangible thing?	Describe what you like doing with it (action words).
...tiques	*Restoring, refinishing, buying, selling, reproducing*

4. Skills With Intangibles

When you look at your skills with intangibles, the object is information, ideas, data, or thoughts.

Skills With Intangibles

Start by describing the intangibles you've worked on or with, or used in the past. Some of the following examples might help jog your memory.

analytical reports	Internet	questionnaires	strategy
company accounts	manuals	records	surveys and reports
drawings/designs	meetings	research reports	systems
facts	pictures	seminars	training sessions
financial records	plans	specifications	user groups
financial statements	policies and procedures	statistics	videotapes

Next, think of an action word that best describes what you like doing with the intangible object above. Use the action words from your list in Exercise 3.1 to help jog your memory.

For example, suppose you said "plans" as the form of information because you are, or have been, responsible for developing and preparing marketing plans, and you think you're good at it. Alternatively, had you not thought of "plans" right away, when you went down the list of action words in Exercise 3.1, you would have stopped at "developing" and "implementing" and thought about all the marketing plans you worked on in the past. Be specific and use "marketing plans" instead of just "plans."

T I P

If you have difficulty coming up with examples of what you like to do with information or ideas, think about how you might use information or ideas. For example:

▶ You use it as a source to accomplish something or to help reach decisions.

▶ You use it in your job to complete a task or reach decisions.

▶ You use it as an output that results from your work.

Consider:

▶ What information do you create at work?

▶ What information do you use at work?

▶ What information or ideas do you give others?

▶ What do you use to manage others?

▶ What do you prepare to give to others?

▶ What do you do to monitor work or projects?

Enter in column 1 the types of information or ideas that you like working with or using, referring to the list of examples on the previous page to help jog your memory. Next, enter in column 2 what you like doing with that information or idea.

What is the intangible?	Describe what you like doing with it (action words).
Marketing plans	*Developing and implementing*

5. Skills With People

When looking at your "people skills," the object is individuals or groups.

Skills With People

Start by listing the type of people or groups you've worked with in the past or want to work with in the future. Use the following examples to help jog your memory.

attorneys	entrepreneurs	managers	production workers	teenagers
accountants	ethnic minorities	men	senior citizens	underprivileged
board directors	executives	military	sports professionals	unemployed
children	handicapped	nurses		university students
departmental staff	healthcare professionals	police/fire	substance abusers	women
doctors		politicians		

Next, think of an action word that best describes what you enjoy doing with the type of people or groups you listed. Use the action words from your list or Exercise 3.1 to help jog your memory.

For example, suppose you selected "politicians" as the group you liked working with, or would like to work with, because you're good at preparing eloquent and persuasive speeches. Alternatively, when you scanned the list of action words, you may have stopped

TIP

If you have difficulty coming up with types of people or groups you enjoy working with, ask yourself:

▶ What type of person do I like to associate with in a work environment?

▶ Who are my friends at work, and what is it about them that causes me to like them?

▶ What type of people do I enjoy associating with outside of work?

▶ What type of people do I miss when I don't have contact with them?

▶ What type of people do I draw energy from when I deal with them?

Then write down specifically what you do with them that triggers the feelings about them that you have.

at "developing," "preparing," or "writing" and thought about how you developed, prepared, or wrote some great speeches. You could even further clarify your preference for speeches with a specific topic, such as foreign affairs.

Referring to the examples in the Tips box on page 50 to jog your memory, list the types of people or groups you like to work with in column 1. Next, enter in column 2 the action words that best describe what you like doing with those people or groups.

What type of people or groups?	Describe what you like doing with or for them (action words).
Departmental staff	*Training and mentoring*

Using skill statements also helps others understand your skills better. Skills with tangibles are sometimes called "hard skills," whereas skills with people and intangibles are often called "soft skills." You can make good assessments of your hard skills by seeing, feeling, or touching the results, but your soft skills can only be assessed by cognitive processes.

6. Job Profile

Another good way to identify your skills is to profile your previous jobs.

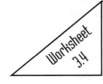

Job Profile

Use the format shown on page 52 and prepare a separate page for each recent job you held. If you held more than one position with the same employer, use a separate page for each position.

Think back into your work history for any job you held and enjoyed, regardless of how long ago you held that job. When you list your skills, focus on those you liked using.

You might now feel you've exhausted all possible ways to identify your skills. Unfortunately, you've only looked at skills from your own perspective. One of the benefits of working with a career coach is his ability to ask probing questions that undoubtedly will uncover skills you didn't recognize. If you're not working with a career coach, find one—a person whom you can trust to be honest and ask you aggressive questions. If you choose not to work with a career coach, you'll need to rely on your spouse, partner, mentor or mastermind group. (See "Create a Support Network" in Chapter 1.)

Job Profile

Job title & employer: Controller – Middletown National Savings Bank
How long did you have this job?   Six years
What were your responsibilities?
Managed 10-person accounting department, including all loan administration activities.
Cash management and hedging of financial securities.
Preparing loan portfolios for discounting and resale.
Construction financing and disbursements management.
Financial statement preparation and reporting.
What skills did you use or develop?
Delegated tasks to team and monitored results.
Trained and supervised subordinates.
Analyzed financial accounts, construction loan applications, and construction loan disbursement requests.
Developed criteria for inclusion in loan portfolio reselling and negotiated transactions with other lending companies.
Analyzed cash requirements and hedging risks associated with foreign loan currencies.
List your most important achievements in this job:
Detected fraudulent construction loan activity involving an officer of the Company, which resulted in his termination and a return of over $300,000 in inappropriate cash advance requests.
Packaged a $750 million loan resale and negotiated its sale recognizing $5 million in profit, largest in the bank's history.
Designed a new construction loan processing procedure which reduced the time to approve construction loan disbursements by 25%, improved control over unauthorized expenditures, and reduced loan administration costs by over $300,000 annually.
Earned the annual Chairman's Award for Outstanding Service for detecting and resolving a fraudulent activity.

7. Interviews

You now need to work with someone else to help you identify other skills. If you think this step is unnecessary or you're hesitant to work with another person in a way that bares your soul, just remember that two heads are always better than one.

You'll not only discover more skills through someone else's perspective, but you'll also get valuable practice talking about your skills in an interview-like atmosphere.

An interview will help you to communicate your skills in ways that others can understand and in a context with which they would be familiar: your skill statement. For example, if you said in an interview that your skill was managing, you now know that's not enough. You need to add what or whom you managed and be prepared for the interviewer to ask clarifying questions such as:

» "Tell me how you manage your staff (or projects)."

» "How do you assign responsibility to staffers?"

» "How do you motivate staffers?"

» "What's the largest number of employees you've managed?"

» "How do you monitor their performance?"

Interviewers won't question all your skills, but they will ask detailed questions to ascertain the reasonableness of your assertion of your top skills. Now that you've explored and discovered most of your skills, you can turn to finding which ones are your top skills.

8. Preferred skills

Determining your preferred skills is achieved through a prioritization process that enables you to make choices between skills to determine which ones you prefer to use most often.

Your Preferred Skills

1. Review the skills you identified when you used each of the previous seven approaches. Mark or highlight those you feel are your strongest skills, and the ones you want to use most often. Try to limit your selection to about 10 to 12 skills from each of the seven approaches.

2. Download Worksheet 3.5 from *www.ExecGlobalNet.com* in the Career Center and make several copies. In the space marked "Area" at the top left, write the title for each of the approaches on individual worksheets (for example: Skills from action words, Skills from achievements, Skills with tangibles, Skills with intangibles, and so forth). Title another worksheet "Summary."

3. Following the instructions on the worksheet you downloaded, prioritize your skills within each area. (See an example of a completed worksheet on page 54.)

4. Transfer the top skills from each Area worksheet to your Summary worksheet.

5. Prioritize the Summary worksheet. Review the results with the top five skills on each of the area worksheets. If you still have skills on these worksheets that you like using more than some on your Summary worksheet, remove

Your Preferred Skills
Prioritizing Choices

Area: Example

Un-prioritized Skills	1	2	3	4	5	6	7	8	9	10	11	12	Prioritized Skills
1. Developing new marketing material	1												1. Developing new marketing material
2. Designing product packaging	(1)/2	2											2. Developing long-term relationships with customers
3. Motivating sales staff	(1)/3	(2)/3	3										3. Making presentations to potential customers
4. Preparing monthly sales reports	(1)/4	(2)/4	(3)/4	4									4. Analyzing and interpreting statistics
5. Developing long-term relationships with customers	(1)/5	2/(5)	3/(5)	4/(5)	5								5. Understanding budgets and finance
6. Making presentations to potential customers	(1)/6	2/(6)	3/(6)	4/(6)	(5)/6	6							6. Designing product packaging
7. Analyzing and interpreting statistics	(1)/7	2/(7)	3/(7)	4/(7)	(5)/7	(6)/7	7						7. Motivating sales staff
8. Understanding budgets and finance	(1)/8	2/(8)	3/(8)	4/(8)	(5)/8	(6)/8	(7)/8	8					8. Preparing monthly sales reports
9.	1/9	2/9	3/9	4/9	5/9	6/9	7/9	8/9	9				9.
10.	1/10	2/10	3/10	4/10	5/10	6/10	7/10	8/10	9/10	10			10.
11.	1/11	2/11	3/11	4/11	5/11	6/11	7/11	8/11	9/11	10/11	11		11.
12.	1/12	2/12	3/12	4/12	5/12	6/12	7/12	8/12	9/12	10/12	11/12	12	12.
A. Un-prioritized skill number	1	2	3	4	5	6	7	8	9	10	11	12	
B. Total number of times that skill is circled	7	2	1	0	6	5	4	3					
C. Priority number	1	6	7	8	2	3	4	5					

Adapted from Richard N. Bolles's The Prioritizing Grid in What Color is Your Parachute?

the last ones from your Summary worksheet and replace them with the new ones. Then re-prioritize your skills on the Summary worksheet. You may have to repeat this process before you feel comfortable with your Summary prioritization. When finished, you'll have a prioritized list of the skills you prefer to use most often.

Do a reality check by reviewing your Summary prioritization with your spouse, close friends, former peers from work, mentor, and career coach. See if they have different perceptions of your skills. If they do, ask them why they see you differently from how you see yourself. Don't worry! Others often see you differently from how you see yourself.

Compare your top skills with the top skills you listed at the end of each of your achievement stories. They should be the same or similar. If not, you'll need to explore the reasons for the inconsistencies. If a career coach is not available to help you through these apparent inconsistencies, discuss them with your mentor or mastermind group, or someone else who knows you well.

Job Responsibilities

Describing job responsibilities is similar to describing skills. Suppose an interviewer asks you what your job was at XYZ Company. If you reply that you were vice president of sales, there would probably be a lengthy pause while she waits for you to finish the statement.

Use the quantification techniques you learned in "Step 3: Bring the Achievement Into Perspective" in Chapter 2 and anticipate the interviewer's clarifying questions that will enable someone who is not familiar with what you did to quickly grasp the significance of your role and your responsibilities. For example, you could say, "I was VP of sales for a $1 billion, high-end office furniture manufacturer, leading five regional sales managers and 125 sales reps and territory sales managers, selling 50 product lines and over 1,200 different products in the U.S. and five overseas locations, including Europe, the Middle East, and Asia." (This is clearly too long, but it illustrates what you could include.)

Use questions similar to the following to help you describe your responsibilities in a way that helps them understand the nature and significance of your role:

> ❖ "Whom did you work for, and what were their job titles?"

> ❖ "How did you get this job?"

> ❖ "Why did you take this job?"

> ❖ "Where did the company have sales operations?"

> ❖ "How many salespeople were there?"

»» "How many people reported to you directly and indirectly?"

»» "How many regional, area, or territory sales managers were there?"

»» "How many sales meetings did you organize?"

»» "How many trade shows did you participate in?"

»» "What was your involvement in setting sales strategy?"

»» "What was your department's budget, and who set it?"

You'll find it much easier to work with someone else who can review your skill and responsibility statements, and ask you to clarify and expand what you mean. If you don't have someone work with you at this stage who can help you identify and describe your skills and responsibilities clearly, you won't respond to interviewers' questions as well as you could if you prepared in advance.

> **TIP** Ask someone who is unfamiliar with what you did to ask you these questions.

Strengths and Weaknesses

Are your strengths the same as your skills? Not necessarily. You have many skills, some you like to use and some you don't. You even have skills in areas where you're merely competent, but not outstanding. Remember the analogy about Kevin, the race car driver, in Chapter 2? Are you a *good* race car driver or a *great* race car driver?

Worksheet 3.5 identified the skills you prefer to use most often: your preferred skills. But are these your strongest skills? Perhaps not. We all have good skills in areas where we don't really enjoy them. If you notice that the skills you prefer to use don't include your strongest skills, it's a good indication that you should be looking at making more than a job change.

Interviewers may question you about your skills by asking, "What are your main strengths?" They often think the words *skill* and *strength* are interchangeable. Marcus Buckingham and Donald Clifton in *NOW, Discover Your Strengths* (The Free Press, 2001) define strengths as containing three components: talent, skill, and knowledge. You may be born with a talent for leadership, but, if you haven't had much leadership experience and made mistakes along the way, you won't be a skilled leader. To be a great leader, you also will need to learn effective management and leadership techniques and principles.

Your preferred skills may be your strengths if they incorporate talent and knowledge. Using golfer Tiger Woods as an example, he may have started with a talent for golf, but he needed to understand the rules of the game, and then had to practice, practice, and practice more, before golf became his strength.

56

You've probably heard the phrase *play to your strengths.* If you want to find your top five strengths (your "signature strengths"), I encourage you to buy *NOW, Discover Your Strengths,* which has a detailed discussion about strengths, or an updated *StrengthsFinder 2.0* by Tom Rath (Gallup Press, 2007), which has a broader explanation of each of your top strengths. They both use the model originally developed by Donald O. Clifton. In both books, read the first part, and then go to their Website and answer the online questionnaire. You'll receive a detailed report describing your top five strengths.

What about your weaknesses? How do you overcome them, or should you even try? The short answer is to forget about your weaknesses, and focus on your strengths. Your strengths are what make you unique and are your strongest selling points. When you look at a weakness, consider whether it's a weakness because you have no talent for that area and are terrible at it, don't know enough about it to be good at it, or don't have any experience (skills) to know whether you could be good at it.

If you don't feel you have a talent for it, don't waste any more time trying to overcome the weakness. You won't. Create defense mechanisms by building relationships with others who have the strengths in the areas where you don't. If your weakness stems from a lack of knowledge, take a course, read a book, or interview others to find out more about it. If your weakness stems from a lack of skill at it, look for ways that you can develop the skill.

Usually, focusing on your weaknesses will not be time well spent, because you're unlikely to turn a weakness into enough of a strength that you will get enjoyment from it. Promote your strengths and mitigate your weaknesses. Interviewers will ask about your weaknesses. Know them, and be up front explaining them. Take the extra step to explain how or what you do to mitigate the weaknesses. Don't say you have "overcome" the weakness, because you generally can't unless it came from additional education, training, practice, or coaching.

> **TIP**
> Never answer questions about your weaknesses by saying you're "too dedicated," "too hardworking," and so on. You'll lose a great deal of credibility if interviewers hear these "positive weaknesses" responses. Besides, they are neither strengths nor weaknesses. They are personal traits or characteristics.

Emotional Intelligence

When you see the word *intelligence,* you probably think about the tests you might have taken in elementary school that measured your cognitive intelligence. You were born with this intelligence quotient, and it won't change significantly throughout your life. It was a part of your "package," much like your personality type as measured by the MBTI questionnaire. (See Chapter 1.)

Your cognitive intelligence is a good predictor of how you'll progress in school, how easily you'll get straight A's, and whether you'll become the next Albert Einstein. Cognitive intelligence is not, however, a good predictor of how successful you'll be in business or how far you'll progress up the management ranks.

Psychologists were researching and defining other types of intelligences in the late 19th and early 20th centuries. Howard Gardner wrote *Multiple Intelligences* (BasicBooks, 1993), identifying seven different types of intelligences. This subject began to gain broad attention with non-academics and business when Daniel Goleman, a PhD and writer for the *New York Times,* published his national best-seller, *Emotional Intelligence* (Bantam Books, 1998).

Without going into too much detail, Goleman popularized the term *emotional intelligence* (EI) in the business world with his later books, *Working with Emotional Intelligence* (Bantam Books, 1998) and, with Richard Boyatzis and Annie McKee, *Primal Leadership* (Harvard Business School Press, 2002). He constructed five components of emotional intelligence, which he later refined into four.

Reuven Bar-On, an academic, had spent years researching and creating a more accurate model of what he calls emotional-social intelligence (ESI) and published *The Handbook of Emotional Intelligence* (Jossey-Bass, 2000) on the theory, development, assessment, and application of EI.

As you might guess, these experts developed tests to assess an individual's level of emotional intelligence: Emotional Quotient (EQ). One of the most commonly used test instruments is Bar-On's EQ-i (for Emotional Quotient-Intelligence). Bar-On developed his model in the early Eighties and revised, refined, and validated it over the next 17 years. It's been translated into more than 30 languages. Bar-On's EQ-i assesses how well you can:

- Recognize, understand, and express emotions and feelings.
- Understand how others feel and relate to them.
- Manage and control emotions.
- Manage change, adapt, and solve problems of a personal and interpersonal nature.
- Generate positive affect and be self-motivated.

The figure on page 59 expands on these characteristics.

It's probably no surprise to you that people join *companies* but leave because of *people,* typically their bosses. Research has shown that low EQ in more than one competency or skill is a major cause of why managers don't manage effectively, leaders aren't able to lead effectively, or people fail to get promoted.

EQ-i Scales and What They Assess

Characteristics	Competencies and Skills
Intrapersonal	**Self-Awareness and Self-Expression**
Self-respect	Accurately perceive, understand, and accept oneself
Emotional self-awareness	Aware of and understand one's emotions
Assertiveness	Effectively and constructively express one's emotions and oneself
Independence	Self-reliant and free of emotional dependency on others
Self-actualization	Strive to achieve personal goals and actualize one's potential
Interpersonal	**Social Awareness and Interpersonal Relationship**
Empathy	Aware of and understand how others feel
Social responsibility	Identify with one's social group and cooperate with others
Interpersonal relationship	Establish mutually satisfying relationships and relate well with others
Stress Management	**Emotional Management and Regulation**
Stress tolerance	Effectively and constructively manage emotions
Impulse control	Effectively and constructively control emotions
Adaptability	**Change Management**
Reality testing	Objectively validate one's feelings and thinking with external reality
Flexibility	Adapt and adjust one's feelings and thinking to new situations
Problem-solving	Effectively solve problems of a personal and interpersonal nature
General Mood	**Self-Motivation**
Optimism	Be positive and look at the brighter side of life
Happiness	Feel content with oneself, others, and life in general

When I hear clients tell me that they are networking but not getting referrals or are getting referrals but not getting the job, I can almost guarantee that part of the problem is related to their emotional intelligence skills. Sometimes it becomes obvious by just observing them while they are networking.

Bar-On's findings suggest that the most powerful contributors to occupational performance are your ability to:

» Be aware of and have a realistic acceptance of yourself.

» Be aware of others' feelings, concerns, and needs.

» Manage your emotions and those of others.

» Be realistic and put things in the correct perspective.

» Have and exude a positive disposition.

Review the list in the previous figure and ask yourself if you think you could have a weakness in one or more of the areas listed. If you don't think there are any, don't get too excited. Most people, when asked that question, don't see themselves as having a problem. If you ask the same question of others who have worked with or for you, you might get a much different answer.

The good news about EQ is that a weakness in one or more areas can be overcome when you are aware of the weaknesses. The key is *your* awareness. You'll probably need someone else to point out what you're doing that is causing the problem. Business coaches are often called upon to help with this major task. Soon after Jack Welch was promoted to CEO at GE, he hired a business coach who shadowed him (followed him around all day) and was able to observe when Jack slipped back into managing his senior team rather than leading them, and could point out the specifics and suggest how he should have acted or reacted differently. Jack learned new skills and, in the process, became a legend.

If you're currently working but not progressing as you think you should, you might have an issue in this area. Don't rely on your employer to come to you to suggest you need some help. Ask your employer if they'll pay for a coach to work with you. Companies often appreciate employees who are realistic about their own weaknesses and ask for help in overcoming them. If you don't think your employer will respond to your suggestion positively, you need to seriously consider whether this is an organization where you will be able to grow and progress.

If your employer won't pay for coaching help, or if you're in transition but feel you could use help in one or more areas, hire a coach on your own. A career coach or mentor can help you become more aware and develop skills to deal with these issues now.

☑ Milestones

The following milestones recap what you need to do to complete this chapter. Include those items you are unable to complete in your summary-level open-items list.

☐ 1.   Complete Exercise 3.1: Action Words (Verbs). Review the list of action words and highlight the ones that match what you currently do or have done in the past. Start your list on a notepad.

☐ 2.   Complete Worksheet 3.2: Skills From Achievements. Review the analyses of achievements you prepared in Chapter 2 and concentrate on identifying your skills. Highlight your skills and list them in the right margin of the analyses. Summarize the five most important ones at the bottom. Add all your skills to your notepad list.

❑ 3.   Complete your analysis of Worksheet 3.1: Skills With Tangibles. Add your skills to your notepad list.

❑ 4.   Complete your analysis of Worksheet 3.2: Skills With Intangibles. Add your skills to your notepad list.

❑ 5.   Complete your analysis of Worksheet 3.3: Skills With People. Consider whether to expand this review by looking separately at individuals and groups. Add your skills to your notepad list.

❑ 6.   Complete Worksheet 3.4: Job Profile sheets for all recent jobs. Add your skills to your notepad list.

❑ 7.   Complete a fifth achievement story.
Title:_____

❑ 8.   Complete a sixth achievement story.
Title:_____

❑ 9.   Complete a seventh achievement story.
Title:_____

❑10.   Review your three new achievement stories, looking for your skills. Highlight your skills in the text, and list the skill or a skill statement in the right-hand column. Summarize your top five at the bottom and add all your skills to your notepad list.

❑11.   Complete Worksheet 3.5: Your Preferred Skills for each skill area from your individual notepad lists and for the summary level. (Download the worksheet at *www.ExecGlobalNet.com* in the **Career Center** and make copies.)

❑12.   Review your final summarized list of prioritized skills with others who know you well to make sure they see your strongest skills as you do. Incorporate any suggestions from them or confusion on their part until you're confident others will understand and quickly grasp the significance of the statements.

❑13.   Review your most recent job profiles and describe your responsibilities using the same techniques you used to quantify your achievements.

❑14.   Compare your current career track or job search with your top preferred skills. If the skills employers would consider most important for the position you're seeking aren't the same ones on your top preferred skills, it's time to start thinking about making a career change.

❏15.   Read *NOW, Discover Your Strengths* or *StrengthsFinder 2.0,* and complete the online questionnaire. Compare your five signature strengths with your top preferred skills and with the top five you listed on your individual achievement stories. If you see inconsistencies, explore the reasons with your mentor, mastermind group, or talk to a career coach.

❏16.   Review the "EQ-I Scales and What They Access" figure and reword each statement as if you are saying it about you, such as: "I..." or "I am..." for each of the Competencies & Skills. Substitute the words *one's* with *my* and *oneself* with *myself.* The Intrapersonal Characteristics are all about you. The Interpersonal Characteristics are about your interactions with others. Stress Management, Adaptability, and General Mood are about you.

Section II

Identifying
and
Evaluating Your Employment
Options

Career 4 Options

You can't get there from here unless you know
where there is!

Chapter Overview

In this chapter, you'll take a fresh look at your career options. Even if you decide to pursue your current career path, looking into alternatives and understanding how to target and evaluate companies and industries will give you a psychological boost and enhance your job search.

Specifically, you'll:

» Recognize when and why you should consider investigating other career options.

» Learn how to identify and target industries and companies more successfully.

» Learn how to evaluate whether a particular company or industry is right for you.

The main sections in this chapter include:

» When you should think outside the box about your career.

» Techniques to identify and target industries and companies.

» Milestones.

Whether you're pursuing your current career path or considering a career change, you must have a clear focus and be able to convey it as a single, well-defined career objective to recruiters, potential employers, and others you want to help you.

If you're the least bit unclear in your discussions with them, they'll be confused and won't know how to help you. For example, if they think you're trying to keep your options open by looking for a consulting opportunity and an employed position at the same time, they're not likely to help you find either.

When You Should Think Outside the Box About Your Career

Without thinking about it much, you may have decided to look for another job in your chosen functional area because that's the next logical step for you. Whether you're in transition (out of work) or working while considering other options, take this opportunity to step outside the box and look at your career options.

You'll reap two benefits by stepping outside the box: You'll either confirm that your career path is what you want most, or you'll discover things about yourself you hadn't previously considered—which may lead you to look at other options.

The following situations could indicate you may need to consider a career change:

» You've worked for one employer for more than 10 years.

» You have broad experience in different industries, rather than extensive experience in one industry.

» You haven't had a promotion within the past five years.

» Your industry experience is in a declining market or in an industry that is moving overseas.

» Your functional area of experience isn't unique.

» You're approaching, at, or past the magical age of 49.

» You're not computer-literate.

» You don't have a good or large contact network.

» Your functional area is increasingly being outsourced.

» Younger and less-expensive candidates can readily perform your current or most recent job.

As you progress in your career and obtain more experience, you naturally gain more knowledge about different functions, industries, and people than was available to you when you started. Most people make three or more career changes in their working lifetime.

Making job and career changes can be positive—if you do it right. If you don't, the results can be disastrous. Here are some situations that, if they relate to you, mean you'll likely have a much more difficult job search:

◆ **Job hopping.** If you jumped from job to job every few years, employers and recruiters will think you took jobs without evaluating them properly, or you bore easily and won't be a reliable employee, or your job performance must have been below par, causing you to keep moving.

◆ **Checkered work history.** If you changed industries too frequently without a clear plan, employers and recruiters will think you don't put enough thought into your jobs and can't decide what you want. This is not a good characteristic of strong managers or leaders.

◆ **Broad industry experience.** If you have broad experience in diverse industries, you'll find yourself at a disadvantage when competing with candidates who have their predominant experience in the employer's industry.

◆ **Stayed too long.** If you stayed too long at an employer or in an industry when all signs indicated you should have made a change earlier, employers and recruiters will question whether you have the vision and capability to make important decisions (because management is about making decisions, anticipating problems, and having a strategic vision).

Employers and recruiters look favorably on executives who seem to be in charge of their careers and know what they want and why. If you've stumbled along the way, you'll have to prepare a justification for your work history so others don't draw wrong conclusions.

You'll also find that your job search becomes more difficult each year after you reach 40 and even more difficult from 49 on. Consequently, take the suggestions in this chapter and this book seriously.

A Shared Experience

I left public accounting as partner of a Big 8 accounting firm at what I thought was my prime, age 49. I had no idea finding a new job would be as difficult as it turned out to be. I purchased a few job search books, including one purportedly targeted at executives. Following the advice for executives, I mailed more than 1,000 letters, accompanied by my resume, to employers and recruiters. After several months, I had nothing to show for my efforts except a large stack of thank-you-but-no-thank-you responses.

When I later switched careers and started my search firm in the UK, I vowed not to discriminate against candidates based on age, since I suspected my own age might have been an issue in my job search.

After a year or so in the search business, I began to notice that a high percentage of executives in their 50s had stopped looking for challenges. Their objective was to find a stable job without problems or demands so they could safely draw a paycheck until retirement. Because I wasn't a career coach at the time, I didn't bother explaining that those jobs didn't exist anymore!

I also found most recruiters wouldn't give resumes even a cursory review if they thought the candidate was in his fifties. Even when I pressed to include older, more experienced executives in our shortlists to clients, I found clients mentally did the math themselves. They were reluctant to consider candidates in their late 40s and would give only a cursory look at candidates who might be in their 50s.

If you fit this age group, does this mean you should stop wasting time pursuing a job? Not at all. It does mean, however, that you need to use a different approach and not spend a significant amount of time sending resumes and letters to recruiters or employers.

One exception to this: If you have an established personal relationship with recruiters and individuals in companies, then sending them your resume on a speculative basis may be highly productive. If you don't have this kind of high visibility, you're not likely to find a job with this approach.

When writing this book, I assumed most readers wouldn't have that kind of high visibility and would need to find other ways of getting the attention of recruiters and employers. Whether you're searching for a new job or exploring career options, stepping outside the box and examining all your options will be productive time well spent on your part. Consider ALL options, no matter how offbeat some may seem. Some options will eventually be discarded, but be willing to consider them all. Re-examining your career options will not only help you consider new possibilities, but will also validate your decision if you're only making a job change.

Be aware that decisions you make about your career are *lifestyle changes.* Your choices will affect your entire family. Consequently, discuss what you do in this chapter with others who are close to you to get their perspectives.

Use the techniques in the following sections whether you're changing jobs or careers. If you feel stuck at any time and don't know how to move forward, that's the time to consult an experienced career professional. You'll find suggestions on how to do this in Chapter 12.

Techniques to Identify and Target Industries and Companies

People typically make career changes in one of three ways:

◈» Change from one function (what they do) to another within the same field.

◈» Change from one field (their industry) to another within the same function.

◈» Change both function and field at the same time.

The following illustration should simplify understanding these changes:

Ways to Make a Career Change

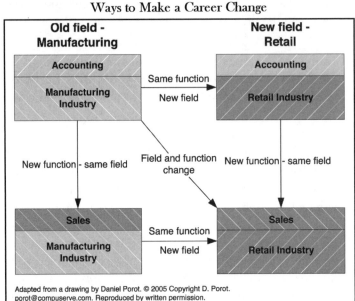

Adapted from a drawing by Daniel Porot. © 2005 Copyright D. Porot.
porot@compuserve.com. Reproduced by written permission.

At some point in your career, you'll need to determine whether to change your function or field. It's not uncommon to change both field and function at the same time, as many of us do early in our careers.

As you progress up the corporate ladder, making a career change becomes more difficult unless it occurs as a natural progression within an employer. For example, if you wanted to move from a CFO role to an operational one, it would be much easier to do it with your current employer, who already knows you and has a good idea of what to expect from you.

If you left your current employer as a CFO to look for an operational role at a different company, that company would be looking for someone with operational experience, not a CFO.

If you want to explore changing your function or field, you'll need to do some research to determine whether the change could be right for you. This will also help you learn if you have a reasonable chance to make the change or if you need additional skills, knowledge, or experience. Let's examine the following techniques to help you identify and target industries and companies:

1. Techniques to research fields.

2. Techniques to research functions.

3. Techniques to research companies.

4. Techniques to test your conclusions.

5. Techniques to find the right job and company for you.

1. Techniques to Research Fields

❖ Use your library as a resource center. Your card will enable you to use the library's Internet research services at no cost. You'll also be able to access selected Internet services that your library makes available through remote access from your home computer.

❖ Look for books, pamphlets, or articles on industries where you think you might have an interest, then conduct research on the Internet relating to news within those industries.

❖ Review the Standard Industrial Classification (SIC) index and look up the industry codes for the industries in which you're interested. You may need to use the North American Industry Classification System (NAICS), which started in 1997, instead of the SIC system. SIC and NAICS codes are available on the Internet and at your local library. Identify the codes for industries that match your interest and look up companies in reference books, such as Dun & Bradstreet's *Million Dollar Directory,* that match those codes. Look up the companies to see what other codes they list, and then find what other industries use those codes.

❖ Talk to people in the industries that are of interest to you. Ask them what skills are in demand, what qualifications are required, and what personal attributes are best suited to that industry. Ask about the transferability of your skills and experience. (We'll cover how to do this in Chapter 8.)

A Shared Experience

At my first appointment with my podiatrist, Arnold Ross, DPM, I immediately knew he was different from all the others I had seen over the years. While they probably all had the same professional training and experience, what set him apart was an obvious passion for what he did, his caring touch, and his personal interest in me.

So, I did what I often do when I meet extraordinary people, I asked him when and how he knew that podiatry was what he wanted his life-work to be. He said while in college and taking pre-med he knew he wanted to do something in the professions that would be very hands-on. At the time, he was pursuing dentistry, but wasn't quite sure it was right for him.

At a chance meeting, a relative asked him what he planned to do with the rest of his life and after a short discussion asked whether he had considered podiatry. He said he hadn't and then began to wonder what else he hadn't considered.

He thought maybe now was a good time to find out more about the different careers in the professions. He called lawyers, accountants, dentists, and various medical specialists and met with them at their offices. He asked them to describe a typical workday, what they liked about it, and disliked. He said they all talked very dispassionately about their jobs, except for a podiatrist who exhibited a great deal of enthusiasm by going in to great detail about what he did and how much he loved it.

Dr. Ross was so taken by the podiatrist's passionate description that he felt that was what he wanted to do. He changed his major and says he's never looked back.

What lessons are in Dr. Ross's story if you're considering changing careers?

» Find what interests *you.*

» Keep an open mind and consider *all* options.

» *Visit* with those doing the jobs, and ask them to describe their day, including what they like and dislike about it.

2. Techniques to Research Functions

♦ List the skills you want to use or develop.

♦ Go to several Internet job posting sites, such as *CareerBuilder.com, Monster.com, or HotJobs.Yahoo.com,* including those that might be specific to an industry or function and search for jobs using the industry and/or function in which you have an interest.

♦ Review job postings that sound interesting to you and see what skills, experience, and qualifications they require.

♦ When you identify a position that requires skills similar to yours, write down how you would reword or translate your skills to match the requirements.

♦ If your skills aren't directly transferable to a new industry you're exploring, look for other opportunities where you could take a position in the new industry as a stepping stone while you develop the new skills that will take you closer to your ultimate objective.

When you complete this process, you should have a list of "A" companies and "B" companies. Your "A" list consists of companies where there's a direct applicability or transferability of your skills and experience. Your "B" list is your backup and consists of companies where your skills and experience should be transferable, but it likely will take some personal connection to convince a potential employer.

You might also prepare a "C" list where the transferability of your skills and experience is still reasonable, but more of a stretch.

3. Techniques to Research Companies

In addition to your contact network, which we'll cover in Chapter 8, you need to use *all* of the following to get the information you need:

◆ Printed reference books at the library.

◆ Library Internet reference sources.

◆ Keyword searching on the Internet for industries and company news.

◆ Company Websites.

◆ SEC filings on *www.FreeEdgar.com* or through the links on their homepage.

Before you start your search for information, make sure you:

◆ Know what you want to learn. If you're not exactly sure what you want, you'll waste valuable time searching down blind alleys. You'll be overwhelmed with information, much of it not useful.

◆ Use the most current sources of information.

◆ Keep a list of where you search and what you find. There are countless sources of information; you want to make sure you keep track of the sources that are useful to you.

Because sources of information are constantly changing and evolving, download a current list of information sources for the United States, Canada, and the UK at *www.ExecGlobalNet.com* in the **Career Center**. (Select the file "Reference 4.1: Where to Get Additional Information.")

4. Techniques to Test Your Conclusions

After you've narrowed your list of potential new fields and/or functions:

◆ Talk to your coach, mentor, or mastermind participants and use your contact network to find others who have experience in the field (or function) you're considering.

◆ Explain that you're exploring a career change. Describe what you've done most recently and what you desire to move toward.

◆ Emphasize that you're not asking for a job but are researching their industry (or function). Make it clear you're gathering information from those who are already in a particular field or job, or who've previously made a similar career change.

◆ Explain that you have a number of questions you'd like to ask that would help you decide whether a change you're contemplating would make sense for you and, if so, what would be involved in making such a change.

TIPS

Here are some examples of questions to ask people already working in the desired job and/or field:

▶ "Can you describe your job for me?"

▶ "What do you like and dislike about it?"

▶ "What's most satisfying about your job?"

▶ "If you had it to do over again, what would you do differently?"

▶ "What qualifications do you think are most important?"

▶ "What additional training do you think I might need, if any?"

▶ "What do you see as the future of this job (position or industry)? How do you think it will change?"

▶ "Is there any technology that might significantly impact this job in the future?"

▶ "What are your thoughts and opinions about my proposed job shift?"

▶ "If there's one thing that should be of greatest concern to me regarding this change, what would it be?"

▶ "Do you know other persons I can talk to who might be able to look at this from a different perspective and help me make a decision, and would you introduce me to them?"

▶ "Do you know others who have made similar career transitions, and would you introduce me to them?"

Add additional questions that pertain to your particular career change circumstances. We'll cover how to find people to talk to in Chapter 8.

In addition to the self-help options described, making a career change is a time when you might benefit from the professional advice of a career coach—someone who has experience working with a number of others who've gone through career changes successfully. I'll cover how to find a career coach in Chapter 12.

5. Techniques to Find the Right Job and Company for You

For most experienced people, identifying the right job or career will be easier than it is for recent graduates or those who don't have a lot of work experience. You've gained skills and experience in different situations that have enabled you to develop likes and dislikes. Before you launch into exploring career options, you need to clarify your likes and dislikes. Exploring your preferences using the following five criteria will help you decide where you want to work:

1. Values and goals.
2. Personal living preferences.
3. Workplace preferences.
4. People preferences.
5. Ideal job profile.

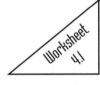 Exercise 4.1: Values and Goals

Review the values and goals that you completed in Chapter 1 in Worksheet 1.1: Identifying Your Values, Exercise 1.1: Known Likes and Dislikes, and Exercise 1.2: Goals Summary. Make additions, deletions, or modifications based on what you've learned so far. You'll review these worksheets again when you've finished this book because you'll have additional ideas and clarifications. Remember that your values and goals are fluid and should be updated frequently to keep your job search on target.

Worksheet 4.1: Personal Living Preferences

You've probably established yourself and your family in a place you prefer to live. This worksheet will help you consider how strongly you feel about commuting times, travel frequency, time away from family, and so forth. These issues are the major factors that can quickly lead to job dissatisfaction, burnout, and stressful personal relationships.

Review each consideration listed in the Personal Living Preferences template on page 74 and check off how strongly you feel about each one. Add others, negative or positive, at the end that you don't see but consider important. Make sure your choices include your *and* your family's preferences.

When you're finished, highlight those preferences that are most important to you because you'll need to be clear about them very quickly when considering a potential job offer.

Workplace Preferences

The next set of personal issues relate to the workplace. It's your responsibility to determine if the company will be a good fit for you. You don't want to wait until you receive a job offer to begin asking questions.

Review each consideration listed in Workplace Preferences on page 75 and check off how strongly you feel about each one. On a separate sheet of paper, add others you don't see but consider important, whether they're positive or negative.

Personal Living Preferences

Preferences	Importance			
	Very Imp. ←	Mixed	→	Not Imp.
Apartment				
At or near mountains				
At or near desert				
At or near beach				
Bustling community				
Climate Dry				
Climate Hot				
Climate Wet				
Close-knit community				
Close to golf course				
Close to park				
Close to public transport				
Close to sporting events				
Close to theater/concerts				
Community of like ethnic group				
Condominium				
Cool climate				
Cosmopolitan community				
Easy access to airport				
Gated community				
Good schools				
House				
Mixed-use planned community				
Near shopping mall				
Older families without children				
Property with a view				
Property with stables				
Quiet community				
Rural area				
Suburban area				
Urban area				
Walking distance to shopping mall				
Young families				

Workplace Preferences

Preferences	Degree You Would Prefer Consideration		
	Must Have ←	Mixed →	Do Not Want
Air conditioning			
Big company or organization			
Cafeteria at facility			
Campus-like or park-like office setting			
Convenient to public transport			
Daycare close to work			
Daycare provided at facility			
Family business			
Flexible hours			
High security			
Modern furniture			
Night shift work			
Noisy office			
One-way commute under ___ minutes			
One-way commute under ___ hour(s)			
Open-plan office space			
Outside sales			
Overtime			
Owner-managed business			
Paid or free parking			
Private office			
Quality furniture			
Quiet office			
Restaurants nearby			
Shared office			
Shopping mall nearby			
Small company or organization			
Tall office tower			
Ten-hour days, four days a week			
Travel in job – define how much:			
Weekend work			
Windows			
Work out of home office			

Review your selections in the Workplace Preferences worksheet and highlight the ones that are "Must Have" or "Do Not Want." Preferably, use a blank ruled sheet and list your "Must Have" and "Do Not Want" in the order of importance they are to you. These will be the ones you will need to consider during the interview process and before accepting an offer.

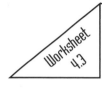

People Preferences

The People Preferences worksheet will help you identify the personal styles of the people with whom you either do or don't want to work. List both positive and negative characteristics that you feel strongly about.

It isn't always possible to choose your colleagues in a new job. What is possible, however, is to be aware of the characteristics of people you would prefer to avoid. Knowing your preferences ahead of time will make you more alert to uncovering the style of the people you meet in your interview(s) and the personal relationships between them. If the traits you're seeking to find or avoid aren't observable, you'll have to ask appropriate questions to uncover them in an interview. (We'll cover how to do this in more detail in Chapter 10.)

There are two ways you can complete the form (See example on next page):

1. List in column 2 the positive character traits that motivate you or that you like in superiors or peers.

2. Identify the negative traits that you don't like in column 1 and then describe in column 2 how you would describe the reverse of those negative traits. This helps you to better phrase the positive characteristics or traits of people you want to work with in your next job.

The following are examples of typical negative behavioral characteristics or traits:

assigns responsibility without authority	fault-finder
back-stabber	grandstander
brown-noser	inconsistent
cheat	micromanager
condescending	narcissist
crisis manager	nitpicker
delegates without clear guidelines	rumor-monger
demands the unreasonable	unable to make decisions
dishonest	uncompromising or unforgiving
fails to show appreciation	unethical or lacking in integrity

People Preferences

Negatives Character Traits I Dislike	Positives Character Traits I Like

Exercise 4.2: Ideal Job Profile

Completing your Ideal Job Profile uses a different approach to finding your work preferences. It will help you describe the characteristics of your preferred job, even if the job isn't an employed position. You may have more than one profile, and one or more could be self-employment options you'll need to consider in more detail.

Your Ideal Job Profile is similar to the job profiles you prepared in Worksheet 3.4 in Chapter 3, except you're now designing your ideal or preferred job (or jobs). Follow these guidelines when you prepare your Ideal Job Profile.

Job Title

Enter a generic position, not an actual job title. For example, if you're designing a job where you would have primary operational responsibility for a business, division, subsidiary, line of business, and so forth, you might choose Chief Operating Executive as the generic position. Show examples of actual job titles, such as COO, SVP, EVP, and GM, in parentheses following the generic position.

Employer Profile

Describe the industry, company size (annual revenue or headcount), stage of company development (start-up, early stage, high-growth, mature, and so on), and company culture. Remember that this is your ideal or preferred profile. It doesn't mean you would automatically exclude all others.

Preferred Responsibilities

Describe what you would like your main responsibilities to include, in terms of what your ideal employer would want or need. Use bullets to list three or four of your most important ones—the ones you would use to decide whether or not to accept an offer.

Skills You Want to Use and Develop

List the skills you have which indicate you can accomplish the responsibilities you described above. Add additional skills you want to develop or strengthen.

Achievements That Demonstrate Your Skills for This Job

Describe one or more achievement stories from your past that demonstrate your skills and passion for the business. These are the statements you would use when marketing yourself.

NOTE: The Ideal Job Profile is a useful exercise whether you're looking for an employed position or considering other employment options, such as self-employment. If you have more than one Ideal Job Profile, make sure each reflects consistent information for the position.

Review your completed Ideal Job Profile with someone close to you who will give you honest feedback. Specifically, ask if she:

» Understands the logic of your ideal job(s) in relation to what she knows about you.

» Thinks your ideal job(s) is (are) realistic.

» Agrees that you have the requisite skills and experience for the job(s).

» Can help you match company names to the job profile(s).

» Can see other options that you might not have considered (industries, businesses, companies).

Next, review the achievement stories you completed in Chapter 2. List your significant achievements in order of those most important to you or that you enjoyed the most. These usually indicate your passion. If you find that something you love doing—your passion—isn't listed on one of your Ideal Job Profiles, you need to spend more time reassessing career options.

> **T I P** Play to your strengths. Don't try to be all things to all people. Your competitive advantage is the uniqueness of *your* strengths and passions.

☑ Milestones

The following milestones recap what you need to do to complete this chapter. Include those items you are unable to complete in your summary-level open-items list.

❑ 1. Complete Exercise 4.1: Values and Goals by reviewing the values and goals you completed in Chapter 1. Highlight those that changed since you completed Worksheet 1.1: Identifying Your Values and Exercise 1.2: Goals Summary. Consider why they changed.

❑ 2. Complete Worksheet 4.1: Personal Living Preferences and re-evaluate those items you ranked "Very Important."

❑ 3. Complete Worksheet 4.2: Workplace Preferences and re-evaluate the items you classed on either end of the scale.

❑   4.   Complete Worksheet 4.3: People Preferences and re-evaluate how you described the type of people with whom you prefer to work.

❑   5.   Complete Worksheet 4.4: Ideal Job Profile and make sure you have identified all the ideal jobs you want to consider.

❑   6.   Compare the Ideal Job Profiles you prepared in Worksheet 4.4: Ideal Job Profile to Exercise 1.1: Known Likes and Dislikes and to your significant achievements in order of those most important to you or that you enjoyed the most. If there are any inconsistencies between these, you need to understand why and what they mean to your job search or career choice decision. Discuss this situation with your coach or mentor, and others in your life you can trust to "tell it like it is" and whose opinions you respect.

❑   7.   Go to your local library and obtain a library card. Inquire at the Reference Desk about printed and online resources that would be helpful for a job search or a career change.

❑   8.   Ask what information would be available to you through the library's online system from your home computer.

❑   9.   Research several companies, industries, and/or functions and start a list of companies comprising an "A" list, "B" list, and "C" list.

❑   10.   When you're familiar with the reference information available to you and able to perform research proficiently, prepare a checklist, detailed plan, or road map so you can work more efficiently on researching other companies.

❑   11.   Use your network of close contacts as a sounding board for ideas as you uncover more information about your career options. Even if you're just making a job change, use your network to help you gather information about specific companies or industries.

❑   12.   Complete an eighth achievement story.
Title: _____

❑   13.   Complete a ninth achievement story.
Title: _____

❑   14.   Complete a 10th achievement story.
Title: _____

❑   15.   Review the analysis of each of your achievement stories. Highlight skills and list them or skill statements in the right-hand column.

❑   16.   Review the top skills you identified in the latest achievement analyses and compare them to your preferred skills you completed in Worksheet 3.5: Your Preferred Skills.

Self-Employment Options

You can't know the best option without knowing all the options.

Chapter Overview

Many executives and managers think they can pursue self-employment at the same time they search for a new job. Those who try are usually unsuccessful at both. This chapter will help you:

» Decide whether self-employment is an option you should consider.

» Understand the different types of self-employment options available.

» Understand if you have what it takes to be successful at self-employment.

» Develop a business plan for your self-employment option.

The main sections in this chapter include:

» When you should consider self-employment.

» Basic considerations about self-employment.

» What are you going to sell?

» Who will be your customer or client?

» How will you brand your business?

» Do you have what it takes to be self-employed?

» Different types of self-employment.

» Creating a plan for your option.

» Milestones.

When You Should Consider Self-Employment

If you aren't finding personal, professional, or financial satisfaction in your current job, the first few chapters helped you reassess your values, goals, personality type, skills, strengths, and what you're passionate about. In Chapter 4, you looked at how to make changes to another employer, field, or industry. If you're still uncertain about whether another job is the right direction your career should take, it's time to explore your self-employment options.

In a robust, growing economy, continuing permanent employment for all may be possible. In recessionary times or even during a sluggish economic environment, however, permanent employment for the middle-aged who are looking for a new opportunity becomes increasingly more difficult as they grow older.

Referring to my "A Shared Experience" in Chapter 4 (page 66), you may not notice that doors are closing if you aren't looking for another job. However, you need to be aware that they are, even if you're happily employed. It's all about the general perception of older workers and has nothing to do with your capabilities. If you're a CEO with a strong track record of success, you're somewhat insulated because your achievements demonstrate what you can do, and your reputation and contacts will enable you to find another opportunity more readily than those who report to you.

If you're below the CEO level and middle-aged, employers consider whether younger candidates could be a replacement. They will compare your salary to a younger worker's, think about how many more years of work they can rely on from you, and how much more you'll cost them in health insurance than a younger worker would.

If you doubt that employers make these considerations, you only have to talk to others who lost their jobs from "restructurings" that eliminated positions held by older workers. The increasing competitiveness of lower-cost countries and what I call the Wal-Martization of American business will continue to place downward pressure on companies to cut costs to remain competitive—or even just to remain in business.

I could spend several paragraphs explaining why employers shouldn't look at it this way. The reality is they do, and neither governmental restrictions, nor you or I, are going to change their thinking. The point is you need to think about it and prepare for alternatives.

If you're middle-aged and in transition and you're not getting interviews, or you're getting interviews but not offers, you may want to explore self-employment.

Basic Considerations About Self-Employment

When considering self-employment, I can't overemphasize *the more you know, the better.* You can never do enough research into self-employment.

If you're leaving employment after a long career, you've probably developed a set of skills or gained knowledge or experience that would be helpful to others. You may have left your last employer with a cash settlement that you might want to use as a springboard to finance a new business. You may even be considering a business in which you're not totally familiar, but you know you can use your skills to develop it.

When starting a new venture, keep in mind the following six keys to a successful business:

1. **Need.** Be certain you fill a need or resolve a pain.

2. **Niche.** Be clear about who your target market is. The narrower you define your niche, the better others will recognize who needs you and be able to refer them to you.

3. **Brand.** You already have a brand. Others who know you well know what it is. Ask them to describe their perception of your brand. Build on that. Don't try to create a new one.

4. **Passion.** You must be passionate about what you do, and others must see it.

5. **Money.** Know your value to others and how you will earn it.

6. **Team.** Build relationships and affiliations with others. Be a resource to them, and use them as a resource for you. Make sure your family is on your team and supports you.

What Are You Going to Sell?

What you sell depends on the type of business you decide to start. One of the most common choices for executives is some sort of consultancy that uses the skills, experience, and contacts they've built over a long career. It may also incorporate a product with which they consider themselves to be an expert.

Similar to a 30-second message you would use for a job search, you'll need to describe what you're selling in a way that others will instantly understand it and be able to decide if it might be appropriate for them.

Think about it as a pain that you resolve for another. Be it a personal or business issue, your message needs to address how you resolve or overcome that pain. Purchasers of business services or products seldom purchase a service or buy a product because it would be *nice to have*, they *could use it*, or they *might want it.* They purchase services or products they recognize they need, or they make these purchases because sellers have convinced them of their need.

You may have great skills and experience that made you successful in your career, but what you're selling today also must be something that's in demand today. For example, if you gained your expertise at developing and marketing VHS-based products internationally, you would have to update that experience to a market that now uses CDs, DVDs, and Blu-ray Discs. You would then need to become an expert with the changes taking place caused by wireless technology, and with whatever technology that follows that.

One of the ironies of moving from employment at a company to self-employment and trying to market your skills and experiences is that potential customers may associate your expertise with yesterday's services or products. Unless you have a way, the desire, and the means to keep current, your expertise may become obsolete sooner than if you had remained employed.

Who Will Be Your Customer or Client?

Vance Caesar, PhD, a noted executive coach and professor, refers to the process of defining your target customer by describing your "Stick Figure." To help you understand this concept, go to any large bookstore and look at magazines on the rack. Pick a few and ask yourself, who is the "Stick Figure" who would read this? As an example, describe the target audience "Stick Figure" for *Seventeen*. It's probably a fashion-conscious, 12- to 17-year-old girl who lives in a middle- to upper-middle-class household and who wants to be seen as being "totally with it" and one of the "in crowd."

The "Stick Figure" is important to *Seventeen* because it informs the publisher of the best place to sell the magazine, how to market it, what stories and articles would be of interest to the person with that profile, what companies would pay to advertise to reach that market, what products they would feature, and so forth. Try to describe the "Stick Figure" of readers of *Field and Stream, Sports Illustrated*, and the *Wall Street Journal*. Wal-Mart and Nordstrom have widely divergent but very clear "Stick Figures," which are significant factors in their success. Macy's and Sears continue to struggle partly because they have not created a clear image of their target customer. Though these organizations may think they have clearly identified their customer, it's not clear to the customers who these organizations want to shop at their stores.

Define your target market precisely because what you sell, how you market it, and how you communicate it to others must enable them to have a clear picture of your customer or client and know whom to refer to you.

A Shared Experience

When writing this book, I had the image of a 49-year-old male executive who wants to take control of his job search. He may also be considering career options. He earns a six-figure income, may be "in transition" and having difficulty, or would like to make a job or career change but doesn't know how to go about it without compromising his current job.

Everything I write in this book is with that image in mind, so I don't try to be everything to everyone. A 20-year-old recent graduate looking for his first serious job out of college will find this book helpful, but he will need to adapt some of the material to recognize his limited work experience. I describe my targeted audience in the Introduction to this book. If you fit this profile, you don't have to worry about how to apply the content to you. I wrote it specifically with you in mind.

Although I didn't initially consider 30-year-olds, I have had several clients in their early- to mid-30s in executive or management positions who didn't earn six-figure incomes and still found the process described in this book directly relevant to their situation. Several of them said they didn't want to wait until they're 49 to figure out what to do with the rest of their lives. They want to do that when they have a better chance of making the change they want. I wish I had that vision in my early 30s!

How Will You Brand Your Business?

Closely aligned with determining your "Stick Figure," you need to brand yourself and your business. When you've determined what you're selling and to whom, your next task is to decide how you're going to tell others what you do, why it's needed, and what sets you apart from others.

Your verbal and written communication needs to set a style consistent with your service or product, as well as your customer or client. Branding your business is not creating a nice visual image that's colorful, flashy, and catchy, but more about creating an image in someone's mind that's consistent with the product or service you offer.

When you buy a BMW, you aren't buying just a car—you're buying "the ultimate driving machine." They reinforce their emphasis on engineering and road-handling by focusing their marketing message on the driving capabilities of the car and the driving experience of owning a BMW. They don't focus on cup holders (a frequent complaint of BMW owners!), the size of the glove compartment, or electronic gizmos. They don't show how easy it is to park; they show how well it handles on the road.

Your brand is not what YOU think it is.
It is what OTHERS think it is.

If you want others to perceive your brand accurately, you must be sure that your printed business card, your verbal business card, your letterhead, your brochures, your proposals, and your products and services have a consistent message that is clear to others. A good book on this subject is *The 22 Immutable Laws of Branding* by Laura and Al Ries (Harper Business, 2002).

New businesses often have difficulty trying to identify what makes their business unique. This is particularly true if you're considering consulting or coaching. People want to know why they should use you and what sets you apart from others. Don't look at others who are in the field to find out what separates you from them. It isn't about them; it's all about you. Your skills, experience, and knowledge, and how you interact with others make you unique. Focus on what you bring to the table, not what others bring.

Do You Have What It Takes to Be Self-Employed?

Here are the 10 most important characteristics you need to be successful in self-employment:

1. Organization.
2. Common sense.
3. Business sense.
4. Enthusiasm.
5. Self-motivation.
6. Commitment.
7. Financial awareness.
8. Business development.
9. Independence.
10. Support.

Let's look at each of these characteristics in more detail.

1. Organization

Organizational skills are essential. You'll have primary responsibility for organizing the business structure, making banking arrangements, developing marketing material, getting business letterhead and business cards, office facilities, and administrative and technical support. You'll also be responsible for developing the business, keeping in touch with potential customers, maintaining computers, telecommunications and office equipment, keeping accounting records, filing tax returns, and so forth.

If you thought you were proficient at multitasking in your last job yet depended on a support network, you'll find being self-employed has its own set of challenges. If you know your organizational skills are lacking and have always relied on an assistant for the "detail" work, you'll find success in self-employment very difficult without that support. A spouse can often help, but, if not, consider finding a "virtual" support person.

If you're not computer-literate and don't understand basic software such as Microsoft Word, Excel, and PowerPoint, you'll be at a serious disadvantage. If you've relied on someone else to send your e-mail or to print your e-mail so you can read it, self-employment may not be a successful option. Being unfamiliar with computers and the Internet will put you at a disadvantage in almost any occupation you choose. If you aren't proficient using computers, e-mail, and the Internet, you'll need to pay someone to do it for you and hope he knows enough to alert you to what you need to know.

If organization isn't one of your strengths, you may find it difficult to develop new business or expand. In the early stages, your sole source of new business may come from people who already know you, but, if they perceive you're not well organized, you won't get the referrals to sustain and grow your business.

If this is not one of your strengths and you still want to pursue self-employment, consider working with or affiliating with others who can provide that support. Clients will soon know if you lack organization, so it's in your best interest to align yourself with those who can provide that support. You might not want to do this permanently, but consider it as a stepping stone arrangement until you can develop a business base and have a better idea about what you can do.

2. Common Sense

This is a difficult area to assess, but, if you're honest with yourself, you're probably the best person to make that assessment. Being self-employed, you probably have (and need!) some knowledge of every aspect of your business, but you don't need to be an expert in all things. This means that your common sense has to help you to make decisions in those areas where you lack expertise but where, nevertheless, you have to make a decision.

Take a cue from angel investors who look to avoid the 85-percenters and the 105-percenters. The 85-percenters are those who can never quite seem to gather all the information they need to make a decision, and the 105-percenters always need just a little more information to make sure they make the right decision.

You'll need to make decisions on the fly, without a lot of detailed analysis, research, or input from colleagues who have expertise in their area. This type of decision-making will be a crucial part of your business risk. The trick is getting the balance right—getting just enough information to be able to make the right decision. You may make many decisions in a new business that, with hindsight, will be wrong. With common sense, you'll learn not to make the same ones again and will find that you make more good decisions than bad ones.

3. Business Sense

A business consultancy exists solely because the person or people providing the service have skills, knowledge, or expertise needed by someone else. If you have recognized expertise in an area needed by others, you have a starting point.

Starting a new business in an area you don't know or in which you don't already have an expertise can be a blueprint for disaster. If you choose to start such a business, you have to spend time learning it. Then you must become proficient in it. Finally, if you're able to hang on long enough financially, you might develop expertise that others recognize and for which they will seek you out.

If you're considering buying a business where you think you can use your skills and expertise more effectively than the current owners and make it more profitable, spend time talking to competitors about the business, hire an industry consultant, subscribe to and research industry or trade publications, and attend trade shows to learn more about it. Another alternative is to work in the business to learn it, even if you have to work for "peanuts." You may find that knowing the business itself may be more important than the skills and expertise you bring to the business. Unsuspecting business buyers often find the business they just bought is in a declining market, or that environmental regulations are making the business unprofitable. You may even find that you will need to implement a new technology to sustain the business, but the business base won't support the investment or the new technology may change the nature of the business in a way you don't like.

> **A Shared Experience**
>
> I know a couple of very successful restaurant owners who learned the trade from waiting and busing tables, washing dishes, helping cooks in the kitchen, and bartending at other restaurants. This was a very low-cost way to learn the business, understand it from the perspective of the workers in the trenches, and decide whether they had the passion to make their new venture successful.
>
> Their experience also enabled them to know where problems were most likely to occur, to learn the "tricks of the trade," and to recognize "red herrings."

4. Enthusiasm

To be successful in any small business, you must have enthusiasm for the work and its products or services. That enthusiasm also must be evident to others. If you like the work but are naturally a dour individual, you'll send the wrong message. Every person you meet is a potential customer or can recommend you to others. Your attitude and your passion also affect your employees, whose support you need and who can put out an upbeat message to customers.

5. Self-Motivation

A small business is dependent on the driving force of its owner. You must have an inner drive that sets the pace for the business and others in it. Opportunity exists, but only if you take advantage of it. You will be the driving force that develops new business. If the opportunity is there and you fail to recognize it, your business will suffer. If you see something wrong in your business, you are the person who must take action and see that it gets fixed and doesn't happen again. If your employees don't have proper training, you have to recognize it and arrange it or you will be the one to suffer.

The biggest need in any new venture is developing new business. You can't rely on others to get the business for you. It will become one of your most important jobs.

6. Commitment

A small business takes total commitment and dedication to be successful. It's important to stay healthy and to allow time for your family. Choosing to spend your time on personal matters or at the golf course will impair the development of your business. Customers or clients want to see total dedication to their work or assignment when you work for them. If not, there are others vying for it who are prepared to put in the effort customers want to see.

Don't expect to start every workday by eating a leisurely breakfast while you read the paper, then walking the dog before getting started around midmorning. Even if you get charged up during the day and are prepared to work past midnight, that's not the work ethic that fits most business situations. If you have others working for you, they'll look to you to set the standard for them.

7. Financial Awareness

How will you price your services? If you are considering a consultancy, will you charge an hourly, daily, or weekly rate, or a fixed price for the project? Do you charge on a retainer or contingency arrangement? Do you price your services low, at market rates, or at a premium? What are market rates? Do you use price to differentiate yourself from the competition to get started?

What costs will you incur to start? Do you rent a full-service office or a small stand-alone office, or work from home? Do you purchase or lease furniture and equipment? Do you charge your client for travel costs, telephone, fax, and printing? How much should you spend for brochures, letterhead, and business cards?

All these issues will depend on the type of business you're considering. The best way to answer most of them is to conduct research of others who are in the business you want to get into. What do they do (from a pricing standpoint)? Why did they decide to do it that way? Did they consider other ways and, if so, what were they? How do they enlist support from others when they need it? Would they consider using your services if they needed help? Would they consider working with you if you needed help? How could you best complement each other?

Budget your cash flow on a monthly basis for the next two years, because you'll need to see the income stream that's required to cover your monthly costs and to sustain your lifestyle. Forecasting your expenses in a business you don't know may be the easy part. Forecasting a revenue stream from it, however, will be tougher.

8. Business Development

This is probably the biggest unknown and the most difficult to estimate. You may have a skill or some expertise that your former employer still needs. They may be willing to use you full-time as a consultant to do what they formerly paid you to do as an employee. It's very risky to let one customer dominate your business, no matter what the relationship. Actively pursue developing business from others.

There will be a very strong temptation to say yes when someone wants your consultancy services full-time. Understand, however, that follow-on work comes from the business development efforts you put in many months before.

Leave at least one day a week available (preferably not a Monday or Friday) to do marketing and new business development. Most clients are aware of your need to continue developing business. If you don't stick to this philosophy rigorously, you may have long periods when you don't have any work.

9. Independence

A frequent complaint from people who have come out of a large organization and gone into consulting is the lack of collegiality in the business. You'll do most things yourself. You'll initiate contacts, type letters, send e-mail, prepare proposals, edit and proof what you wrote, go to the office supply store and the post office, do the work, deliver reports, make statements of recommendation or opinions, develop and nurture relationships with customers, give satisfaction and, hopefully, get paid. You'll need to feel comfortable doing all these things alone.

Although you may be working as part of a client's (or even your former employer's) team, you're always an outside member of the team. If you're a consultant at a client's office doing work, you may feel like part of their team. However, when lunchtime comes, be prepared to be on your own. This can be an unsettling feeling for someone who has always worked in a team environment.

Consultants often form relationships with others so they have someone to turn to when they need help in an area where their own skills are limited. As a consultant, even you will probably need to consult others.

10. Support

The most important item is last. Your family needs to understand what you want to do and why. They must see how important it is to you and how much you want it to succeed. You know it won't be easy on you or your family, but, with their understanding and support, you have a good chance at success. Without it, everyone loses. If your spouse or family doesn't support you, do you really want to jeopardize that relationship to try this option?

If they're concerned about your potential failure, make sure you've involved them in the entire process before you reach your decision. Sometimes all that's needed is for them to feel comfortable that you're doing the research to make sure your ultimate decision is based on merit and not some vague feeling you have.

Different Types of Self-Employment

The most common types of self-employment executives and mid-career managers pursue are the following:

» Consulting and coaching.

» Starting a company.

» Franchise.

» Joining a start-up or early-stage company.

» Buying an existing company.

» Writing and/or speaking.

» Teaching and training.

» Turning a hobby into a business.

» Doing what you always wanted to do when the time was right.

I'll cover consulting and coaching first and in more detail, as that's the most frequent type of self-employment senior-level individuals choose.

Consulting and Coaching

Consulting is where you use your knowledge and expertise to provide a solution to a client's problem. You usually have a deliverable and provide it in the form of a document and/or an implementation plan.

Coaching is where you use your knowledge and expertise to help a client identify and take actions that enables him to accomplish one or more objectives. The major difference between consulting and coaching is that the coach doesn't have the answers; the client does. The coach's task is to help the client find them and then hold him accountable to achieve his objective(s). People in this field call themselves executive coaches, career coaches, leadership development coaches, or other coaching terms that give an indication of their area of expertise.

There are no governmental regulations that cover consultants and coaches because they are not a well-defined group like doctors, accountants, and lawyers.

Many, however, belong to professional associations that require their members to subscribe to a code of ethics or standards of practice.

Consultants and coaches who work alone usually do so as a sole proprietorship. They may operate under a name different from their individual name, in which case, regional laws may require they file a DBA (doing business as) notice in a local or regional newspaper. If your municipality requires business licenses, as most do, they will be scanning the local papers looking for new businesses that need to register and pay a license fee.

If consultants or coaches work in a group, they usually structure the organization as a partnership or corporation, such as limited liability partnership (LLP), limited liability corporation (LLC), Subchapter S-Corporation, professional corporation (PC), or C-Corporation. These types of organizations require registering in the state where they operate and with the IRS. Consultancies typically engage individual consultants on a contract basis, referred to as a "1099 employee" (after the IRS reporting form) rather than employ them.

Because there are no academic qualifications to be a consultant, or professional associations like the American Bar Association (ABA) or the American Institute of Certified Public Accountants (AICPA) that regulate, test, and qualify members, seek out a professional association that has a chapter in your area which would be appropriate for you. They can be an excellent way to find out more about the business you're considering, meet others who are already involved in it, and network on how to develop your business. Occasionally, they can be a source of business.

Starting a Company

Choosing to start a small business generally takes the form of making or selling a product or offering a service. The business may be anything, such as:

- A store or shop selling retail products or services to consumers.
- A niche business selling products direct to other businesses, offering something that more established competitors can't or won't provide. Examples are distributors, resellers, or value-added retailers (VARs), such as those who offer additional support accompanying the purchase of computer hardware or software.
- An owner-managed manufacturing or service business.

People often start small businesses to capitalize on a feature, service, or segment that their former employer wasn't providing effectively, efficiently, or at all. Every recruiter and outplacement consultant I've met who started a business says he learned the trade while working for a larger organization. They left to "start" their own businesses and took many of their clients with them.

Ninety percent of all businesses in the United States are small operations, most of which were started with the owners' knowledge or experience gained from previous employment. You'll improve your success in a small business if you've already worked in the industry, have a thorough understanding of it, have a fat Rolodex of names and addresses of potential customers or clients, and know the future industry trends.

Start by discussing your ideas with your spouse, your mentor, and someone who knows the industry. Visit your local library and review the reference material on the type of business you're considering, review industry publications, and search the Internet for information on industry trends.

Look to bring in another person to help you get started. If you choose to bring in a relative or a friend, be aware there's a higher risk he won't work out than if you brought in someone you didn't know but who had skills and experience that complement yours.

Franchise

Becoming a franchisee enables you to participate in a business that has a proven business model in the marketplace. A franchise is generally a retail consumer business. Examples of some of the many better-known franchises include Baskin Robbins, Burger King, ChemDry, Dunkin Donuts, Subway, and The UPS Store (previously Mail Boxes Etc.).

Some advantages of a franchise include:

◆ A proven business idea that is successfully operating elsewhere.

◆ Results can be measured, quantified, and extrapolated to another location.

◆ A protected business area where others within the same group cannot compete.

◆ The franchiser helps in setting up, training, and providing specialist skills.

◆ Standardized successful business practices create name recognition.

◆ Being part of a large group enhances company image and controls costs.

◆ The franchisor provides technical expertise and leads innovation.

Some disadvantages include:

◆ You will be tied to a branded image without direct control over the quality of other franchisees.

◆ You will be required to put up an up-front cash outlay for the franchise, business assets, and supplies.

◆ You may need to make an additional significant financial investment to cover a rental commitment and initial working capital and may need to obtain financing for this on your own.

◆ You will be required to pay a periodic fee plus a percentage of your gross receipts.

◆ You typically must purchase all your supplies from the franchisor at prices they set.

◆ You will have to depend on the franchisor to implement new technology.

Starting a franchise usually involves your making a substantial up-front cash outlay and obtaining a bank-financed loan. Your initial out-of-pocket cash investment generally covers the franchise fee, the cost of leasing premises, furnishing an office, buying equipment, and preparing promotional material. The additional financing is required to cover working capital until the business becomes cash-positive.

The franchisor will usually send you to a training course (at your expense). You then work with another franchisee for a short period to acclimate you to the business. The franchisor then helps you set up and start operating your own franchise.

Joining a Start-Up or Early-Stage Company

This is a common situation in the technology sector where one or more individuals decide to launch a new business based on an idea they have or on a new technology, often unproven. There could be opportunities for a senior executive to join the company to fill out the management team so it can secure seed funding to launch operations or to obtain angel funding to take the company to a higher level.

Early participants usually work for equity, not salary. If you join a very early-stage company with some financial backing, salaries for executives typically will be limited to the mid-five figures. If you come from a large company background, you'll probably encounter some reluctance to consider you because too many executives with this background fail to adapt to a small company with limited resources.

Buying an Existing Company

If you're looking to buy an existing business that you don't know very much about, be very careful that you read the real signs of why the seller wants to "retire" (often the stated reason). It may be because it's a dying industry, the equipment is obsolete or at the end of its useful life, a new technology could potentially overtake the business, the owner is unable to find and retain experienced labor at a competitive price, cheaper foreign manufacturers are taking over the industry, or potential laws may require the business to relocate or incur significant costs to meet new environmental requirements.

Talk to your banker about the opportunity you're considering, even if you don't plan to involve them in the purchase. They may know something about the industry from other customers that could be helpful to you.

In a small business, you're likely to have employees who can do some tasks that you either can't handle or aren't good at handling. As with a consultancy, you'll need all 10 personal characteristics to be successful in a small business. If your business is to prosper and grow, one of your biggest challenges will be to hire, lead, manage, train, motivate, and retain the *right* people.

You can find businesses for sale by contacting business brokers in your area. Your banker, accountant, and attorney should also be able to lead you to the best sources for finding companies for sale.

Writing and/or Speaking

Becoming an author and/or speaker is a business that will require a long lead time to develop material and obtain speaking gigs. Writing articles for publication in trade journals and a local newspaper is a good place to start. Writing an article and trying to get it published in a major newspaper will be a challenge because most papers will only accept articles from syndicated writers. They don't want to be sued for something you said that offended someone or turned out to be incorrect.

If you have a passion to write a book, be forewarned that it can easily take years of dedication. This book took me several years to complete. Admittedly, I didn't spend every waking moment on it, but it was a major focus during that time.

Start by writing articles for trade magazines and local newspapers and see what reaction you get. Using a professional editor to review and edit your work will enhance the success of getting your work published. If you have some initial success at this, consider writing a smaller version on the subject you want to focus on and have it self-published. You can then use that book to help you get speaking engagements as an author and sell copies at events. This can help you to establish your credibility and give you confidence.

Teaching and Training

I find many individuals want to leave the corporate life and give something back by teaching or training. If you have an advanced degree, you can pursue teaching at a major university. If you don't, there are many other universities and colleges that would welcome you for your expertise and even pay you (but not much).

Inquire at local universities and community colleges about extension courses they offer adults who want to get specific training in a subject that isn't an academic program and doesn't lead to a degree. You'll find courses covering many of the nuts and bolts issues of doing business ranging from accounting for non-financial business people, preparing business plans, preparing marketing plans, film production, import/export regulations, and so forth. More than likely, they'll have a program that covers what you are already an expert at, and they may have a need for someone like you to teach it.

Training consultants work for companies, universities, and colleges. Refer to the section on consulting and coaching for suggestions. If you want to pursue this, look into joining the American Society for Training and Development (ASTD; *www.astd.com*), a national organization. Get involved in a chapter near you, and network to find out if this option is one you want to pursue.

Turning a Hobby Into a Business

If you don't want to continue doing what you've been doing in the corporate world and aren't motivated to find a business that capitalizes on your work skills and experience, look inward and ask yourself what you enjoy doing when not working. People often create a profitable new career by turning a hobby into a business. Many of these new careers require skills with tangibles, like woodworking, metal working, ceramics, painting, or buying and selling antiques.

Start by talking to others who are in the business of doing what you think you'd like to do. (I cover how you can gather this information in more detail in Chapter 8.) If you doubt that you're expert enough to convert your hobby to a business, talk to people who are doing it as a business to find out if it's an option you want to pursue. If it might be, ask if they would let you work for them for a while so you can understand the business better. Offer to work for free if they're not willing to pay you. If they see that this new career is right for you, they may ask you to join them on a permanent basis or collaborate with you on some basis, if you want to specialize in something unique but complementary to their business.

Doing What You Always Wanted to Do When the Time Was Right

Suppose you don't have a hobby that you think is convertible to a business, but you've always had a burning desire to do something else, if only the time would present itself. Without knowing what options you would consider, all I can do is give you some examples of what others have done so you can see the potential.

For example, if you take time off to do some traveling, think about how you could make it interesting to others. Journalize your trip and write an article or story about it. Focus on one of the countries you visited. Focus on some aspect of people or their life, and compare and contrast that to the people in each of the other countries you visit. If you say that you don't know what would be of interest to readers, don't worry about that. If it really interests you, you'll be passionate about it, and it will be of interest to others.

Consider starting or joining a nonprofit organization where you can add a service or capability that you know others need. Look for corporate or government grants or get a company to sponsor the program. Talk to people in government about programs that aren't working very well and how you might be able to help.

Board Service

Executives often ask about how they get on boards, thinking it might be something they'd like to do after full-time employment, so I'll briefly mention board service, even though it isn't self-employment.

If you're interested in serving on a public or private company board and aren't already on a board, you'll find this a very difficult option. In years past, the CEO and chairman of the board, typically the same person, chose board members from his personal contacts and colleagues whom he knew would be generally supportive.

Since the introduction of the Sarbanes-Oxley legislation in 2002, there's a more transparent approach to selecting directors. Although public companies are the focus of the Sarbanes-Oxley legislation, private companies and not-for-profit associations are beginning to feel some of the impact of Sarbanes-Oxley on their boards.

If you're interested in getting on a board, ask others who are on boards about their experiences of being a board member. For guidance on how to get your first seat on a corporate board, read *Into The Boardroom* by D.K. Light and K.S. Pushor (Beavers Pond Press, 2002).

Creating a Plan for Your Option

The above self-employment options include some guidance on how to get information that might help you decide whether you want to consider any of them further. Keeping that information in mind, go to *www.ExecGlobalNet.com*, click on the **Career Center**, and download "Resource 4.1: Where to Get Additional Information." You can use the summary to help you do your research depending on the self-employment option you want to pursue.

Look for books that are devoted to the specific type of business you're considering. Contact Service Corps of Retired Executives (SCORE; *www.score.org*), an organization funded by the U.S. Government Small Business Administration (SBA) that offers free services to individuals who want to start a business.

Starting a new business without a plan is like driving with your eyes closed.

Before you begin to launch a new business, you must prepare a business plan. This is a crucial step if you're considering starting a business, whether the new business will be a sole proprietorship or you include others. Having a plan won't guarantee success, nor will the lack of one guarantee failure. What it will do is to help you decide whether this is a good option for you and whether it's financially viable. If you need bank financing to commence operations or to fund operations until you're cash positive, the bank will require a business plan.

A business plan will help you through the thought process of starting a new venture to assure you've covered the significant points. You can find good examples of how to prepare a business plan at these three Websites: *www.inc.com*, Guy Kawasaki's *www.garage.com*, and the SBA's Website, *www.sba.gov*. When you've done your research and think you've found what you want to do in your new self-employment career, use the following sections as headers for your business plan. I've included an explanation of each section.

I recommend you start by preparing a two-page Executive Summary of your plan. If you can't prepare a summary at this stage, you probably need to spend more time thinking through your potential business. When you complete your summary, prepare your plan by covering the following sections:

1. What Is the Business?

Describe the business similarly to a verbal business card. If you met someone who asked about your business, what would you tell them? Don't limit your discussion to just the 30-second pitch. That will be in your Executive Summary. But in this section, describe it in a way that someone who doesn't know anything about the business would understand it, at least conceptually. Don't be vague to "protect your business concept." If you can't grab the interest of others in this first section, you should reconsider whether you really have a business.

2. Who Needs the Business and Why?

Describe why your target customer needs your product or service. What need is not being met that your business will fulfill? What pain exists now that your business will resolve or minimize? This section must support the first section, and it must describe a compelling reason why there's a need for the business.

3. Industry/Market Characteristics and Size

Describe the industry or market. What's the current state of the industry or market? How mature is it (the market, not the customer)? How does it work? Who are the competitors? How big is your target market (the people who are most likely to purchase your product or service)? What's the market potential? Describe if it's fragmented and, if so, why? How will technology influence your product or service? How will it affect your target market? What's the labor pool that supports the industry? Why are others who are currently in the market not meeting the need?

4. Operating Strategy

Describe how you'll operate the business: Will it be a partnership, sole proprietorship, limited liability company, franchise, and so on? If others will be involved, what will their roles be? If you have individuals who have agreed to participate, how does their background support their role in the business? Include brief summaries of the bios of the management team. Put resumes in an appendix.

Prepare a timetable to show when you start, what needs doing by whom and when, when others need to come into the business, and what their roles will be.

5. Marketing Strategy

How will you brand your business so that you have something unique that sets you apart from your competition? Describe how you'll promote the business and develop new customers. How will competitors currently in the market react/respond to your business? Describe why you can do something that others haven't done and how you can protect/insulate your business from competition. If there are no or only limited barriers to entry, what will keep others from taking your business? What's your Plan B?

A Shared Experience
A colleague of mine, Margaret Meloni, a former IT project manager, left the corporate world because she found her real passion was coaching project managers. She spent considerable time developing her client base, but found the process very slow. She started teaching project management skills at an extension program with a major Southern California university. The pay wasn't the motivator, but the contacts she makes teaching her course has elevated her exposure in the community and has had a significance impact on her ability to connect with people in her specialty who are looking for a coach.

Include estimated sales by month and how you expect to generate sales (direct mail, telephoning, direct visits, and so forth). When making sales estimates, don't use market-penetration-percentage assumptions in your calculations. Use a bottom-up approach, such as how many widgets you will sell by month, and how you support that rationale. The more realistic your assumptions, the more believable they will be to others who need to make decisions about you and the likely success of your venture.

If you're looking for an investment from others, you'll enhance the potential success of your endeavor in the eyes of potential investors if you can get some form of written confirmation from potential customers. Lenders or investors don't take "guesstimates" very seriously.

6. Financial Forecast

Prepare a financial forecast, showing revenue, costs, and capital purchases separately, net cash flow, and the remaining cash balance or cash requirement. Indicate whether you're using an accrual or cash basis of accounting. If you aren't looking for outside investors, prepare a three-year forecast showing the first two years monthly, and annually for the third year. If you'll be looking for outside investors, prepare a five-year forecast, showing the first two years monthly, and annually for the third, fourth, and fifth years.

Explain how you intend to support the startup costs. If you'll need outside financing, what are your plans to raise it? Prepare supporting notes explaining assumptions for sales recognition and reasons for each significant element of cost or capital asset expenditure. Include only an annual summary for each three- or five-year period in the body of your business plan, and put all detailed monthly schedules and assumptions in an appendix.

Putting Your Business Plan Together

A comprehensive business plan should be no longer than 25 pages. Put all supporting information, schedules, and so forth in a separate appendix. When you've finished your plan, revise your Executive Summary to reflect the information you collected from your research.

When writing your business plan, avoid making sweeping, generalized statements about market size. Be realistic, and err on the side of conservatism rather than glowing potential. If you use industry-standard acronyms, include descriptions of what they mean, as others who read your plan may not be familiar with the terms.

Don't be a name-dropper and infer that Bill Gates or Cisco is a potential associate unless you have a relationship with them and have an indication of their interest in participating. Avoid superlative adjectives because they're judgmental and not objective, and the reader may conclude that you're padding your plan.

Focus on the positive aspects of your business, not the negative aspects of others. It's acceptable to make a comparison to another organization that doesn't do exactly what you do.

Review your Executive Summary and, if appropriate, your business plan with a trusted advisor, your mentor, or someone you think would understand your business and the market, and will give you honest feedback. If you don't know anyone who fits that description, talk to your accountant or attorney. They can usually refer you to someone they know who can help.

When you've completed your reviews and modified your plan and/or summary as necessary, send your Executive Summary to those you want to consider participating or investing in your venture. Investors won't be interested in reviewing your entire business plan unless your Executive Summary elicits an interest in them.

Investors

The management team typically provides initial funding for start-ups and early-stage companies. As they either run out of money or need additional funds, they turn to the three "F's": family, friends, and fools (a typical reference to this stage of funding). If the business has raised an acceptable amount of money (as defined by later-stage investors) from these sources, the business can then look outside its circle of personal contacts for investors with no connection to the business or the management team.

This next stage will either be a corporate backer, an angel, or angel groups who pool resources to invest in promising technology. Angel investors typically don't invest unless the company is already in business, has a prototype or proven business concept, or has established a compelling reason to believe the entrepreneur, such as an academic who has done some proof of concept. In addition, angel investors don't typically invest in companies unless there's a quick exit strategy (usually within two years), which typically means that a corporate investor will participate, or one or more venture capitalists (VC) will provide follow-on funding.

Most VCs aren't interested in business models that don't have the prospect of hundreds of millions of dollars of revenue within five years. VCs hope to be fabulously successful 10 percent of the time, and that one in 10 will make up for all the others that fall flat. If your idea doesn't have the potential to generate hundreds of millions of dollars within five years, you should probably explore other types of funding, such as corporate investors or a strategic alliance with a corporate alliance partner. Keep in mind venture capitalists fund only about 3 percent to 7 percent of all new businesses.

To find out what other entrepreneurs are doing to raise money in your area, contact attorneys, accountants, commercial insurance agents, and recruiters for recommendations on where you can network to make the best connections for your new business.

✔️ Milestones

The following milestones recap what you need to do to complete this chapter. Include those items you are unable to complete in your summary-level open-items list.

Check off the following when you have completed each item:

❑ 1. Are you clear about the specific reasons why you want to consider self-employment?

Describe your reasons.

_____

_____

❑ 2. Do you have the personal characteristics indicative of those who are successful in self-employment? If not, how will you compensate for the ones you don't have?

Describe the characteristics you don't have, and indicate how you will compensate for them.

_____

_____

❑ 3. What is the service or business that you plan to offer through self-employment?

_____

_____

❑ 4. Describe your target customer or client.

_____

_____

❑ 5. Explain why your target customer or client needs your services or products. (What's their pain that you can resolve, or what unfulfilled need do they have that you can satisfy?)

_____

❑ 6. Describe how you envision branding your business.

_____

_____

_____

❑ 7. You are prepared and willing to invest the mental and physical effort you'll need to stay the course to build a business. This can take up to two years. You've discussed your thoughts with your spouse, partner, advisor, confidante, and/or coach and have their encouragement and agreement to support your decision.

❑ 8. You have investigated and defined the appropriate business structure your new business will take (corporation, sole proprietor, partnership, and so on).

❑ 9. You've prepared a preliminary Executive Summary for your business and discussed it with your spouse, partner, advisor, confidante, accountant, lawyer and/or coach, as appropriate. You've prepared a list of their questions or concerns and you plan to resolve those you need to clarify when you prepare your business plan.

❑ 10. Sketch out your business plan and be ready to complete it when you've finished this book.

As you read the next chapter on resumes, think about the concepts as they relate to your business. You probably won't prepare a resume, but you will need a bio, and you may need a brochure, depending on the business you start.

Complete the remainder of this book, paying close attention to Chapter 8 (networking) and Chapter 9 (communicating). They'll help you be more successful whether you're looking for additional resources (financial or human) or you're trying to develop business. Chapter 10 (interviewing) will be helpful to you if you plan to interview others who will be joining your business.

Section III

Marketing Yourself Effectively: What, Why, and How

6 Resumes

I'll decide within 30 seconds whether to
continue reading your resume.

Chapter Overview

Your resume is a paradox. It won't get you a job, yet it's unlikely you'll get one without it. This chapter will reveal the purpose of your resume from a reader's perspective and help you prepare a resume that shows who you are, what you want, and why someone should consider you.

The main sections in this chapter include:

- ❧ The purpose and importance of your resume.
- ❧ How others will use your resume.
- ❧ The different resume formats you can use.
- ❧ Putting your resume together.
- ❧ Techniques for consultants and engineers.
- ❧ Milestones.

If you've ever gone to a bookstore to buy a book on resumes, you've probably left muttering to yourself, "How can there be so many books about resumes, and how do I choose the right one?"

Let's start by reviewing some of the more common *misperceptions* about resumes:

- ◆ There's one right way to prepare a resume that works for everybody.

- ◆ Resumes possess a magical ability to help you land the job of your dreams.

- ◆ Interviewers will have actually read your resume before they interview you.

" I THINK YOU WILL FIND IT EXTREMELY INTERESTING "

Illustration by Simon Meyrick-Jones.
Used with permission.

104

◆ You must have a resume to get a job. (This last one is not, as it might seem, a contradiction to the second sentence of this chapter.)

I'll deal with these misperceptions in this chapter.

The Purpose and Importance of Your Resume

Companies spend millions of dollars preparing brochures about the services or products they offer. If they designed their brochure to tell you *everything* about their company and the services or products they offer, it would be so lengthy you'd never read it—hence, the brochure wouldn't convince you to use their products or services.

To get you to read it, they keep it tightly focused on the main features, with just enough about the benefits of their product or service to entice you to contact them for details.

Your resume is like a brochure. It should focus on the main features and the benefits of hiring you. It should tell the reader just enough for them to want to know more. The analogy in the following figure will help you visualize the purpose of your resume. It illustrates how you might decide to buy a book compared to how a reader of your resume might decide to meet and/or interview you.

A Book From Your Perspective	Your Resume From an Employer's Perspective
Does the title and subtitle attract your attention?	Does the position and industry where she wants to work match what we want?
Does the table of contents, highlights, or testimonials suggest that this book might be what you're looking for?	Do her capabilities—skills and achievements—indicate she possesses the skills and experience that are of interest to us?
You buy the book and begin to read it. If it's well-written and holds your attention, you finish reading it.	We begin to read the rest of her resume. If it's well-written and holds our attention, we finish reading it.
You finish the book and conclude it was worth reading. You tell others positive things about it.	We like what we read in her resume and think we should meet and/or interview her. We may also tell others in the company positive things about her and share her resume with them for their opinions.

Using this approach to prepare your resume will be an extremely important step, because the information you develop and the way you present it in your resume will enable you to:

» Perfect your personal 30-second sales pitch—the "elevator speech"—so you tell others the same message that's in your resume.

» Focus on and confidently verbalize your key strengths, which are consistent with the three strongest skills you list on your resume.

» Tell credible and memorable achievement stories, which are consistent with what you describe in your resume and demonstrate the skills and experience you offer an employer.

» Exude a feeling of confidence knowing your resume is an accurate reflection and a powerful statement of what you want, can do, and have done, and is consistent with what you tell others.

» Affirm your chosen career objective (or highlight why you may need to consider other career options).

How Others Will Use Your Resume

Because you don't always know who will be reading your resume and what they will be looking for, here are four basic objectives of your resume:

1. Communicate what kind of a resource you can be to an employer.

2. Tell them enough about you to entice them to contact you for an interview or more details.

3. Provide a documentary statement supporting a decision to employ you.

4. Induce key people to pass your resume along to those who could consider employing you.

Next, let's look at how others will use your resume under different situations.

Situation 1

You send your resume to a recruiter or employer in response to an advertisement or a job posting on the Internet, or speculatively.

● Step 1. Your resume is used to screen you out.

The person who receives your resume, typically a junior-level clerical person, spends less than 30 seconds finding reasons *not* to consider you. For example, she can't understand what you want, your past experience isn't comparable with the position they have, your resume contains misspellings and grammatical errors, or it's too long or too busy.

❯ Step 2. Your resume is used to screen you in.

If you make it past the initial screening, someone with experience at reviewing resumes will quickly look at yours, looking for the skills, experience, education, and so forth they seek. If she doesn't *immediately* see what she wants, she'll screen you out.

❯ Step 3. Your resume is reviewed for specific skills and experience.
If you reach this stage, someone who knows more about what the employer wants will read your resume. The focus at this stage is to identify the strongest candidates with the industry-specific skills and experience the employer wants.

❯ Step 4. Your resume is used to facilitate an interview.

If you're among the top five to 10 candidates, you'll probably receive a phone call. You'll be asked about your skills, experience, education, and other specific job requirements.

Situation 2

You've approached a potential employer through one of your contacts. You've spoken with them about what you can do for them, and they ask for your resume.

❯ Your resume is used to facilitate an interview.

An employer reviews your resume, sees it supports what you told them, and arranges an interview.

Situation 3

You've had discussions with an employer you already know or through an introduction by one of your contacts.

❯ Your resume is used to substantiate a decision to employ you.

An employer is considering making you an offer but wants to support the decision by obtaining and checking the details in your resume. Or the employer may make you an offer contingent upon reviewing your resume and completing background checks.

Situation 4

Your resume is requested by someone you met through one of your contacts or from someone you met through networking.

❯ Your resume is used to make evaluations about you.

Others will use your resume to understand what you're seeking so they can match it with an appropriate opportunity, should they become aware of one. They may also forward your resume to someone else who may have or know of an opportunity.

The Different Resume Formats You Can Use

Knowing the purpose of your resume and understanding how others will use it gives you the background information you need to consider when deciding which format might work best for you. The four different resume formats are:

1. Targeted.

2. Functional.

3. Chronological.

4. Combination.

I'll review these formats over the next several pages, and provide the pros and cons of each from the perspective of employers and recruiters:

Targeted Resume

What's Unique About It

Begins with your skills, experience, and achievements as they relate to a specific company. You follow this with a summary of your employment history, education, and anything else you think might be of interest to the specific company.

When You Might Consider Using It

Can be effective when you know the position and company where you want to work, and you want to focus their attention on your skills, experience, and achievements relating to the position and their industry. Employers and recruiters accept the targeted format if you're making a classic vertical career progression or the employer has already made a decision to employ you. It can also work to your advantage when you don't want the reader to focus on your skills, experience, and achievements in a different industry.

Pros

You focus the readers' attention on the skills and experience that are relevant to the position, their industry, and their company. If you're changing industries, the targeted resume makes that change difficult to discern.

Cons

Some employers and recruiters don't like targeted resumes because it's difficult for them to match your skills, experience, and achievements with a specific employer. The targeted resume shows only your last position at each company, making it impossible for them to see your progression within each company. They know they'll have to talk to you to clarify your experience.

An example of a targeted resume is shown on page 111.

Functional Resume
What's Unique About It
Emphasizes your skills and experience by functional area, not by where you gained your skills and experience. Follow this with your work history in summary fashion.

When You Might Consider Using It
Can be effective when you're making an industry change and want to focus the reader's attention on specific skills and experience, such as if you have a technical background and want to bring out your non-technical (or soft) skills and achievements. Useful if you don't have a clear career path in one industry or if you're transitioning from a non-commercial type of employment, such as government or military, or you're returning to work after an extended leave of absence, such as caring for an ailing family member or raising children.

Pros
You focus on demonstrating to others the skills and experience you bring to the table by using memorable achievement stories that demonstrate what you've actually accomplished. You focus the readers' attention on what's most important about you and what you have achieved for others (and can do for them) and minimize when and where you did it.

Cons
Some recruiters and employers don't like functional resumes because it's difficult for them to match what you did, and when, with your employment history. They must contact you to get the additional information they need.

An example of a functional resume can be found on page 112.

Chronological Resume
What's Unique About It
Shows your work/career history in reverse chronological order, starting with your most recent position and working backward. Within each position, you describe what you did and what you accomplished.

When You Might Consider Using It
An ideal choice for those making a classic vertical career progression within one industry.

Pros
The chronological resume format is the most widely used. Employers and recruiters prefer it because they can quickly focus on and review your career progression to see what you did, and when and where you did it.

Cons

The chronological resume format is retrospective. It assumes you want to continue in the same functional area and industry. If you want to make a career change, have made such changes in the past, want to change industries, or have experience in more than one industry, the chronological resume format highlights inconsistencies in a classic career path and puts you at a disadvantage with employers and recruiters who are most often looking for continuity.

An example of a chronological resume is shown on page 113.

Combination Resume

The first three resume formats are distinctly different from each other and, as such, are considered basic formats. Wanting to be different, people often merge one or more of the strengths of the three basic formats into one, called, naturally enough, a combination format.

The "Big Three" of outplacement companies—Right Management, Lee Hecht Harrison (LHH), and Drake Beam Morin (DBM)—have developed their own combination resume formats that their job-seeking clients use. The downside to this, however, is that, because recruiters see many resumes, they soon learn to identify which ones are the products of the outplacement companies and quickly know which candidates are out of work.

So, why is that an issue you might ask? Recruiters are often wary of candidates they know are working with an outplacement company because they also know that outplacement companies are eager to get their clients into any new job as quickly as possible (a key metric of their success by the companies that hire them). If they are a retained search recruiter (more on this in Chapter 7) working on a senior-level position, the recruiter knows that their corporate client will be less enthusiastic about a candidate who is not currently working.

Before I explain how I suggest you prepare your combination resume, let me use an analogy that might help you see it from a broader perspective as I see it. Let's say you go to a new restaurant that recently opened that you don't know anything about. They give you their extensive menu that covers breakfast, lunch, and dinner. You look at all the choices and wonder, "They certainly can't be great at everything. I wonder what their specialties are." If you see some dishes that say "Featured," "Specialties of the House," "Signature Dish," or are in boxes, have stars, or larger print to make them stand out, you can quickly grasp which ones are likely to be the special ones for this restaurant. If you don't see anything highlighted and you're still curious, you might ask the waiter or waitress which dishes are their specialties, which ones are they known for, or which are the most popular.

Targeted Resume

Adam D. Vantage
52 Deer Field Lane, Newtown, CA 90025
Tel: (123) 555-7890 • Cell: (321) 555-0987
Email: advantage@abc.com

EMPLOYMENT OBJECTIVE

Customer Service Manager for a complex, integrated, high-volume electronic office equipment supplier.

CAPABILITIES *[Limit examples to three]*

- Broad familiarity with complex, integrated, high-volume networked office equipment: copiers, fax machines, printers and point-of-sales machines.
- Using technical language with technical staff and translating significance of problems to non-technical customers.
- Convincing customers to upgrade to more sophisticated and profitable replacement machines.

ACHIEVEMENTS (or ACCOMPLISHMENTS)
[Limit examples to three]

- Managed customer service department with a staff of 15 for a $300 million office products company specializing in high-volume copiers, printers and integrated fax machines
- Supervised maintenance department with a staff of 20 for $50 million computer printer distributor
- Reduced product rework time from 20% to 3% within six months of accepting position with office products company

EMPLOYMENT HISTORY

Northern Office Machines Co., Toledo, OH   July 2003 – Date
Customer Service Manager

HP - Landsdown Sales Div, Lincoln, NE   June 1997 – July 2003
Customer Service Supervisor

Sony (USA) Inc., Sioux Falls, SD   Oct. 1994 – May 1997
Customer Service Representative

EDUCATION & QUALIFICATIONS

MBA, Northwestern University, Chicago, 1999
B.Sc., Marketing, University of Nebraska, 1994

PERSONAL

Invented and hold patent No. 5,345,975 for an integrated interface control mechanism, which speeds up the printing and dissemination of data over high-volume communication networks.

[Condensed to display on a single page.]

Functional Resume

Adam D. Vantage
52 Deer Field Lane
Newtown, CA 90025
T: 123-555-7890 • E: advantage@abc.com

WORK EXPERIENCE

Project Management	SVP-Project Manager, supervising all aspects of an $800 million construction project, including interface, scheduling and quality control of six subcontractors.
Administration	Coordinated administrative activities of a facilities management service organization for a multinational staff of 3,000 on a Middle East construction project, including housing, food, transportation and pay. Maintained a perfect safety record during the 30-month construction period.
Electricity	Coordinated electrical contractors installing residential, commercial and industrial wiring, appliances and equipment.
Civil	Senior engineer responsible for design and development of commercial, industrial and residential buildings in the UK, Austria, Saudi Arabia, Bahrain, Thailand and Indonesia.
	Special knowledge of construction methods in locations affected by high water tables or subjected to periodic flooding.

EMPLOYMENT HISTORY

July 00 – Date	Northern Technicians Ltd., Birmingham, AL Senior Vice President - Project Management
Sept. 98 – June 00	British American Constructors Ltd. Senior Project Administrator
March 94 – Aug. 9	Brown & Root (UK) Ltd., London Civil Engineer
1986 – Feb. 94	Various electrical and civil engineering positions in U.S. and internationally.

EDUCATION & QUALIFICATIONS

M.Sc. (Civil), University of Birmingham, 1989
B.Sc., Electrical Engineering, University of Birmingham, 1986

OTHER

Married with three grown children (will only relocate with spouse on long-term project assignments)
- Fluent in Arabic
- Technical speaker on international project management issues in the Middle East

(Condensed to display on a single page.)

Chronological Resume

Adam D. Vantage
52 Deer Field Lane, Newtown, CA 90025
T: 123. 555.7890 • E: advantage@abc.com

WORK EXPERIENCE
Northern Packaging Co. Inc., Sunnyvale, CA   March 2002 – Date
Finance Director

Directed all administrative and financial functions for this $200 million plastic packaging manufacturer and distributor until its acquisition by Global Distribution. Managed staff of 24 plus two divisions operating in Northern California and Oregon. Company grew 18% annually with profits exceeding 15% every year. Major achievements:

- Initiated and coordinated the strategic acquisition of Kilt Packaging in Oregon, which enabled us to expand our market share and dominate the packaging market in the Northwest.
- Developed integrated direct costing process that increased productivity and profitability by 6% annually.
- Negotiated profit-sharing program with union, covering all employees that resulted in productivity increases of 13% and a 30% reduction in quality complaints from customers.

Landsdown Manufacturing Co., Fresno, CA   Jan. 1996 – Feb. 2002
Financial Controller

Started with this $25 million manufacturer of plastic and paper packaging machinery as Senior Accountant upon graduation. Promoted to Financial Controller reporting to the Finance Director. Managed all accounting functions, including a staff of 12 and six at a branch packaging facility. Coordinated product costing, productivity ratios and branch consolidation. Major accomplishments:

- Developed an improved product costing system that eliminated two accounting staffers and reduced reporting time by 30%.
- Improved branch accounting by developing standardized reporting procedures and simplifying the information requirements.
- Simplified financial consolidation and reporting, enhancing information to management.

EDUCATION & QUALIFICATIONS
MBA, University of San Jose, McKay Business School, 1999
B.Sc., Business Administration (Accounting), University of San Francisco, 1995

OTHER
Instructor in Advanced Accounting, University of San Jose.
Actively mentor entrepreneurs of small business start-ups in manufacturing process controls.

(Condensed to display on a single page.)

Now, put yourself in the position of the restaurant's owner. Wouldn't you want to draw your customers' attention to the items on your menu that are your particular specialty, you're most proud of, and the raison d'etre rather than the ones you think you're just okay at?

A chronological resume that doesn't highlight what's most important about you and what you want is similar to the menu analogy. By now, however, you probably have a pretty good idea about what you think you want and what you're good at, and you even have some achievement stories that support what you say are your strengths. If you don't fall into one of the limited situations where one of the three basic formats may be best for you, I recommend you use a combination format that I think is best.

Keeping to the same structure as I've used for the basic formats, here is my view of a combined targeted and chronological resume:

What's Unique About It

Combines the targeted and chronological formats; shifts the focus from a retrospective to a prospective view. It makes a positive statement about what *you're* looking for and highlights your key strengths and achievements. Your work history follows this in reverse-chronological order.

When You Might Consider Using It

Whether you're making a classic job change or changing careers in a function or industry.

Pros

It quickly and very clearly focuses readers' attention on the job *you* want, *why* you're qualified for it, and *demonstrates* your skills and experience through achievement stories.

Cons

If you don't prepare my combination resume format correctly, employers and recruiters will simply ignore what you're trying to emphasize and go directly to the chronological work history.

My format sends the following very powerful messages about you:

❖ You're in charge of your career.

❖ You know what position you want.

❖ You're clear on the industry in which you want to work.

❖ You know the skills substantiating why you're qualified for what you want.

❖ You can support your skills and experience by describing achievement stories that demonstrate them.

If you are to take full control of your job or career search, your resume must direct the attention of the reader to where you *want to be,* not where you've *been.* You also need to attract and retain the attention of the reader.

Having owned an executive search firm where I worked with other recruiters, I've come to accept that recruiters are linear in their thinking and have incredibly short attention spans. They're usually under a lot of pressure to find that unique needle in the haystack their client wants.

Let me share a very typical scenario about how recruiters and employers work when you send your resume to them, as described in Situation 1 earlier in this chapter (page 106). Because you're not the only person sending a resume, you should assume the recruiter or employer is receiving hundreds, and sometimes thousands, of resumes. As a result, he needs to focus on what *he* needs to know as quickly as possible—not on what *you* would like to tell him.

If your resume leads with, "I am looking for a senior management position in a growing company," few recruiters or employers will take the time to figure out what kind of a position you want and what kind of industry experience you have.

First, companies don't have "senior management positions." Companies have positions with titles like CFO, vice president of sales and marketing, and so on, which identify their expertise within a specific functional area. These positions may also be "senior management positions," but only the functional title is in the minds of the employer or recruiter reviewing resumes.

Second, companies are not "growing companies." They're fashion retail companies, industrial equipment manufacturing companies, food and beverage retail companies, and so forth. They usually think their industry AND their business are unique. Some of them may also be "growing companies."

Now place yourself in the shoes of the recruiter or employer reviewing thousands of resumes. You can only spend a few seconds to find the candidate's job function and industry experience. If you can't locate these two pieces of information immediately, you'll probably discard the resume. Remember Step 1 in Situation 1 (page 106) where your resume is used to screen you out?

If you pass Step 1, you move on to Step 2 and Step 3, where recruiters and most employers will take only another few seconds to find the answers to the following six basic questions:

1. Who are you, where do you live, and how do I contact you?
2. What do you want?
3. What do you bring to the table?
4. What is your work history?

5. What is your university degree, and what certifications do you have?

6. What else is important about you for the job?

I'll expand on each of these six questions and link them by number to my combination resume example at the end of this section.

1. Who Are You, Where Do You Live, and How Do I Contact You?

If you don't provide this information in a manner that's easy to find and understand, you're shooting yourself in the foot. Make it simple for them to contact you quickly by showing your name, mailing address, telephone number, and e-mail address. Resumes that say "Name Confidential" without full contact details are usually discarded.

2. What Do You Want?

❖ Use a header such as "Employment Objective" or "Career Objective" and, in one sentence, describe the *position* you want, the *industry* or *business,* and the *location* where you want to work. Be as specific as possible. Make sure your stated objective is in agreement with your 30-second elevator pitch—what you tell others when asked what you're looking for or what position you're seeking.

❖ Don't use a vague reference to a position, such as "senior management position." Describe the exact position you're seeking. If you use "Chief Financial Officer," recruiters will know that could also mean "VP Finance." Alternatively, you could play it safe and use "Chief Financial Officer /VP Finance," or even "chief financial executive position."

❖ Don't use a vague reference to the industry or business, such as "a growth-oriented business." Be precise. Companies and their recruiters think their industry, and perhaps even their specific business within the industry, is unique.

❖ If location is an issue, state your preferred location. If you already live where you want to work, it's probably safe to exclude mentioning location. If you live on the East Coast and you will consider positions on the West

> **TIP**
> I've had recruiters who excluded candidates from consideration just because they didn't live near the job on the assumption that, if the candidates were open to relocating, they would have said so.

Coast, for example, you should state the breadth of locations you will consider.

❖ Recruiters often tell executives not to include a career objective in their resume, explaining that they'll read the resume and find out what the person *should* be doing based on what she's doing now or has done in the past. Besides, they reason, most people only make a generalized statement that doesn't say anything. If you're making a vertical job change and want the recruiter to decide your career path for you, then you can leave your career objective off. But if you want to make a *career change,* want something *specific,* or just like the idea of *being in charge* of your career, then don't let others make decisions about what's best for you—*tell them.*

3. What Do You Bring to the Table?

Companies hire for skills and experience first. Here you need to make two sections: one that lists your key strengths (your skills) and another that proves it (achievements that demonstrate your skills).

❖ **Key Skills:** Using bullet points, list your top three strengths—no more than three. If you list more, the reader likely will ignore them all or question your objectiveness. When you've listed your three strengths, review them to make sure they answer the following questions: "What am I really good at?" "What am I known for by others?" and "What would others say I am really good at?" Although I suggest you call this section "Key Skills," it really reflects your top three strengths. Remember the distinction between skills and strengths in Chapter 3: talents, skills, and knowledge? You want to show what you're good at doing, like doing, and want to do. When you think you have your top three, confirm them with someone who knows you well, such as a former colleague or your significant other.

❖ **Achievements:** Your achievement stories will leave the biggest impression on the reader because they're memorable and credible, and they *demonstrate* your skills. Review both the skills and achievement sections to make sure they complement and support each other. Include up to three achievements (or accomplishments) from prior jobs. Use bullet points so you keep your statements brief. Start each with a verb (for example, "Restructured Sales and Marketing organization, resulting in a 40% annualized increase in revenue over three years."). Your achievement stories will cause the reader to think about positive traits and characteristics that you probably possess without you even having to mention any. When they tell others about you, it will be the achievement stories they'll tell, not your list of skills (or strengths). For more help on how to write about your achievements, refer back to Chapter 2.

4. What Is Your Work History?

❖ Use a title such as "Employment History," "Work History," "Career History," "Work Experience," or "Professional Experience"—something that your chosen occupation or profession easily recognizes. For example, if your experience was in the legal profession, you'd probably use "Professional Experience." Employers and recruiters will examine your career path, looking for a logical career progression. If it isn't there, you'll need to deal with this issue in a cover letter.

117

◆ List your most recent employer first. Start with the employer's name and the city where you worked, followed by your most recent position. Show beginning and ending *month and year* for each position, even for different positions at the same company. Recruiters and employers need this information because they're looking for gaps in your employment. If they don't see the month and year, you can be sure they'll ask for the dates early in an interview.

◆ If you're unemployed, show the last date of employment in month and year. Don't show your most recent employment end date as "Date" or "Present" and then, in an interview, try to explain that you haven't updated your resume. Interviewers will see through that as a misrepresentation on your resume and your statement as a lie.

◆ If the industry isn't readily apparent by the company name, give the company's industry and size (such as "$400 million manufacturer of sports apparel"). Describe your responsibilities, starting with a verb such as *created, managed,* or *developed,* not "Responsibilities included..." Include any lesser achievements not shown in the previous section.

◆ Show your most recent employer and position on the first page so recruiters and employers can find it quickly. Putting this information here also forces you to be brief with your skills and achievements. Show earlier positions in reverse chronological order and continue on the second page.

◆ Because an interviewer will probably ask you how you found each job and why you left, mention if you were headhunted by a recruiter or recruited directly by management. It enhances others' perceptions of you. If you left an employer to further your career, include a statement about why you left (such as "Left this company to take a more senior position with more career potential").

◆ Briefly summarize employment more than 10 years earlier by listing the employer, the highest position you attained, and the dates of employment (here you can limit the dates to year only, such as 1995 to 1998 instead of March 1995 to December 1998).

5. What Is Your University Degree, and What Certifications Do You Have?

◆ Education: List, in the following sequence, the degree, the name of the institution, city, state if not obvious, and date you obtained your degree. Leave the date off if it's more than 10 years ago.

◆ Professional qualifications or certifications: If the abbreviation or acronym is not universally familiar, spell it out and enclose the acronym in parentheses.

NOTE: Do *not* include company training or evening classes unless they resulted in an industry-recognized certificate of technical proficiency. A one-day course on management techniques will not be viewed positively. A long list of courses may cause the reader to question how you can do any work if you're taking so much training or why you've needed so much extra education or training.

6. What Else Is Important About You for This Job?

❖ Include other skills (for example, foreign language proficiency) or involvement in activities that would be of interest to a prospective employer and are clearly relevant to the position you're seeking or the industry in which you want to work.

❖ Don't list sports, hobbies, or any organization that implies a religious, political, racial, or ethnic connection, unless that involvement would improve your prospects with the person reading your resume and with the organization. Omit age, marital status, children, health, and so forth from your resume unless the position is an overseas assignment where your residency status would be an important issue.

> **TIP**
>
> Mentioning that you play racquetball, to demonstrate that you are active physically and competitive, may be misinterpreted that you are not a team player. I've encountered this logic more than once in discussions with employers and recruiters.
>
> Including statements to emphasize some aspect of your ability or character can often have unintended consequences.

Following are two examples of my recommended resume formats. (See pages 120–123.) The numbers in this section are keyed to the first resume example.

Putting Your Resume Together

The first five chapters have dealt with preparing you to create your resume by showing you how to:

❖ Clarify and take charge of your employment objectives so they're consistent with your values and goals.

❖ Recognize and describe significant achievements from your career, which demonstrate your capabilities, your passion for success, and what kind of a resource you'd be to a prospective employer.

❖ Describe your preferred skills by identifying your skills and prioritizing them for the main ones you prefer to use.

❖ Review your career path and explore other career options you might not have considered previously.

For illustration only. Do not use a border on your resume.

Adam D. Vantage ❶
52 Huntsfield Lane
New Town, NY 90025
Tel: (123) 555-7890
Email: AdamV@Vantage.com

Use 12 pt type for your name and 10-pt for address and contact details.

EMPLOYMENT OBJECTIVE ❷

Or "CAREER OBJECTIVE" Use one short paragraph!

Chief Financial Officer position for an expanding plastics/paper manufacturing company with annual revenue in excess of $500 million located in the Northeast.

KEY SKILLS ❸

Or "CAPABILITIES" Use no more than three bullets.

- Developing workable, cost-effective, accounting solutions for mid-sized companies with limited personnel resources
- Managing, training and motivating staff
- Balancing demands for IT resources to achieve maximum utilization

ACHIEVEMENTS ❸

Or "ACCOMPLISHMENTS" Use no more than three bullets.

- Developed a simplified accounting system that reduced headcount by 10%, improved the quality of information, and reduced financial reporting time by two days.
- Developed program for training staff and implemented succession training for junior managers.
- Rationalized IT services focusing on production and sales information, which influenced a 20% productivity improvement and enhanced customer targeting.

WORK EXPERIENCE ❹

Or EMPLOYMENT EXPERIENCE or PROFESSIONAL EXPERIENCE

Northern Packaging Inc., Buffalo, NY   April 99 – June 08
Chief Financial Officer – July 05 to June 08
Overall administration of financial organization for this $300 million plastic and paper packaging manufacturer until its acquisition by Global Distribution.

Managed all personnel and IT functions, including staff of 24 plus two divisions operating in the Northeast. Company grew 18% annually with profits exceeding 15% every year. Negotiated financing package with bank that reduced annual cost of capital by 1.5%.

Group Financial Controller – Jan. 01 to June 05
Promoted to this position upon acquisition of Smallco Products. Architect of divisional reporting and monitoring system for Smallco and another company already owned by Northern.

Adam D. Vantage
Page 2

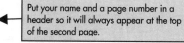

Put your name and a page number in a header so it will always appear at the top of the second page.

WORK EXPERIENCE (CONTINUED)

Northern Packaging Inc., Buffalo, NY (Cont'd)   April 99 – June 08
Financial Controller – April 99 to Dec. 00
Joined this plastics and paper packaging manufacturer upon its
acquisition of Northeast Packaging Co. Rationalized IT
resources for the operations, sales and finance organizations.
Organized data-processing function and recruited IT Manager.

Northeast Packaging Company, Albany, NY   Jan. 94 – March 99
Finance Director

Joined this $20 million local paper packaging manufacturer as
Senior Accountant. Developed computerized accounting system
and introduced IT systems, replacing outdated manual
processing systems. Initiated discussions for the sale of the
company when owner decided to retire.

Arthur Andersen & Co., New York, NY   Oct. 91 – Dec. 94
Audit Staff

Joined this Big 6 international certified public accounting firm to
obtain CPA qualification, gaining experience in the paper
packaging industry.

EDUCATION AND QUALIFICATIONS ❺

MBA, University of New York, Graduate Business School, 1992
B.Sc., Finance, University of New York, 1991
Certified Public Accountant, New York, 1993

OTHER ❻

- Member of the Board of Directors of the National Paper Products
  Assn. (NAPPA)
- Fluent in French; speak limited German
- Author of several articles covering Total Quality Management
  (TQM) in the paper industry
- Part-time lecturer on Mergers & Acquisition Strategy at University
  of New York

Shirley Thomas
1325 E. Napster Dr., Silicon Valley, CA 94345
Tel: 415-555-3689 ♦ Email: sthomas@legacy.com

EMPLOYMENT OBJECTIVE

A CTO/VP of Technology position in a well-financed, fast-growing, e-commerce company with a team-oriented culture.

CAPABILITIES

- Developing technology to solve strategic business problems
- Architecting systems
- Developing software products and Web-based operations

ACHIEVEMENTS

- Created the software "Office Assistant" concept and implemented it in Microsoft Windows.
- Managed a team that built a complex supply chain communications infrastructure and an exchange in one month. Delivered the production software running on in-house Web servers in another two months, on time and on budget. Product accounted for 30% of the company's sales.
- Hired 25 Developers, QA and Network Administrators for a dot-com start-up in less than three months during a very highly competitive job market.

PROFESSIONAL EXPERIENCE

BizTrade.com, Eureka, CA - CTO   March 04 – Present

Offered the CTO position after a short consultancy period for this B2B supply chain services start-up. As part of executive team, took the company from an idea to a Web-based ASP with 75 employees.

Managed the technology development, including software, hardware, communications, infrastructure, vendors and 27 technical people, as well as being prominent in planning, budgeting, recruiting and mentoring.

Macro Discovery, Las Vegas, NV - President   Jan. 00 – Feb. 04

Started a custom software development and consultancy firm, including Internet development. Projects included automated commodity trading systems, NBA, NFL, MLB, NHL and MLS game blackouts, 401K Administration Systems, Email, Workflow, and Imaging Systems for small and large companies.

NorthStar Motors, Detroit, MI   Jan. 97 – Dec. 99
S/W Specialist & Proj. Mgr

Developed a Windows-and-Unix-based National Automated Electronic Software Distribution and Installation product, which earned a patent. Managed four developers. Enhanced the installation programs for NorthStar Advantage EX, an inventory management information system. Used C & C++, and MFC.

Shirley Thomas   Page 2

DMJW, Chicago, IL   Jan. 94 – Dec. 96
Director of Software Development
Directed the company's software development effort from concept to
delivery including recruiting, planning and budgeting. Managed seven
programmers. Presented the product overview and vision for large
customers. Developed multi-platform networked multimedia products.

BMW, Advanced R&D, Chicago, IL
Sr. Programmer & Software Architect   July 91 – Jan. 94
Developed a front-end newsletter layout and publishing graphics
workstation on 386-PCs, using C++. Invented a unique graphical tool for
formatting and manipulating feature story layouts.

Xerox Corporation, Mountain, NJ   March 88 – July 91
Senior Programmer
Developed the Interpress Programmer's Library, Diablo 630 & Xerox
2700 to Interpress converters, as well as an Interpress printer driver for
Microsoft Word in C/MSDOS. Co-designed the Arabic & Hebrew bi-
directional multi-language text-handling for Xerox workstations (in
MESA). Designed various algorithms to handle the never-before-
discovered problems of computerized bi-directional text.

CIA, Langley, VA – Research Scientist   Jan. 85 – Feb. 88
Developed a full screen bi-directional Arabic & English text editor and a
device-independent text formatter. Built bilingual system programs for a
custom built CP/M environment (in C and ASSEMBLER).

George Washington University, Washington DC
Graduate Teaching Fellow   1984 – 1985
Taught graduate and undergraduate digital computer design courses.
Created a CP/M compatible operating system for slave Z80 computers,
MP/M interface, program transfer and execution utilities for a multi-
processor system (in Z80-ASSEMBLER).

EDUCATION AND CERTIFICATIONS
- MBA in Business Management, Northwestern University, 1991
- M.Sc. in Computer Science, George Washington Univ., 1984
- B.Sc. in Electronic Communications Engineering, University of
  Pennsylvania, 1982
- Microsoft Certified Professional – 1996
- University of Phoenix, Faculty Certification – 1996

TEACHING EXPERIENCE
- "Information Technology and Computer Programming,"
  Michigan State University, 1992 – 1993
- "Computer Design and Computer Programming," George
  Washington University, 1984 – 1985

You now will begin to put your resume together for a trial run. You shouldn't send it out yet, as you'll need to do some test marketing first. You may decide, if you choose self-employment, you really don't need a resume. What you might need instead is a bio or even a brochure. I'll help you through the discovery process and show you how to test your resume in the following chapters.

Step 1: Gather the Information You Need.

Start by taking an inventory of your career. This will be an in-depth look at your past. Look at what you did and achieved in school, and where you volunteered outside work or participated in associations.

You'll use some of the information in your resume, and some you'll need for an interview or when completing an employment application.

Personal Information Inventory

Complete the Personal Information Inventory, which helps you gather all the information you will need to prepare your resume, respond accurately to interview questions about your past experience, and facilitate completing an employment application.

Step 2: Select the Resume Format That Will Work Best for You.

Unless the targeted or functional formats work best for your situation, I recommend you use the combination format that I've described in the previous section. I know it works because my clients tell me so. They know it works because employers *and* recruiters complement them on their resume. The comment I hear most often is "a powerful resume."

Step 3: Get Your Resume in Sync With Your Message.

Your resume will be the benchmark against which people evaluate you, even if you've spoken with the recruiter or employer in advance of providing your resume. If your message or interview answers aren't completely consistent with your resume, the interviewer will question your integrity and forthrightness, and wonder whether the resume or the interview reflects the *real* you.

Make sure your resume is an accurate reflection of you!

Illustration by Steven Lait.

124

If you obtained an interview solely on the strength of your resume, the interviewer will typically use it to delve into and test its accuracy

> **TIP** If you find you're telling others something different from what your resume shows, then you haven't yet finished your resume. Your resume *must* mirror what you say to others.

and integrity. Your verbal statements and representations must be consistent with what your resume reflects.

If, on the other hand, you obtain an interview through a referral (I'll cover how you can do this in Chapter 8), the interviewer will use your resume to substantiate what someone else has said about you. If your resume isn't consistent with that, you'll probably no longer be a candidate *and* you will have compromised the integrity of the person who made the referral.

Step 4: Connect the Dots for Transferable Skills and Experience.

If your work experience cuts across a range of industries, you may feel your breadth of experience puts you in good stead because you bring a range of industry experience many others probably don't have. You would be wrong!

A Shared Experience

When I left public accounting after 15 years, my experience was in a range of manufacturing companies, long-term civil and construction engineering management services, rental cars, transportation, food manufacturing, industrial construction, resort development, and some other minor industry assignments. I thought, "Wow, do I ever have good experience!"

That wide range of experience became a yoke around my career. I found that employers wanted executives who had most, if not all, their experience in their industry or business. I soon realized they were comparing me to other candidates whose experience was predominately in their industry, and their feeling was that someone with substantially all their experience in their industry would be better able to hit the ground running than I could and, therefore, could be more effective, sooner.

While I was managing my search firm, I also observed our clients were consistent in only wanting to see candidates from their industry. Even clients whose businesses were simple to understand believed that their business was unique, and people from outside it would have trouble adapting.

This seemed much too restrictive and unreasonable until I realized that the people who were making these decisions had all, or substantially all, their own experience within their industry. Because they lacked experience in other industries, they had trouble understanding how people from another industry could adapt to theirs.

Employers and recruiters will attempt to stereotype your experience. This will make it difficult to make a career change, if that's your goal. It won't be a problem if you're making a classic career path change either vertically (a promotion) or horizontally (a similar job-to-job change).

The economy also influences how employers and recruiters view your industry experience. In an expansionary economy or during booming economic times, the employment market will be strong, and qualified candidates in a particular industry might be scarce. During these times, employers and recruiters won't be as concerned about the breadth of your experience. In fact, they may even rationalize it as being a good thing. (Shouldn't they always think like that?)

In recessionary economic times, or when the economy is flat and the employment market weak, lots of candidates are looking for new opportunities. During these times, focus on your strongest industry experience, because you'll be competing with many others who have all their experience in the same industry, as well as those who are looking to transfer their skills from one industry to another.

Employers and recruiters typically use resumes to identify people whose skills and experience come closest to the skills and experience the employer desires. In their minds, the ideal candidate is one who already has successfully done at another company what they want done—the achievement story.

When trying to promote your skills and experience gained in one industry for a different industry, use terminology and examples that relate to the industry you're targeting in language people in the different industry understand. Connect the dots for them, because they won't make the connection from your industry to theirs on their own.

> **T I P** If the industry you're focusing on is the same as your experience, recruiters and employers will be more receptive to you. If you're making an industry change and think your skills are transferable to another industry, you'll need to rely much more on your contacts for referrals.

If you're making an industry change, you won't be very successful just sending your resume to employers or recruiters, even if you enclose a cover letter explaining how your skills and experience relate to their industry. You'll need to expand your network of contacts to include those in the industry where you want to work.

I'll cover how you can successfully use your network to make career changes in Chapter 8. I'll help you create letters that will enhance your ability to connect successfully with key people who can help you make the transition to another industry in Chapter 9.

A Shared Experience

When I left public accounting as an audit partner, I followed the advice in job search books and prepared my resume to send to employers and recruiters. I also sent it in response to advertisements for CFO positions. The Internet was in its infancy at the time, so that wasn't an option.

Because most of my career to that point was in auditing, I said I was looking for a "senior management role in a growing company." This seemed logical to me at the time, as CFOs were part of the senior management team.

After about a month, I received a terse letter from the VP of Human Resources stating I wasn't qualified for the position of CFO because I wasn't an accountant and didn't have a degree in accounting—two requirements for the position.

Naturally, I was taken aback. How could someone not know that auditors were accountants because they audited the accounting systems of companies and knew more about accounting than most CFOs? Didn't the VP of HR also know that you don't get degrees in accounting? You receive degrees in business administration and choose an area of emphasis, such as accounting.

What I failed to understand at the time was that I hadn't prepared my resume for the reader. I should have tailored my response and connected auditing to accounting so an uninformed reader would quickly see and understand the connection. I also should have highlighted the accounting emphasis of my business administration degree.

Step 5: Get Feedback on Content and Context From Those Who Know You.

You only need one version of your resume for the following reasons:

◆ It needs to be ready to send to others on short notice without significant modification.

◆ If you micromanage the text for each person you send or give it to, it will become *very* difficult remembering which version you gave to whom.

◆ You create unnecessary confusion in an interview if your verbal responses are different from what's in your resume.

◆ Someone may receive two different versions and will wonder which one is the real you.

There could be times, however, when you *might* want to re-order the sequence of skills or achievement stories when you know an employer is looking specifically for that skill or experience.

Admittedly, every opportunity you pursue could be different, and you do need to address what's most important to the employer or recruiter. That, however, is the purpose of a cover letter.

> Your resume should be an accurate reflection of you. If
> you find you need to constantly change your resume, you
> don't yet know who you are, and neither will anyone else.

You wouldn't send your resume to someone in an envelope without a cover letter, would you? Cover letters provide a personal introduction with targeted information (such as referrals) that you can't include in your resume. (I'll discuss how to prepare cover letters and what to put in them in Chapter 9.)

Resume Checklist

When you've completed a first draft of your resume, review it against/fill out the Resume Checklist.

Resume Checklist

Check the following points before sending out your resume. Remember: Content is king!

Content:

❏ When you've finished your resume, have someone who knows you well read it and ask him if it fairly reflects who you are.

❏ Does your Employment Objective clearly identify the position, industry, size of company you're interested in, and where you want to work?

❏ Have you prioritized your skills and achievements, showing the most important first?

❏ Are your skills and achievements relevant to the position you're seeking?

❏ Have you avoided the use of traits and characteristics?

❏ Do your achievement stories demonstrate your skills?

❏ Have you avoided the use of any jargon, clichés, colloquialisms, unfamiliar acronyms, and hyperbole?

❏ Have you excluded non-occupational information, such as marital status, hobbies, religious associations, and personal interests, that aren't relevant to consideration for employment?

❏ Did you include awards or certificates that exhibit exceptional performance or commendations?

❏ Have you included other information, such as foreign language skills, involvement on boards, or other activities or interests, that might be of interest to a potential employer?

❏ Did you omit names and contact details of references? (When employers want that information, they'll ask for it.)

❏ Does your resume clearly answer the six basic questions: Who and where are you? What job do you want? What skills and experience can you bring to the table? What have you achieved? Where did you do it? What else do I need to know about you that you consider important?

Resume Checklist

❑When you read your resume, can you say, "This is me, and *others who know me will agree?"*

Structure:

❑Have you used a very simple layout for your resume? Using tables, boxes, and unusual symbols doesn't always translate well to different versions of word-processing software or even different versions of the same software.

❑Did you use bullets and short phrases to describe your skills and achievements and limit them to no more than three each?

❑Are all sentences short and to-the-point?

❑Have others who *don't* know you very well read your statements and clearly understood what you meant?

❑Have you avoided introducing more than one thought in each sentence?

❑Have you avoided ALL references to *I, me,* or *my?*

Appearance:

❑Did you limit your resume to no more than two pages?

❑Did you use a serif font (like Times Roman), type size preferably 12-point, but no less than 11-point? Serif type fonts are warm; sans serif fonts (like Arial) are cold.

❑Have you left one-inch margins around the paper?

❑Did you single space?

❑Have you used **bold** only for major captions, like section headings, names of employers, and job titles?

❑Have you avoided *italics?* Italics may not scan accurately, and it may not translate well when converted to different word processors or versions of the same one.

❑HAVE YOU AVOIDED USING EXCESSIVE CAPITALIZATION, AS IT IS HARD FOR OTHERS TO READ?

Other considerations:

❑If you mail your resume, use a good smooth white or off-white bond paper and matching envelope. Avoid using linen or other rough-textured paper because the printed images often smear when mailed.

❑If you mail your resume, enclose a cover letter and use a standard #10 letter envelope. Fold your letter and your resume together so when they're unfolded, the resume is behind the letter.

❑When creating an electronic version of your resume, use Microsoft Word document format (used by most recruiters and employers) or rtf (rich text format). Be cautious when using the latest version of software as companies are often slow to upgrade.

When you have others review your resume, limit the review to two or three people who know you well and ask them to focus on the content not the format. Don't ask recruiters and others to review your resume, because you'll get a different perspective from everyone you meet. It seems everyone thinks they're an expert at preparing resumes!

If you've followed the guidelines in this chapter, and the content in your resume is an accurate reflection of you, you're finished with your resume.

A Shared Experience

A client laboriously completed his resume using the combination format and reviewed it with some colleagues who knew him well. After some minor modifications, he and his friends agreed it was an accurate reflection of him and a powerful statement about him. They were even more impressed with him after seeing his resume.

He then made the mistake of sending it to a recruiter friend who worked for an international search firm and asking for his comments.

The recruiter came back to him with only a couple of suggestions. First, he said he should eliminate the career objective section because recruiters would probably look at what he had done in the past and decide what he should be doing anyway. The recruiter acknowledged that my client's career objective was different from what he had assumed for him. I explained to my client that this was precisely why he *needed* the career objective statement.

Second, the recruiter said he should provide more details on his technical experience so recruiters wouldn't have to contact him to get the information. I explained this was the main objective of the resume: to get the employer/recruiter to contact you!

His resume wasn't supposed to tell them everything they wanted to know. It should only tell them enough so they want to contact you for elaboration. The light finally clicked in his mind that his resume had achieved its purpose very well.

Techniques for Consultants and Engineers

Consultants and engineers usually struggle over how to prepare a resume that highlights the extent of their projects in a two-page resume. In my search practice, I vividly remember receiving resumes of five, 10, 15, even 18 pages.

Consultants and engineers typically prepare chronological resumes and list their projects in that order, frequently duplicating similar work as they include all their projects.

If you're a consultant or an engineer and your work experience is project-based, prepare a combination resume format highlighting your key skills and most successful projects. Supplement your resume with an attached list summarizing your projects by industry, function, or other broad category.

Here are some general guidelines and formatting options that will help you decide how best to show your experience.

Consulting

Consulting projects typically are short-term and may be in the same or similar areas of expertise. Group these projects by areas of expertise, disciplines, or some other similar grouping and combine them into as few sections as possible, without losing the distinction between the projects.

Don't list individual projects that are the same or similar unless there's a valid reason to do so (such as the magnitude of the project or the name-recognition value of the client or customer). For example, you might summarize projects in one paragraph covering financial applications and in another for HR applications.

Alternatively, you might choose to list the different types of projects individually under a major heading for financial applications and then list those that are HR-related applications.

Engineering

Engineering projects typically are longer-term. You can group projects as above for consultants, or you can group them chronologically or by project type. For example, list them chronologically with a description of the time frame, the client, your role, and the nature of the project.

Alternatively, group them by type, such as Commercial Construction, Refinery Construction, and so forth, and then list the individual projects chronologically within the major types.

Two examples of supplemental resume attachments for consultants and for engineers follow on page 132.

Consulting Projects Summarized by Project Type

Adam D. Vantage

Project Summary

Sales Order Entry System
Developed PC-based sales order entry system for $1 billion
international document courier company. System enabled
company to track documents until received at final destination.

Call Center Help Desk
Created an integrated call center help desk for three divisions of
a $600 million electrical appliance manufacturer which reduced
a $20 million overhead budget by 5% and increased call
response time by 12 minutes, thereby improving customer
relations and reducing customer complaints.

Purchasing and Warehouse Control
Redesigned purchasing and warehouse procedures in Germany
for a €500 million European distributor of imported machine
tools. System improvements simplified procedures and
shortened ordering time by two days. Warehouse stock levels
were ultimately reduced by 35%.

Engineering Projects Summarized by Date

Adam D. Vantage

Project Summary

Aug 05-June 08 Johnson & Johnson, Jersey City, NJ
Project Manager responsible for installation, testing and
commissioning of a $950 million commercial building
with six direct and 250 indirect reports.

Mar 05-June 05 S.A. Bechtel Co., Jubail, Saudi Arabia
Senior electrical engineer responsible for quality
control of all electrical and HVAC installations of a
$300 million manufacturing facility.

Jan 03-Feb 05 Jacobs Engineering, Inc., Khamis Mushayt,
Saudi Arabia
Consulting electrical engineer responsible for electrical
testing, commissioning and documentation of H.T.
/M.V. back-up diesel power supply system for a $1.5
billion desalination plant.

Oct 99-Nov 02 Jersey Consulting Engineers Ltd., North Sea
Electrical engineer responsible for initial design,
installation, testing and commissioning of HVAC and
the HALON 1301 fire protection system for an
offshore oil platform, requiring HAZOP qualifications.

☑ Milestones

The following milestones recap what you need to do to complete this chapter. Include those items you are unable to complete in your summary-level open-items list.

☐ 1. Complete Worksheet 6.1: Personal Information Inventory. You'll use the information you gather for this form to prepare your resume, help you prepare for interviews, and provide information you'll need for employment applications.

☐ 2. Prepare your resume using the format that will work best in your situation.

☐ 3. Review the six questions employers and recruiters want answered in your resume, and make sure your resume answers those questions.

☐ 4. Does the opening statement in your resume mirror what you say in the "elevator pitch" you use when networking?

☐ 5. Have you limited each of your three key strengths to as few words as possible and only one sentence?

☐ 6. Have you limited each of your achievements or accomplishments to no more than four lines?

☐ 7. Do your achievements demonstrate your key skills?

☐ 8. Have you limited your skills and achievements to no more than six bullet points in total?

☐ 9. Have you limited the text of your skills and achievements so that your most recent employment begins on the first page of your resume and includes at least one paragraph of text?

☐ 10. Have you considered summarizing your employment over 10 years prior to your current job if you're short of space?

☐ 11. Have you reviewed your resume with your career coach, mentor, spouse, and/or colleagues who know you well and addressed the modifications and clarifications they suggested?

☐ 12. Have you reviewed your resume with a personal reference at your most recent employer, and does she agree with the statements you make?

☐ 13. Have you given those whom you plan to use as references a copy of your resume and reviewed it with them?

☐ 14. Complete Worksheet 6.2: Resume Checklist.

The Job Market

You can't win the game if you don't know the rules.

Chapter Overview

Would you play a game if you knew you only had a 5-percent chance of winning? You might think these are reasonably good odds if you're a gambler, but would you want to spend 90 to 95 percent of your time pursuing a job search if you knew that what you were doing only had a 5- to 10-percent chance of success? In this chapter, you'll learn:

» How the job market really works at the executive and manager level.

» The different approaches to the job market you need to consider, and how to maximize your effectiveness when you use each one (knowing the game and the rules).

» The six different ways employers try to find executives, and why you want to be in the first five.

The main sections in this chapter include:

» Job fairs and trade shows.

» Government career centers and job clubs.

» Print advertisements and Internet job postings.

» Internet job search Websites.

» Contacting recruiters.

» Contacting employers.

» Your Website.

» Networking.

» Milestones.

Many resume writers and career coaches will tell you it's a numbers game and you need to send "a powerful letter and resume" (which of course they'll help you prepare for a fee) to a large number of recruiters and employers. Unfortunately, it's not a numbers game, because you probably won't find your next job by sending letters and resumes.

More than 85 percent of executives and managers find their next job through someone they already know or met through the networking process. Although networking will be the most important and probably most successful activity for you, you need to know the various job search approaches that are available to you (playing the game) and how to maximize your effectiveness when you use each one (knowing the rules of the game).

Illustration by Steven Lait.

The job search process and job market were much simpler and more direct when you were a recent graduate in your early 20s. Now, when you're an executive or manager, the job search process isn't so transparent. Though there's no clear and simple process that works for executives and managers, there are approaches you can use that can be effective.

Before you dismiss some of the approaches described in this chapter with "that one isn't appropriate for me," read the suggestions for each one and consider how you might get something useful from it. I often hear executives tell me how they made a contact that turned out to be useful later when using one of the approaches they initially thought would be unproductive.

Job Fairs and Trade Shows

Job fairs attract large numbers of job seekers who want to discuss employment opportunities in specific fields or industries. Although this approach may be the *least* effective for you at a senior level, here are some good reasons to attend job fairs and trade shows:

» To gain a better understanding about an industry you're exploring.

» To connect with employees at several different companies within an industry.

> **TIP**
>
> These fundamental truths about finding another job should be kept in mind at all times:
>
> ▷ There's not just one way to find a job.
>
> ▷ You never know where your next job will come from.
>
> ▷ You never know who knows whom and who will be the person to connect you with the person who can employ you.
>
> ▷ The more approaches you use effectively, the more successful your search.

> ❧ To gain a better understanding of how a company might approach recruiting senior personnel.

> ❧ To hear rumors about people leaving, companies with open positions, or companies searching for someone.

> ❧ To determine the names and positions of persons who have the power to employ you at your target companies.

Trade shows are designed to help companies enhance their visibility within their industry and promote their products to potential purchasers. They don't focus on job or career issues. Sales and marketing people predominate at trade shows, but senior management often attend.

Attend trade shows as a way to gather information and research an industry or a company. Before going, call the trade show organizer (usually found through the Internet) and get a list of the current or prior year's exhibitors. Go with the intent to make contact with someone in a target company who might be able to give you inside information on their structure, approach to hiring, or current or expected opportunities, or help you connect later with the person who has the authority to make hiring decisions.

Government Career Centers and Job Clubs

Inquire at a state or local office of a government unemployment department. Many have job-search programs, and some have special programs for executives. Employers often post jobs at these facilities, even at executive and manager levels. You can also gain access to various restricted job-posting Internet Websites at no cost. The more senior your position, however, the less likely the government job centers will be an effective resource for you.

To use the services of most government programs, you'll be required to register and participate in their programs, which may be similar to those offered by outplacement companies. If you're planning to file for unemployment, you'll have to register anyway.

Print Advertisements and Internet Job Postings

Companies and recruiters often place job advertisements in newspapers, journals, and trade publications, on the Internet, and on their own Websites. The simplicity and speed with which jobs appear on the Internet often makes it difficult to know the actual source of a job and how many times the same job appears on more than one site. For example, one major Internet job board scours the Internet looking at employers' Websites for jobs and then copies them onto its own Website.

If you respond to advertisements or job postings on the Internet, use a cover letter to serve as a bridge between your resume and the requirements outlined in the job description. Be aware, though, that when you post your resume on the Internet, you lose control of it, and anyone can view it.

Although you will find many jobs posted on the Internet for staff-level positions, you'll not find many at the executive level. Executives in the United States won't find many jobs posted in newspapers either. The *Wall Street Journal*'s Tuesday edition is the only national print publication that carries advertisements for positions at senior levels, and even then you may only see a couple of pages of ads. Their Internet job site *www.careerjournal.com* includes jobs posted by employers, but most are for manager and non-managerial positions.

Executives in the UK have excellent alternatives. *The Times* and *The Financial Times* are both national newspapers, and *The Times* devotes an entire section on Sundays that can run as long as 35 pages containing senior-level jobs at positions equivalent to CEO on down. *The Financial Times* does the same on Wednesdays for financial services industry positions, and on Thursdays for accounting and auditing-type positions.

In the United States, you often find advertisements in print publications that reflect a generalized description of a position and almost no information about the industry. The ads direct your response to a P.O. box. All too often, these aren't real jobs, but attempts by a recruiter to collect resumes to fill a database for future prospecting. Placing an advertisement for a job opening that doesn't exist is illegal in the EU and many other countries, but it's common practice in the United States.

> **TIP**
>
> If you see an advertisement where the description seems close to your employer or a position in your company, be careful. It may *be* your employer. Companies occasionally post jobs to see if they receive resumes from their employees who might be looking.
>
> One of my clients had lost his job because he responded to an advertisement for a more senior position, only to find that the position was with his employer. And until he applied for that position, he was actually being considered for promotion into that role.

Because advertisements typically result in a large number of responses, those who are likely to be more successful will be younger and less expensive candidates, for whom the position would be a step up.

Age discrimination may be illegal, but there are subtle ways employers use to accomplish the same thing. Advertisements mentioning the level of experience required as "from four to six years" are actually telling you if you have seven or more years of experience, you're "overqualified"—a euphemism meaning you're too old.

Your success rate at finding a job at the executive or manager level in the United States from an advertisement in the press or on the Internet will be in the range of 3 to 5 percent. If you choose to respond to an advertisement, Chapter 9 covers how you can improve your odds, and Chapter 11 covers requests for providing your salary history (often requested in advertisements).

Internet Job Search Websites

The three types of job search services on the Internet relevant to executives in transition include:

1. Fee-based programs.
2. Fee-based Websites.
3. Free Websites.

I'll explain how each of these work, so you can decide whether they might be an option for you.

Fee-Based Programs

The following two organizations specialize in the recruiting industry and offer services to executives:

◆ **Kennedy Information** (*www.KennedyInfo.com*) publishes an annual *Directory of Executive Recruiters,* known as the "Red Book," and other directories of professional service providers. You can purchase the "Red Book," and have them send your resume to a select number of recruiters that match your search criteria. The book is the most comprehensive and up-to-date listing of retained and contingent executive recruiters for the U.S. market. Most libraries carry the book, although it probably won't be current.

◆ **Association of Executive Search Consultants** (AESC; *www.aesc.org*) is the trade association for the executive search industry. They maintain a database of executives that's available to their executive search member firms at no cost. You can create a profile and post your resume if you earn more than $100,000 and pay a fee. You also get access to their recruiter database and for an additional fee can participate in a forum with other executives for one year. Access to the database is restricted to search firms that are members of the AESC, and, because the membership fee is substantial, only larger firms tend to be members. Go to *www.BlueSteps.com* to post your resume.

Fee-Based Websites

The three best-known fee-based Websites are:

◈ *www.ExecuNet.com*

❖❯ *www.ExecutivesOnly.com*

❖❯ *www.NetShare.com*

These sites allow you to use their services and post your resume for a specific number of months for a fee. They claim they'll make it available to their confidential list of recruiters and/or employers. These sites are legal in the United States, but illegal in the EU and many other countries.

Although I don't encourage paying a fee to anyone who promises to market you to a select group of recruiters, I know that recruiters will use any means to find candidates, especially when they're having trouble finding qualified candidates from their traditional search sources. Some of these Websites sponsor networking functions in locations where recruiters and career coaches have agreed to host the events.

Free Websites

Two free Websites for executives are:

◆ *www.ExecGlobalNet.com*—ExecGlobalNet is a Website I created as an employment matchmaker between executives who are looking for new opportunities and employers/recruiters who are looking for executives. The main feature of the site is your creation of an anonymous profile that employers and recruiters can search and examine without knowing your identity, whom you work for, or where you live. The site doesn't require resumes. By using a unique profile format that protects your identity, ExecGlobalNet is the only Website secure enough for those not actively looking, but still wanting to consider other opportunities without compromising their current job. ExecGlobalNet's consultants work as an unbiased go-between to make sure you're right for the job and the job is right for you, while also protecting each party's identity from the other until we're told to disclose it. The Website contains a range of information that's helpful to those more experienced who are exploring new opportunities, such as full-size copies of many of the worksheets that I use in this book, additional resources that I can keep more current than if they were included in this book, answers to typical job search questions, and direct access to a career coach when you need it.

◆ *www.ExecSearches.com*—This site specializes in executive, fundraising, and mid-level jobs in non-profit, government, healthcare, education, and other non-profit organizations. You can search jobs, create a profile, and post your resume at no cost.

You can create a profile and/or post your resume on a large number of other Websites that don't specifically target executives, such as trade and professional association Websites and, of course, *Monster.com*. Consider these as an option *only* if you're currently unemployed and don't mind posting your resume where control over it will be out of your hands. Some sites allow you to keep certain details confidential. To find current sites, go to *www.Google.com* or *www.Yahoo.com* and enter search criteria, such as "executive jobs" or "executive job search."

The following Websites provide career information and links to other career-related Websites that might be useful:

» *www.jobhuntersbible.com*

» *www.rileyguide.com*

» *www.quintcareers.com*

The links and suggestions on these sites are more general in nature and may not focus on what's unique for executives and managers. These Websites also suffer from the same problem that occurs when you buy a book—that is, the information is not always current.

Despite the allure of using resume and job-posting Websites on the Internet, it's not very effective for senior-level job seekers. It works much better for those who are younger and in lower-level positions. Although accurate statistics aren't available, some industry sages estimate that less than 5 percent of senior-level people find a job on the Internet.

Many people at staff-level and even entry-level management positions do find jobs on the Internet, perhaps more than 10 percent. I believe this percentage will increase over time, and the Internet will become a much more significant source of jobs for this group in the future.

At the executive and manager level, however, it's my opinion that you will *not* find the Internet to be an effective way to find a meaningful job. Employers must hire the right manager or leader, and the Internet can't provide the quality control that recruiters and referrals can offer.

A Shared Experience

While conducting research of companies who were recruiting for senior-level positions on the Internet, many told me the exercise wasn't productive. They said they spent hours reviewing "tons" of resumes from candidates who lacked their industry experience, or the company would have had to pay relocation costs, or their resume presentation was so poor, they were excluded.

I was intrigued when one HR person said she found her last two CFOs on Monster. The first one didn't work out, so she advertised again, but that one didn't work out either. She said they were going to advertise again on Monster, though, because they had such large responses the first two times they advertised, and she was sure they were going to get the right person eventually.

It's my belief the HR person who was trying to recruit the CFO was inexperienced and assumed that, if she could recruit staff on the Internet, why not executives and managers? I tried to explain the cost to the company of not getting it right the first time—in money, lost time, opportunities not taken, etc.—but she seemed intent on using the Internet to find someone so she could save the cost of engaging a recruiter.

I wondered whether her objectives were the same as the CEO's!

Contacting Recruiters

I know what you're thinking: "A-ha—finally! Now I'll learn how to work with recruiters to find my next job."

There's a lot of misunderstanding about what recruiters do. Most executives, and employers for that matter, don't know how recruiters work or what's going on behind the scenes. Because I've owned an executive search firm and worked with both retained search and contingency recruiters, I'm going to share with you what goes on in the recruiter's office.

If you remember nothing else from this section, remember this:

> **Recruiters work for employers;**
> **They don't work for job seekers.**

There are two basic types of recruiters—retained and contingency—and each type works very differently.

Retained Recruiters

Retained recruiters often call themselves executive search consultants, headhunters, executive recruiters, or just plain recruiters. Retained recruiters typically work at C-level and senior-manager levels at salaries above the low $100,000s.

Retained recruiters exclusively work on retainer with companies. They usually collect their fee in three installments: one-third at the beginning, one-third after a month or two or upon presentation of a shortlist, and the final one-third after another month or two or, rarely, when the company hires a candidate. Retained recruiters typically collect their full fee regardless of whether they're successful at finding a suitable candidate for an employer.

Retained recruiters begin each engagement by assigning a search consultant. The search consultant or another person in the firm, sometimes called a researcher or associate, will interview company personnel and prepare a detailed description of the position, called the "brief," and they call this process of gathering the information "taking the brief." The company usually reviews and approves the brief.

The search firm's researchers then conduct research to identify target companies with names of possible candidates, which they call the "search list." Sometimes the recruiter reviews the search list with his client before he begins contacting names on the list.

The search firm scans their internal database to see whether they can add any additional candidates to the search list. The search consultant or a support person then begins contacting people on the search list by telephone to prescreen them as to their qualifications for the position and interest in it. The call goes something like this:

"Hi. I'm John Applegate with Executive Search Consultants.
We've been engaged to find a VP of marketing with experience
in the retail home furnishings business. You were referred to
me as someone who might know of a potential candidate who
might have an interest in this unusual opportunity."

You've probably received calls similar to this. The wording may have been slightly different, but you get the gist of the conversation. The recruiter isn't asking if you're interested; he's asking in a non-committal way for you to think of someone. He anticipates that, if you're interested (the real reason for the call), you'll ask some clarifying questions. If you respond that you might be interested, he knows he's done his homework well, and a short screening will follow before he decides whether to have a more in-depth interview.

The recruiter will attempt to invite all potential candidates to interview during a two-week window so he can meet everyone within a short time. At the conclusion of the interviews, the firm will put together a shortlist of top candidates they think are qualified and should be a good fit for the client's corporate culture. They present this list to the company for consideration, along with a resume for each candidate and the recruiters' interview notes and evaluations.

Most search firms' procedures will differ slightly from the previous scenario, and the firms will promote their differences to their clients as a sign of what makes them unique.

A Shared Experience

When I started my own search firm, I wanted to learn the ins and outs of the business as quickly as possible, so I prevailed on my recruiters to let me sit in on their interviews with candidates.

I also asked our clients if I could sit in on their interviews with the shortlist candidates, ostensibly so I could assess the thoroughness and quality of our own interviews and assessments. At the same time, I was able to find out how they interviewed and assessed candidates and what they considered most important.

After participating in these interviews over seven years, I developed a detailed and thorough understanding of how the recruitment process really works, and how recruiters and employers make their decisions about candidates.

Some maxims I learned from observing candidate interviews by recruiters and employers are:

◆ Employers seek candidates with the skills and experience they want. This may be different from what they really need and what the recruiter may believe they need.

◆ Employers believe their industry, and very often even their company, is unique, and they're hesitant to consider candidates with industry experience outside their comfort zone.

◆ Employers have a very strong preference for candidates who, with their most recent employer, have already done what they want done at their company.

◆ Recruiters work for employers and focus their search on what the employer wants. They're not willing to spend time considering, let alone present to their client, candidates who don't fit the profile of what the client wants.

◆ Because employers are paying substantial fees to their recruiters to "search out and find" the best candidates from their competitors, they are not generally receptive to candidates who are currently unemployed.

Companies do, however, sometimes make conscious decisions to look outside their industry. A good example was when IBM hired Louis Gerstner as CEO. Though he didn't possess the technical knowledge or experience, he did have significant turnaround experience, and that was the driving issue for considering candidates outside the IT field.

Contingency Recruiters

Contingency recruiters differ from retained recruiters in that they typically work below the executive or C-level, at salaries up to the low $100,000s, and they collect their fees only when they present a candidate whom the company subsequently employs.

Contingency recruiters maintain databases of managers, directors, and some executives, and keep extensive lists of people they meet. When a company calls wanting to fill a position through a contingency recruiter, they may give the recruiter a short window of exclusivity, such as 30 days, or they may call several recruiters at the same time. Consequently, because time is critical, these recruiters can't spend time taking a brief, researching candidates or interviewing them.

If the recruiter believes she has candidates that come close, she'll e-mail or fax candidates' resumes to the company and let them decide whom they want to see. If you've sent your resume to more than one contingency recruiter, the company may receive your resume from more than one recruiter. The first one who sent it is the firm that earns the fee if you are hired.

Contingency recruiters typically refer to themselves as recruiters or even as executive recruiters. They're not keen to promote the *contingency* part to candidates. The only safe way to know for sure is to ask them if they work on a retainer or contingency basis.

Working With Recruiters

Recruiters will only be interested in you if your skills and experience match what a client wants in connection with a specific assignment. Alternatively, they *may* be interested in you if they believe they may have an assignment in the future that might require your skills and experience.

A Shared Experience

During my years in executive search, I could see why some recruiters began to develop inflated feelings of self-importance. People always wanted my attention to tell me what they did and, not so subtly, to tell me they were thinking of making a job change. I thought, "They must figure I have a pocketful of jobs just waiting to hand out when the right person came along."

A typical recruiter may only handle about 20 to 30 assignments a year, and only rarely will they be for the same position in the same industry requiring the same skills and experience. Every assignment turns out to be unique.

In my seven years in executive search, we never had two assignments that were the same and no one from our stockpiled database of 8,000 executives and managers ever made it to a shortlist.

Recruiters I know who have about 100,000 executives on their databases often tell me they can't remember the last time they placed an executive who came from their database. The size of the database isn't what's relevant. Every assignment is unique and requires a precise set of skills, industry experience, and cultural fit that has to match a client's demanding expectations.

If you were headhunted for your last job, it's natural for you to expect the same recruiter will also help your find your next job. That probably won't happen.

If you have a personal relationship with a recruiter, she may be more comforting and tell you she'll "keep a look out for you," but realistically, recruiters rarely share their client assignments or candidates with other recruiters and employers rarely share their potential employment needs with recruiters until they've decided to engage one.

"Okay then," you decide. "I'll just send my resume to the 20 largest search firms, who probably handle most of the executive search assignments anyway." Just when you thought the information about recruiters couldn't get any worse, it does. My extensive research shows that the top 20 search firms actually handle less than 15 percent of the total executive search business!

An estimated 20,000 recruiters at over 6,000 smaller "boutique" search firms handle 85 percent of the executive search business. Some industry sources estimate the boutique search firms generate, on average, less than $2 million in annual billings each. Assuming a typical fee per assignment of $50,000 (33 percent of a $150,000 salary), the average boutique search firm handles about 40 assignments per year. This means that, if you wanted to get reasonable exposure to your resume, you'd have to analyze an estimated 20,000 recruiters to decide which recruiters should be on your mailing list.

Your chance of finding a job by contacting recruiters directly has a success rate of less than 10 percent (according to Richard Bolles, author of *What Color is Your Parachute?*). Because I do hear the *occasional* story of an executive who found her job through a recruiter, the following box suggests some techniques if you choose to send them your resume or post it on their Website.

Techniques When Posting Resumes on Recruiters' Websites

1. Include a cover letter as the first page of your resume, and be concise and specific about what you want, using the three components of your elevator pitch: position, industry, and location. Recruiters, like employers, are trying to fill a specific position in a specific industry.

2. Don't try to be all things to all people. If you broaden your interest in different industries or functions, you reduce the chance they'll consider you even for the job for which you're most qualified.

3. Acknowledge that you're aware recruiters work for employers; they don't work for you to help you find a job.

4. Point out that, if a recruiter doesn't have an assignment that matches your career objectives, he has permission to keep your resume. *Specifically mention* that you don't want him to forward your resume to any potential employer without your permission.

5. Their Website will tell you whether you can post a Microsoft Word, .rtf, or a .txt version. Some sites don't take resumes, requiring you to complete an online profile instead.

(Chapter 9 will give you suggestions on writing cover letters.)

So, how *can* you develop relationships with recruiters? Attend business and community events in your area. Make sure you meet as many people as you can. Recruiters attend as many events as possible because they'll be networking to drum up business from potential clients. Meet them and engage them in short conversations, making sure they know who you are and what you're looking for, but let them continue to network for business. If you know other executives who are working, introduce the recruiters to them—they are potential clients! The recruiters will love you and remember you!

You want recruiters to know who you are and what you want. If they see you networking at other events, they'll begin to remember you and realize you have your act together by doing what you should be doing. This will enhance their estimation of you, and, if they hear of a position that sounds right for you, even if that position isn't with their client, they'll throw your name in the hat, knowing that you could become a potential client for them someday.

Contacting Employers

You'll face three major challenges when contacting employers:

1. Which of the hundreds of thousands of employers do you target?

2. How do companies approach the recruiting of executives and managers?

3. How do you find the person in each company who would know about opportunities at your level and be in a position to consider you?

Despite these challenges, it will be far easier for you to find them than it will be for them to find you. You can identify most public and many private companies through various printed and online directories.

The difficulty will be finding subsidiaries, divisions, branch offices, and entities owned by domestic and foreign companies, as every company seems to use a different method when recruiting experienced and senior people, depending on whether the company is large or small, a parent, subsidiary, division, and so forth.

In addition, the recruiting process can even be different between functional departments (for example, between sales and finance) and divisions or subsidiaries within the same company. In larger companies, for example, the HR department at one company may have responsibility for managing recruitment, but another company in the same industry may not involve HR until after the company extends an offer, and then only to send the offer letter.

Once you know that each company has a unique way of recruiting senior talent, you understand why approaching companies can be time-consuming and complex.

Even if you're able to find out how the company handles senior-level recruiting internally and can identify the person who has direct hiring authority, you'll still have to figure out how to get past the gatekeeper and reach the person who makes decisions. If you don't get it right, your letter and resume will go to the HR department and die an untimely death.

The more targeted and purposeful your approach (as opposed to a mass mail/e-mail approach), the greater your chances of getting your information in front of a decision-maker and obtaining an interview. Chapter 8 describes how you can use your contact network to reach decision-makers, and Chapter 9 gives examples of how to prepare letters that get the attention of decision-makers.

Before you contact employers, you need to know which of the following two assumptions you'll make:

1. **A Known Need:** An employer needs to fill an existing position, or they have identified a new position they now need to fill.

2. **An Unknown Need:** An employer has not yet identified the need to have a certain function performed.

Let's look at how your approach would be different under each of these assumptions:

A Known Need

When an employer knows he needs to fill a position, he generally looks for candidates by following the sequence of methods shown in the following figure.

How Employers Find Executives and Managers	
1st	Promote or transfer someone from within.
2nd	Employ someone they already know from a competitor or who is known to them as an industry expert or a trade show speaker, or has written an article that is relevant to their industry or the position.
3rd	Employ someone recommended by an employee or someone connected with the company (for example, a shareholder or director).
4th	Employ someone recommended by someone known to the company (supplier, customer, friend, acquaintance).
5th	Employ someone who has made himself known to the company in the right way at the right time, such as from networking or a letter.

(Continued on next page.)

6th   Employ someone found by using one or more of the following methods:

▶ Placed advertisements in newspapers or trade journals.

▶ Posted a job opening on the company's internal or external Website.

▶ Searched Internet resume-posting Websites for candidates with the skills and experience the company needs.

▶ Used a federal or state government-sponsored job referral program.

▶ Used a recruiter.

There's a major distinction between the first five steps and the sixth one. In the first five, one or more of the following is present:

» The employer already knows one or more potential candidates.

» Someone they know and respect can vouch for the person.

» Some initial screening and interviewing may have already taken place.

» The employer generally has a degree of comfort with a candidate or candidates at this stage.

If the employer is unsuccessful at finding a candidate from one of the first five methods, he must then turn to sources "below the line," where potential candidates come from sources that may be untested, unreliable, or biased. Employers typically choose to use a recruiter when they:

» Lack skills internally to recruit senior-level personnel.

» Don't know how to find what they want.

» Need help in deciding what they really need.

» Can't allocate the resources internally to handle a major recruitment effectively.

» Can't risk disclosure that they're recruiting, either for competitive reasons or because they don't want a person being replaced to know about their intentions.

Recruiters often develop close professional relationships with their clients, becoming trusted advisors to management. Unfortunately, there are also recruiters who are more concerned with collecting their fee than their client's best interests.

If the employer becomes aware of you from any of the top five sources, you'll only be competing with yourself, or at most a couple of others. If the employer becomes aware of you from any of the sixth sources, you'll be competing with an unknown number of other candidates, and you'll have to sell yourself first to a recruiter, then to an HR department person, and/or finally to the decision-maker.

> **TIP** Employers sometimes choose a lesser-qualified candidate known to them from one of the first five sources, rather than take a chance on outside sources.

Recruiters fail to place candidates with their clients approximately 30 to 40 percent of the time. The reasons for these failures are most often because the employer decides to promote someone from within, they're not comfortable with the candidates submitted by the recruiter, or the employer makes an internal reorganization, eliminating the position or combining it with another function in the company.

An Unknown Need

Like most people searching for a new job are, you're probably looking for a similar position or a step up at a different company; you're not looking at companies where the position doesn't exist or the company hasn't yet come to the realization that it needs someone to perform the function.

Well-established Fortune 500 companies will probably already have the position you want, but many young and early-stage growth companies often don't.

If you're getting interviews and think you're doing well in them but not getting the job only because they're looking for younger candidates, try looking into smaller and younger companies that don't yet have that position, but will need it at some point during their growth. You're a valuable resource with experience and skills, and you have achievements to prove it.

Large companies are often reluctant to employ those who are older and more experienced (those in their late 40s and in their 50s). Smaller and younger companies, on the other hand, often look for seasoned executives with lots of experience in their industry and consider a little gray hair to be a positive trait.

If you have a background in a large, well-respected company with a name such as GE, P&G, 3M, Dell, or Johnson & Johnson on your resume, you might find a receptive audience at many smaller, younger companies. Before you approach them, however, you'll have to fine-tune your message so it overcomes their perception that you might have difficulty making the conversion from a big company environment, where you had a team to support you, to a small company where you won't have the same level of support.

A Shared Experience

In my networking, I often ask people how they found their jobs. The most frequent response is through a referral from someone they already knew or met in their networking.

The second-most frequent response, surprisingly, is from approaching a company that didn't have their desired position and convincing them they could use their experience to help the company do something better, like grow their business, be more efficient, or improve their time to market. They used their achievements to back up what they said.

I believe the ones who successfully made the transition to a smaller, younger company were probably unsuccessful at finding a job on their "A" list of large companies.

The "A" list of companies you prepared in Chapter 4 probably includes only companies that already have the function you performed at your most recent employer.

Consider including smaller, younger companies in your "B" or "C" list, who don't currently have your function as a separate position or department or it appears combined with another function or department. If you can't find that information from your research, use your contact network to help you. (Chapter 8 explains how to do that.)

If you can't determine whether an organization has your function, you may have detected an organizational weakness the company hasn't identified or doesn't yet consider a high priority. That's your opportunity to show them why they need that function, and why you're the one they need. This can be a successful way to make a career change into smaller and fast-growing companies. (Chapter 9 includes some examples of how you can present your case.) The following techniques will prepare you to contact companies.

How to Prepare to Contact Companies

1. Research company information using:

   - ⟫ Company Website.

   - ⟫ Library (for background information and current news about the company).

   - ⟫ Internet search engines such as *www.Google.com* or *www.yahoo.com.*

   - ⟫ FreeEdgar (for Securities and Exchange Commission [SEC] filings by the company [for example, Form 10-K]).

   - ⟫ Your contact network.

2. Determine how the company is organized and how it recruits executives at your level/function using:

   ⟫ Library research for news on recent management changes. (Articles often describe how they did it and whom they used.)

   ⟫ Direct contact by calling the CEO's office to ask an executive administrative assistant how they typically approach senior recruitment.

   ⟫ Direct contact by calling someone who used to work at the company.

   ⟫ Your contact network.

3. Research names of senior employees and the decision-maker by using:
   ⟫ Company Website.

   ⟫ Company's SEC filings (Form 10-K).

   ⟫ Direct contact by calling the company to ask who holds the position. If they won't tell you, ask the receptionist to transfer you to the person. You'll most likely reach the person's assistant and can ask for what you need.

   ⟫ Your contact network.

4. Find the hook:
   ⟫ Define what you can bring to the table (your achievement story).

   ⟫ Define what you can do for the company and why it needs you.

   ⟫ Ask selective contacts in your network if they have other ideas about possible hooks.

Would you like to uncover the "Hidden Job Market" or the secret "Unadvertised Job Market" that you've probably heard about? Some career services companies, consultants, and career advisors claim they have access to the hidden or the unadvertised job market, and they will market you for a fee.

Don't fall for that.

Almost *every* open position that a company needs filled is a hidden and unadvertised job, whether it falls under the known need or unknown need described earlier in this chapter. Every time an employer finds someone from one of the first five options in the chart on page 148, the job was hidden and unadvertised.

When an employer engages a recruiter to conduct a search for an executive, the job is also in the hidden or unadvertised job category. Sometimes, employers use a recruiter who uses both executive search and advertising to find executives. Although this is uncommon in the United States, there are a large number of recruiting firms known as search and selection (advertising) in the UK that use both executive search and advertising to find executives.

Bottom line: You *already* have access to this "Hidden Job Market" if you follow the advice in this book. Although it may sound enticing to have your own personal search agent look for jobs for you, neither employers nor recruiters are receptive to other people calling to market or promote you.

Your Website

If you're currently in transition with a technical background and you're looking for a position in the technology or media industry, you might want to create a Website where you can expand on your skills and experience, and include your resume.

If you decide to create a Website, keep the content focused on the reason for the Website: getting a job. Limit it to highlighting your skills, experience, and achievements. Don't show pictures of your dog, your family at Disneyworld, your hiking trip to Mt. Kilimanjaro, etc.

Based on my experience in executive search and knowledge of how recruiters and employers work at the executive and manager level, I believe the Internet is not yet the place where you will find your next job—whether it's sending your resume to Websites or posting your resume on your own Website.

One of the techniques recruiters and their researchers use to find candidates is to search the Internet looking for people with the skills and experience their clients want. If your Website contains informative articles or stories identifying your skills and experience that demonstrates your achievements, recruiters and researchers will want to talk to you. A Website with a long list of all your skills and experience will have the same effect as if you were to put them on your resume. More is less!

Having a Website containing your resume can be an advantage when you're networking. Rather than carrying your resume around, which I don't recommend anyway, you should have a personal business card with the URL of your Website where those who are interested in knowing more about you can go for more information. A Website also enables others to find more about you when it's convenient for them and if they are referring you to someone else, that person can find out about you very easily 24/7!

Not having a Website probably won't have a significant adverse effect on the success of your job search. Having one, however, gives you additional means for others to find out about you and, the more ways you can connect with others, the more successful your search will be.

Networking

Networking is *THE* most successful technique you can use to make a job or career change—but only if you do it properly. Chapter 8 is devoted to networking because it's the most important and powerful technique you can use.

☑ Milestones

The following milestones recap what you need to do to complete this chapter. Include those items you are unable to complete in your summary-level open-items list.

❑ 1. Investigate job fairs and trade shows that are of interest to you within a reasonable commute. Inquire as to the exhibitors and audience to determine if you should attend.

❑ 2. Attend trade shows and industry conferences. Be visible, expand your network, and inquire about opportunities in general, who's hiring, who's downsizing, and what's the latest news on the industry and companies in it.

❑ 3. Investigate whether government-run career and job centers are conveniently located to you and what resources they have that could benefit your search.

❑ 4. Read newspapers and trade periodicals on a regular basis to keep up-to-date on topical events. Keep abreast of job-related information and industry news.

❑ 5. Attend seminars or workshops that update your skills and expand your knowledge in areas where you have a particular interest. Use this opportunity to build your network.

❑ 6. Consider writing articles for publication in industry- or function-specific publications to get your name recognized as an expert.

❑ 7. Get involved in nonprofit, community, trade, political, special interest, and/or professional organizations where you can be active, visible, and expand your network.

❑ 8.   Create your profile on *www.ExecGlobalNet.com.* The process you'll follow will help you focus your search.

❑ 9.   Go to *www.ExecGlobalNet.com* and look in the **Career Center** for "Resource 4.1: Where to Get Additional Information." Investigate the sources that are relevant to your situation.

❑ 10. Go to a regional or local library and ask at the reference desk for the information they have online. You should find a wealth of information you can't access on your own. Ask what information sources you can access remotely from your home computer through a library card.

❑ 11. Identify the recruiters in your area who cover your industry or job function. Call them and ask where they recommend you network.

❑ 12. Send your resume to a select group of recruiters, limiting your time devoted to this to no more than 10 percent of your total search time. Do a little each week.

❑ 13. Identify where you plan to concentrate your time by week. Which events seem to provide the best opportunities for you? Schedule your time around these events. Act as if you're currently employed and your job is to attend these events. Get involved and be active in not-for-profit organizations, connect with others, and expand your network.

❑ 14. Consider creating a simple personal Website that features your skills and experience and demonstrates them with your achievement stories. Include articles you've written showcasing your industry or functional expertise and include your resume in a downloadable format, such as Microsoft Word, .rtf, .txt, or .pdf.

Section IV

Mastering the Different Ways You Communicate With Others

Networking

If you want others to help you, you must first get them to want to help you.

Chapter Overview

If you were starting a business, how would you promote its features and benefits to potential customers? The challenge remains the same if you're searching for a job. How will you promote your skills, experience, and achievements to your potential customer—the employer? This chapter will:

» Introduce you to a simple three-phase approach that will improve your success at networking for employment.

» Show you how to broaden your contacts well beyond those you already have.

» Increase your effectiveness at getting your contacts to want to help you.

» Improve your ability to ask the right questions to get the help you need.

The main sections in this chapter include:

» Why you must network and be effective at it.

» Build an effective network in three easy phases.

» How to use questions to get your network to want to work for you.

» Networking requires a personal commitment.

» Suggestions on where to network.

» Milestones.

Having a contact network alone won't help you find a new job or career unless you can get your contacts to *want* to help you. The effectiveness of your network will be the defining difference between success and a long, drawn-out and potentially unsuccessful search.

Most people think networking for employment is the same as networking for business. They're quite different, and, if you don't understand the differences, your network won't work for you. The guidelines in this chapter focus on networking for a job or for exploring a new career, not networking for business.

> **Networking** for employment is a process that facilitates connecting you from where you are to where you want to go in the shortest amount of time possible.

Why You Must Network and Be Effective at It

Research indicates that people who used networking as part of a well-organized and planned job search were successful at finding their next job more than 85 percent of the time.

Other research indicates that, when employers need to recruit management talent, they turn to executive recruiters 64 percent of the time.

What these seemingly contradictory statistics mean is that employers are only able to find senior-level talent using their own sources about one-third of the time. When they're not successful, they turn to recruiters two-thirds of the time. The five different ways companies try to find senior talent on their own are listed in Chapter 7 (page 148).

Some people might think contacting recruiters makes the most sense, because they handle two-thirds of all management recruitment. *You* know that wouldn't be effective, because you'd have to find and then attract the attention of that one recruiter out of more than 20,000 who would be conducting the right search for you. Then, if you're currently unemployed, you'd have to compete with other candidates who are currently working.

You'll stand a much better chance that companies will consider you if you use your network of contacts to connect with the appropriate person in the company. Using this approach increases your potential success at finding your next job up to 85 percent.

A Shared Experience

I often hear about executives who want to change jobs while they're still working and make the mistake of sending their resume to one or more recruiters, asking them to be discreet in helping them look for a new job.

Unfortunately, they don't know how recruiters work and don't realize that companies pay recruiters to find people.

As expected (and as you should now know), though the recruiters say they'll "look" for opportunities for these executives, they're also starting to look for their replacements. If they find a replacement first, they present that candidate to the company—which obviously says it doesn't have an open position.

The recruiter will then "discreetly" inform the company that he has knowledge that their employee is "on the market," and that he has the perfect replacement.

The recruiter may not be successful in placing the "perfect replacement candidate" but, as expected, employees often lose their jobs when confronted with the evidence.

Knowing which approaches might work for you is only part of the process. You'll also need to know how to build your network and use it effectively. Because networking will be key to your success at finding what you want, it's crucial that you get it right.

If you're making a *job* change: The contacts you meet and add to your network will help you gather information about your target companies and help you connect with the right people: those who are able to make decisions about employing you.

If you're making a *career* change: The contacts you meet and add to your network will help you connect with people who understand whether your anticipated change is right for you. They can evaluate the reasonableness of your thinking and the likelihood of success in making such a change, and they can introduce you to others who may help you find out what you need to know.

Build an Effective Network in 3 Easy Phases

Networking for business is generally easy and straightforward. You meet someone; discuss the features, benefits, and price of a product or service; and then exchange business cards.

When I started my search firm and networked for business, I observed executives who were networking for jobs and noticed the ones who seemed most successful. I asked them how they approached networking and why. Although their explanations varied, they all seemed to share a common theme:

→ "If I want others to help me in my search, I've got to create a relationship with them that makes them *want* to help me."

→ "Once I've created that relationship, I need to make sure they know what I want and why my skills and experience qualify me for it."

Using this new insight, I created a graphic representation with an explanation of the three phases I observed so others could quickly grasp its concept and remember the process more easily.

I use the acronym IOU to represent the three phases: **Initiate, Obtain,** and Use. The acronym IOU helps you remember these phases.

First, let's examine each phase so you're clear about the purpose of each one and can see why you must follow them sequentially.

158

Phase 1: Initiate

The **Initiate** phase is when you're introducing yourself to people with the intent to initiate relationships and develop rapport with them. This phase is similar to what you often do in a social setting.

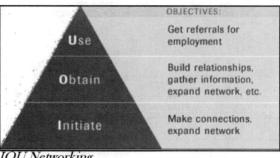

IOU Networking

You'll spend the largest amount of your time in this phase and will have to "kiss a lot of frogs," because you'll find you won't like some people, some of them won't like you, you won't find any common interest, or the other person simply won't be interested in you.

Phase 2: Obtain

In the **Obtain** phase, you're building on the relationships you successfully created in the **Initiate** phase so you can obtain support, encouragement, information, and referrals. You need to be careful not to move too quickly from **Initiate** to **Obtain,** because you could lose a potentially valuable contact if you haven't built the relationship first.

In some situations, however, you may find you can proceed more quickly from the **Initiate** phase to the **Obtain** phase, such as when you're at events designed to help people who are in transition connect with each other quickly.

Phase 3: Use

If you've successfully initiated and built relationships during the first two phases, you'll be able to proceed to the Use phase. Here, you'll be asking your contact for referrals that will directly or indirectly result in your connecting with a person who has the power to employ you.

The acronym IOU is a reminder that when you successfully find your next job or a new career, you owe a huge thank you to those who helped you get there.

Let's turn to specific objectives you should pursue while in each phase. I'll suggest some techniques you can use that will help you achieve your objectives.

How to Use Questions to Get Your Network to Want to Work for You

The Networking Objectives Matrix lists your six basic networking objectives and shows the phases when it's most appropriate to use them.

Networking Objectives Matrix			
	Phase		
IOU Networking Objective	1 Initiate	2 Obtain	3 Use
1. Initiate relationships.	✓		
2. Expand your network.	✓	✓	✓
3. Obtain referrals.	✓	✓	
4. Obtain support and encouragement.		✓	
5. Obtain information for research.		✓	
6. Get referrals for employment.			✓

Because you could have similar objectives in more than one phase, I'll suggest some ways you can successfully pursue each of the objectives and provide some explanations for how you might adjust your technique, depending on where you are in the process.

1. Initiate Relationships.

This objective seems to be the most difficult for many who held positions where opportunities for networking weren't an integral part of the job. Even if your job required you to network to develop business (for example, sales), networking for employment will be much different.

When initiating relationships during a job search, bear in mind that your goal is to create a relationship with someone (perhaps not even the person you initially meet), leading to a recommendation for employment for a job or a new career.

Illustration by Steven Lait.

If you rush this critical objective and aren't successful at creating the relationship, you'll never know what you may have missed—perhaps another connection, a needed insight, or a referral to someone else whom you couldn't reach any other way. Take your time and do it right.

When you attend an event, arrive early so you can get a lay of the land and converse with those who also came early. Your conversations will be more relaxed with fewer distractions. As others arrive, you have an opportunity to bring another person into the conversation and re-introduce each other.

If you arrive late, you'll enter a room where small groups have formed and conversations are already taking place. This can be intimidating and make it more difficult to find a group where you can break in, introduce yourself, and join the conversation. This is particularly important if you are the least bit shy or uncomfortable or inexperienced with networking.

Start by introducing yourself. Depending on the event, you might want to add your occupation/job and industry experience. Lead with questions that elicit a conversation, such as:

❖ "What do you do?"

❖ "What's your business?"

❖ "How long have you been in business?"

❖ "How long have you been a member of (the organization)?"

❖ "Why are you attending this event?" OR "What brought you here?"

❖ "Have you heard this evening's speaker before?"

❖ "Do you know anything about the speaker?"

❖ "How did you get started in your business?"

❖ "How did you choose your career?"

❖ "Who are you with?" OR "Who do you work for?"

❖ "What's the situation in your company since the (current economic situation, recently announced merger, or some other development [based on what you know or have read about the company])?"

❖ "What impact do you see on the industry because of (a topical issue that might affect employment)?"

If you're attending an industry/trade show, do the following before you go:

❖ Get a list of companies and attendees. Use last year's list if the current year's isn't available. What companies and job titles of the attendees are on the list?

❖ If there's an industry focus, is it familiar to you, or do you need to research it before attending?

❖ Anticipate what you think will be the objectives of those attending.

❖ Be clear about what your networking objectives will be, but be prepared to modify them based on circumstances.

❖ Check the schedule and note the networking times so you can plan your minutes most effectively.

◆ *Don't* take your resume with you. You want to build your network and develop relationships. If you give them your resume too soon, it's obvious the conversation is all about you and not about them. You risk losing the opportunity to have a further conversation with them.

◆ Arrive early, before the crowd develops, so you can engage people in discussions and avoid competing with others for their attention.

While you're at the event:

◆ When you meet other attendees, introduce yourself and then ask about them. What do they do? Don't start by discussing your job or career search. You're in Phase 1; focus on developing relationships and expanding your network.

◆ Bring up some topical event that can serve as an icebreaker. Ideally, this could relate to the subject of the event or the type of people at the event.

◆ Ask what, in particular, brought them to the event—part of their job, new employee who needs to get up to speed, they've lost some people and need to do double-duty, and so forth. (If you don't ask, you never know what answer you'll get!)

◆ Ask about their employers or jobs and determine how that relates to the topic of the event.

◆ If you're attending an event that companies attend to promote their products and services, it will become obvious to them pretty quickly you're not there because of your interest in what they have to sell. After introducing yourself, ask for permission to have a conversation; for example, ask, "Do you have a few minutes for me to ask you some questions?" If they say, "Not now," ask if you could talk to them later and, if so, when and where would it be convenient. Offer to meet where you can buy them lunch or a cup of coffee.

◆ Try to find commonalities in your experience or skills that could create a connection between you and your networking targets.

◆ If you've created a dialogue, your questioning likely will have elicited some questions about you. If not, the person probably isn't interested, and you should excuse yourself to find someone else with whom you can have a discussion. Don't be afraid to end an encounter and move on if the discussion isn't getting the results you want.

◆ If you're able to develop an informal connection with someone, and if it's appropriate *and* you feel comfortable asking, explain why you're there. Ask if she has any thoughts on who else you might speak with at the event. If she doesn't show an interest or make any suggestions, thank her for her time and politely excuse yourself.

◆ If you develop a rapport with someone who seems genuinely interested in you and your situation, exchange business cards and ask if he would be willing to meet you another time so you can pick his brain some more.

◆ If someone asks for your resume, explain that you didn't bring it because your intent was to gather information that might help you make job or career decisions. Get his business card and assure him you'll send a copy of your resume tomorrow. When you send your resume, enclose a cover letter thanking him for his time and interest. Add something that helps him remember you from the dozens of others he might have met that day, and clarify any points you couldn't make when you met. This also gives you an opportunity to follow up with him in the future.

At some events, such as those designed to help executives in transition, you might be able to accelerate moving from the "I" to the "O"—initiating relationships to another objective, such as asking for a referral to another for information. But you must feel confident that the other person is ready to move on. If you're eager but you're not sure the other person is ready, you're better off not rushing it.

When you meet someone who agrees to talk with you further:

◆ Thank him and exchange contact details. Say you'll call him later to set something up. Don't try to schedule meetings at networking events.

◆ When you call, thank him again and schedule a time to meet. Mention that you'd like no more than 20 minutes of his time. If he agrees, confirm the date, time, and length of the meeting by sending an e-mail or letter within a couple of days after your telephone conversation. If your meeting is more than a couple of weeks away, send a reminder e-mail or call and leave a message a few days before your meeting.

◆ Suggest meeting for breakfast, coffee, lunch, or an afternoon break, as it may not be appropriate or convenient for them to meet you at work. Dinners are not usually an effective environment at this stage, and they can become expensive quickly. A dinner may be appropriate after you've developed a relationship and have met previously.

Be careful about trying to move too quickly when you first meet. You're likely to lose the contact if the other person thinks you weren't genuinely interested in what he had to say, but only interested in getting a meeting to ask for a favor. This is an all-too-common mistake, and one that's extremely important for you to avoid.

2. Expand Your Network.

Your circle of family, friends, colleagues, and acquaintances are the contacts at the core of your network. Those who know each other are your **Power**

Contacts, because they know you *and* each other. If two of your contacts refer you to the same person, that new person will view you much more comfortably.

You're probably familiar with the theory of "six degrees of separation," which holds that you're only six acquaintances away from anyone else in the world. In a job or career search situation, however, if you choose your contacts carefully, you only have about three degrees of separation.

Beyond three degrees, the quality of the referral often becomes more tenuous and less effective because you're expecting people to put their reputation on the line to recommend you to others.

The illustration (at right) shows how your network can expand like the ripple effect from a drop of water. One contact leads to another, which leads to another, and so on. People often comment on how contacts at the third degree of separation had a connection or a similar interest that created a close and strong relationship.

Never discount a contact who you think won't be helpful in your job search because she just might turn out to be the one who refers you to the person you want to con-

Expanding Your Network

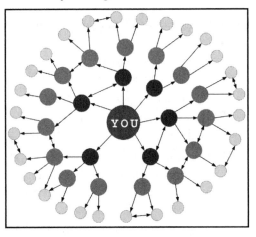

tact. The more people in your network who know you and are familiar with your job or career objectives, the greater your chances of finding the job you want in the shortest time possible.

3. Obtain Referrals.

This is the next hurdle. You've successfully established a relationship with someone, and now you want to ask for a referral. People often fail at this stage because they don't have a clear picture in their minds of what they want from a referral. Is it simply to expand your network, to conduct research, or to find someone who'll support and encourage you?

If you were to ask me, "Could you refer me to someone else?" I'd probably respond, "Possibly." Now what? If I don't know what you want, I won't be able to refer you to the person you need. This may seem obvious, but you only have a few seconds to tell me what kind of a referral you want.

If you don't start thinking about it until we're having our conversation, or if you seem the least bit unclear as to what you want, I'm probably going to respond that I don't think I can help you, when in fact I possibly could. You've made an unfavorable impression, and I'm not likely to go out of my way to help you.

When you network, you won't know whom you'll be meeting or what kind of a contact they'll be. Consequently, you'll have to identify what you think the different options could be, and then decide what you would ask under each set of circumstances.

This may sound overwhelming, but in reality, you'll only have a few options, such as to find:

» A mentor to support and encourage you.

» Someone who works in the industry you want to transfer to.

» Someone who has made a similar job or industry change as you are considering.

» Someone who has worked at and knows about an employer you plan to target.

Prepare a list of questions you think applies to your situation, then review your list before you meet or attend an event. You'll impress those you meet if it's obvious you're clear on what you want from a referral.

Okay, one of your contacts has agreed to refer you to someone else. Now what? Here are some suggestions on how to approach the referral:

◆ Call the referral and mention you're calling at the suggestion of the referrer. Be prepared for the referral to ask you when and where you last spoke to the referrer and, perhaps, some other questions about the referrer to test whether you're telling the truth.

◆ Explain in general terms the purpose of your call, taking no more than 30 seconds—for example, "I'm considering making a career change from the X industry to the Y industry, and John suggested I talk to you because you're an expert in the Y industry and could give me the insight I need."

◆ Do *not* attempt to conduct an interview on the telephone. Try to schedule a meeting (breakfast, coffee, lunch). You want to start with some **Initiate** objectives, because the referral doesn't know you and may be uncomfortable giving you any serious help until he feels he knows you better.

◆ If the referral presses you for your questions so he can answer them on the phone, explain that you haven't compiled all your questions yet because you only called to see if he'd be willing to meet, and you were hoping to schedule a meeting. You might add that you'll be doing further research before you meet that will result in targeted questions.

165

◆ If the referral agrees to meet, always send an e-mail or letter, or call to confirm your scheduled meeting a few days before the meeting. Remember: Your personal agenda isn't his.

◆ If, instead of agreeing to meet you, the referral suggests you talk to someone else he knows, get his permission to use his name as a referral. Ask if he'll call or e-mail the other person to let them know that you're doing research, for example, and will be calling them.

When you meet your contact or referral:

◆ On the day of your meeting, make sure you arrive early. If you're meeting at his office, he'll probably have informed the receptionist or his assistant and ask to be alerted when you arrive. If you arrive right on time, he won't have heard from his receptionist or assistant and may assume you aren't coming or will be arriving late. As a result, your meeting might be delayed or even pre-empted. Always *plan* to arrive 15 to 20 minutes early.

◆ Spend your early time to get comfortable with the surroundings. This is an excellent time for you to practice what to do when you arrive at a company for a job interview. Look around and assess the company environment and culture based on what you see.

◆ When you meet the person, thank him for taking the time to see you and reiterate the purpose of your meeting.

◆ Reconfirm your referral's time availability. Many people forget how much time they committed and overextend themselves, or sometimes something more important will come up that takes precedence over your meeting. If this person is a referral, spend a few moments reminding him about the person who referred you. Try to understand the relationship between them so you'll understand the strength of the referral.

◆ Have your notebook handy with your questions, and make sure he can see you really do have a list. Mention you'll take notes during the conversation. If you agreed to a 20-minute meeting, by the time you finish pleasantries and discussions about the referrer, you'll only have 15 minutes left. If you take three minutes explaining your background and what you're looking for (job title, industry, and location), you now have only 12 minutes left to get the answers you came for. Be very sensitive to the time.

◆ Ask the most important questions first, not necessarily in the order you listed them. One of the vagaries of these initial meetings and interviews is that a question you so meticulously created before the interview suddenly seems inappropriate, unnecessary, or out of sequence.

◆ When your allotted time is up, thank the interviewee for his time. If you were unable to ask all your questions, ask if you can meet again to finish your questioning. If he says it's okay to continue the meeting, finish your questioning. When you're done, thank him again for his time and comments. Ask if he could suggest someone else you might contact. Let him know the purpose.

◆ If the referrer asks for your resume, mention that you're in a research mode to gather more information so you can make more informed decisions about your job or career change. You didn't bring a resume with you because it isn't complete. If he would like to see one, tell him you'll send a draft when you get home. Ask if he prefers you send it by e-mail or mail. If he chooses email and asks you to send it to his company e-mail address, reconfirm his choice; some employers scan e-mail messages for the word "resume" and company firewalls often delete attachments. When you return home, send a thank-you e-mail or letter, enclosing your resume (only if it was requested). In your email/letter, reiterate what you're seeking, what questions you're trying to answer, or what issues you're trying to resolve.

◆ If the referral tells you he "may have a potential opening for someone like you," thank him for considering you. Mention that you're flattered, but that you need to complete your research. Ask when he plans to make a decision about the position, because you might be interested, and you'd like to know how long the opportunity would be available.

4. Obtain Support and Encouragement.

You'll have two basic groups of contacts in your network. One will be those closest to you or with whom you have a very close relationship (I'll refer to these as friends), and the other group will be those who help you answer a question, clarify an issue, and/or send you on to see another person (I'll refer to these as acquaintances).

Your friends will serve as your personal champions. They know you best. You can ask them questions about whether they really think the career option you're considering is right for you. You can rely on this group to tell you what you need to know—not what you want to hear—and you can trust that their information will be in your best interest.

Most of your friends have known you for several years, and some are familiar with you in a work setting. A few will come from your networking, particularly as a result of two or more of your referrers as noted in Number 2 previously on expanding your network.

To create a relationship as a friend, you'll have to open up and be receptive to criticism and hearing what you need to hear. Your friends need to know enough about you to be able to talk about you in a way similar to how you would do it yourself.

Keep your friends informed on how you're progressing on a regular basis. Keep them aware of whom you talk to and what you learned, what you'll do next, and when. You want them to be your coaches, and you want them to see themselves that way. A coach doesn't tell you what to do, but supports, encourages, and holds you accountable for what you say you'll do.

Nurture these relationships. Meet your friends occasionally for breakfast or lunch, but keep the conversation focused on your search. Make commitments to them about what you'll do, gain their perspectives, and ask if they see something you might be missing. Encourage them to hold you accountable for achieving your objectives.

If they're new friends, make them feel like they've known you for years and can vouch for what you tell others. Consider getting some or all of the people in this group together at one time and introduce them to each other so they know who else supports you. By doing that, you help them expand their own networks.

Don't expect your friends to help you if they don't know enough about you. Make sure they have a current version of your resume, and review it with them in detail so they're comfortable talking about you when someone calls for a reference. You're responsible for making sure your friends believe:

» You've communicated your goals and achievements succinctly and clearly.

» Your career goals are consistent with your skills and experience.

» You're qualified for the job or career opportunity you want.

» Your achievements demonstrate your skills and experience.

» You and your job-search or career-change goals are in alignment with each other.

» They are comfortable being in this group and being your champion.

» They can talk to others about you with conviction and assurance that they know you well.

5. Obtain Information for Research.

Your second group, your acquaintances, will be those you meet with the intent to obtain something that helps you make decisions or clarify your strategy. Richard Nelson Bolles, in his career book, *What Color is Your Parachute?* (Ten Speed Press, published annually) refers to this process as Informational Interviewing.

Partly because of the success of Bolles's book, too many people have misused the intent of Informational Interviewing as a ruse to get themselves in front of someone to ask for a job.

Rather than saying you're doing Informational Interviewing and then see people roll their eyes, explain that you're conducting research, and make sure you have a clear idea of what you want. For example, when you're conducting research, you're looking for answers to the following:

» Information on an industry or organization.

» Referral to someone who's made a career change similar to the one you're contemplating.

» Help and suggestions on how to translate your experience in a specific industry to a new one that your contact knows.

» Knowledge of opportunities within an industry or a specific company and how you can position yourself to pursue a job or career change.

» Referral to someone in an industry you want to transfer to so you can discuss the appropriateness of your skills and experience as they relate to that industry, and whether you can translate your experience to their industry.

» Referral to someone who can answer questions about your relocating to a specific area.

Using the examples of how to approach a referral in the previous sections, make sure you clearly communicate what you want to talk to her about and why.

Give her an estimate of how much time you think you'll need (a 15- to 20-minute meeting is common) and ask if that's okay for her. If it isn't, ask how much time she can give you.

When you go, have an agenda with your questions. Make sure they are open-ended and can't be answered by a yes or no. If you ask broad questions, you may find you get all the answers you wanted, including some you hadn't thought about. Here are some examples of questions you can ask:

◆ "Can you tell me about your position (or job)?

◆ "Can you tell me about your company (or division or subsidiary)?"

◆ "Can you tell me about your industry?"

◆ "What do you like most and least about your job (or company or industry)?"

◆ "What are some of the pros and cons of your job (or company or industry)?"

◆ "What would you consider to be your company's 'hot buttons'?"

◆ "How did you go about getting your job?"

◆ "What specific skills and experience are required for your job?"

◆ "How is your company organized?" OR "How are companies in this industry typically organized?"

◆ "What do you think are the most important skills or skill sets for someone to have?"

◆ "What's the typical career path for people in this field (or industry)?" (There are often classic career paths in some fields—for example, from sales associate to territory sales manager to regional sales manager to national or product sales manager to VP Sales. You'll want to assess whether and how that might restrict you if you're making a career change.)

◆ "How would you view the transferability of my skills to this industry?"

◆ "I'm researching whether I can transfer my skills and experience in my own industry to [name of the new industry]. Do you know anyone I could talk to who has made a similar change?"

◆ "What educational requirements or qualifications would be needed for this new job?"

◆ "How would you suggest that someone with my skills and experience go about making a job or career change to your industry?"

◆ "Could you refer me to someone else who might be able to help me decide about this planned career change?" (Even if the person was able to help you with answers to many of your questions, ask for referrals so you can expand your network.)

◆ "I'm exploring a [job title] position at [employer], but I haven't been able to find [the name of a person you want, how they handle recruitment, who's responsible for a division, etc.]. Can you help me?"

◆ "Do you know companies in this field?" If so, "What do you think would be the most appropriate way to contact ABC Company?"

◆ "Do you know someone at XYZ Company to whom you could introduce me?" If not, "Do you know someone else who might have contacts in XYZ Company to whom you could introduce me?" (The person you want to reach for a referral doesn't necessarily have to be a company employee.)

◆ "Do you know anyone else I could talk to who might be able to assist me in making my career transition?"

◆ "What trends do you see that might affect the job (or company or industry) that I should consider?"

At the end, ask if there is anything you didn't ask that she thinks you should know.

Be mindful. The purpose of your meeting is to obtain information, viewpoints, ideas, and referrals that will help you make decisions. Also, you're seeking to make contact with others who can get you closer to a target company. Don't attempt to get referrals for employment during an initial meeting.

However, if you and the referral develop a good relationship during this meeting, it's an opportunity to ask her if she'd be willing to meet again after you've completed your research and have a better idea how you plan to make your transition. At that meeting, if she feels you're on target, ask her if she would be willing to introduce you to someone for possible employment. If you're successful at this, you will have moved her from an acquaintance to a friend.

This leads to the next objective: get referrals for employment.

6. Get Referrals for Employment.

You've invested a lot of time in your contacts: getting to know them, getting them to know you, and educating them about what you do, where you've worked, what you've achieved, and what you want to find. If you've built that relationship properly, you should now be able to leverage your relationships into referrals for employment.

This objective is only appropriate in the Use phase because you're asking your referral to use all the information she now knows about you and put her reputation on the line to refer you to someone for employment. You may be comfortable with the relationship to ask her, but, if she isn't comfortable with you, she's not going to risk her reputation to refer you to someone who can employ you.

You also need to be sure that the person you'll be asking to refer you for employment is the one you want. Do you know her well enough to know whether the person she'll refer you to respects her and her judgment? Are you certain she carries enough weight to influence a potential meeting with your target person (that is, the person who can employ you)?

You may have only one opportunity for a referral to your target person. If that referrer isn't the right one, your target person probably won't be receptive to a second attempt from another of your contacts.

When you're confident you want your contact to make a referral, here are some examples of what you can ask her to do:

» Refer you to your target person by calling him on your behalf or sending him an e-mail or letter introducing you.

» Refer you to another person external to the company who can introduce you to your target person.

» Introduce you to someone within the company who can facilitate your connecting with your target person.

You may encounter situations where your contacts don't have a direct link to your target person, or don't have any ideas that could help you. It will be up to you to connect the dots for them by giving them various options they haven't considered.

Thinking about what you should have asked after you leave your meeting won't be of much help to you. More importantly, your lack of preparation could weaken your contact's confidence in your thought process and capabilities.

Although asking for referrals assumes you're in the Use phase, you might be able to ask for a referral in the Obtain phase. You'll need to feel you've developed a strong enough relationship where the other person will feel comfortable making a referral.

Here's an example of how you can ask your contact a series of questions, assuming she answers each question with a no: Let's assume your contact knows that you're looking for a Chief Production Officer position in the XYZ industry in the Chicago area, with a particular interest in Albatross Industries. You could ask, "Do you know anyone at Albatross whom I might talk to about a potential opportunity there?"

If your contact answers with a no, follow with, "Do you know someone else who might know someone at Albatross?"

If your contact answers with a no, you can ask, "Do you know anyone who works for a competitor of Albatross?"

If your contact answers no, you can revert to an Obtain phase type of question and ask, "Do you have any thoughts on how I might connect with someone who works at Albatross?"

If she tells you nothing comes to mind, but she'll think about it and let you know, you could suggest that she also think about companies in Albatross's supply chain. For example, whom do they buy from (significant vendors) and whom do they sell to (significant customers)?

When you're trying to come up with your questions, assume she'll answer negatively to each one and be prepared to ask a follow-up question. If you don't, I guarantee you'll think of at least one question later that you'll wish you had asked.

Networking Requires a Personal Commitment

Asking the right questions is a major part of successful networking for employment. Equally important, though, is how you come across to others when you network. If others perceive that you're just going through the motions, they won't see you as being personally committed.

When you ask questions, make sure you're interested in the answer. If you ask illogical questions or follow-up questions that are inconsistent with your line of thought, your contact may conclude you're not interested in him and just asking questions to appear interested. When your contact responds to a question, think about what he said and not about the next question you want to ask.

Show others you're genuinely interested in them by being an active listener. Here are some suggestions:

» Look at them while they speak.

» Show genuine interest in their comments by nodding and making encouraging acknowledgments (for example, "Uh-huh. You're right"; "Yeah, I see what you mean"; "Really?"; "That's interesting"; "Oh?"; and "I see").

» Watch other people's facial expressions, arm gestures, and body language for signs of enthusiasm, boredom, or indications that they want to leave and talk to someone else.

» Listen to (don't just hear) what they have to say and respond appropriately.

» Gauge the effect you're having on people. Are they backing away? Do they seem distracted or preoccupied with something else? Are they looking around, trying to catch another person's eye? Are *they* responding like an active listener?

» Be sensitive to their needs. Don't tie up too much of their time. If it seems appropriate to move on, thank them for their time and perhaps ask to exchange business cards.

The following two figures on page 174 highlight those techniques that increase—or decrease—the effectiveness of your networking.

Techniques That *Increase* Networking Effectiveness

▶ Concentrate on building relationships with those who have an interest in you and who'll commit to help.

▶ Explain with laser-like clarity your career objectives (position, industry, and location).

▶ Be respectful of your contact's time.

▶ Prepare in advance for every meeting. What do you want to know or accomplish?

▶ If you go to an event, arrive early. You can make better connections if fewer people are competing for attention.

▶ Read the news *every day.* Know what's topical.

▶ Stay abreast of current events in your industry or functional area.

▶ Look for personal similarities in your experience or skills that might match your contact's background.

▶ Show that you're in charge of your search and use your contact as a resource, not as someone on whom you can unload your excess baggage.

▶ Listen and be prepared to switch your IOU networking phase to match the situation.

▶ Be receptive to opinions or suggestions you might not have thought about on your own. You *want* different perspectives.

▶ Have business cards handy but *never* a resume, unless you're asked to bring one.

▶ Have a positive attitude about being unemployed and cast it as an opportunity. Don't try to ignore it.

▶ Get agreement as to how often you should call. Call when you have something you want to know or need help to accomplish. Always have something specific to discuss.

Techniques That *Decrease* Networking Effectiveness

▶ When asked what you want, be unclear and unfocused.

▶ Ask for a referral without building a relationship.

▶ Show insincere friendliness rather than treating contacts as professional advisors.

▶ Show narcissism or egoism. Talk about what *you* want without listening to what *they* say.

▶ Ignore their advice without explaining why.

▶ Don't keep your contacts informed about referrals they've given you.

▶ Don't contact referrals in a timely manner.

▶ Overstate or mislead others about your relationship with your contacts.

▶ Arrange a meeting for some **Obtain** phase questioning, and then at the meeting explain that you're really looking for a job and give them your resume.

▶ Call your contacts frequently without having a real purpose.

▶ Complain about your last employer and how hard it's been for you to find a new job.

▶ Carry several copies of your resume with you to hand out to people you meet.

Suggestions on Where to Network

Networking requires a *serious* investment of your time to make and develop new contacts. You *must* get out, network, and meet people. As you do, you'll meet others doing the same thing. Share your experiences with them, and they'll share theirs with you. The **Career Center** on *www.ExecGlobalNet.com* includes a list of networking organizations that you might want to consider to get you started.

Here are suggestions regarding where to network:

❖ Identify as many networking groups in your location as possible, attend each one, and evaluate their potential to help you.

❖ Groups that focus on developing business are great if you want to start and grow a consulting practice or a small business, but they aren't very effective if you're trying to find a job.

❖ If you're trying to shift to a new industry, focus on attending functions or groups in the new industry.

❖ Ask your friends and former colleagues for suggestions on where to network.

❖ If you're a member of a national professional association, check out the association Website to see if they have a local discussion group or chapter where members meet and exchange information.

❖ Search the Internet. Try Google, Yahoo, and other directories and search engines.

❖ Contact business networking organizations. There are venture capital and technology-related networking groups around the United States.

❖ Contact your local chamber of commerce for referrals to organizations in your area.

❖ Contact the banquet office of local hotels and ask for the names of groups that book events on a recurring monthly basis.

❖ Contact a local university and ask the business school or graduate school for names of networking groups. Ask the department that covers your field of interest for names of networking groups in your functional area.

❖ Contact outplacement firms near where you live and ask where they encourage their clients to network. Some sponsor networking events where they invite employers. Some also allow non-clients to attend in order to encourage more employers to attend.

◆ Contact recruiters in your area, tell them what you're looking for (job, industry, and location), and ask them where *they* network or if they can suggest where you might network. Recruiters network to develop business, and, because they often specialize by industry, they're usually familiar with the best places to network for that industry.

◆ Seek out nonprofit associations and organizations in your community and volunteer to use your expertise to help them accomplish some objective or to serve on the board or committees. Commit to take charge of your area of responsibility with gusto, be active, and stand out as a breath of fresh air and someone who gets things done.

◆ Offer to lead a seminar or workshop on a subject in your area of expertise for a group and notify your local newspaper. Many newspapers have calendars of events covering subjects that would be of interest to their readers. Contact the chamber of commerce, library, or community service clubs (Rotary, Kiwanis, and so forth) in your community for suggestions on a venue.

◆ Use Internet networking sites, such as Linkedin, Plaxo, and others, to look for connections to companies. Be careful about making others aware that you are looking to make a job or career change as that information may find its way to your current employer.

It's preferable to network in the location where you want to work, but sometimes that's not realistic. For example, if you want to relocate to Southern California and you live on the East Coast, your networking on the East Coast won't be nearly as effective as if you were networking in Southern California.

If you're looking for opportunities at other locations, you'll want to focus on asking questions about companies that might be opening or expanding a facility where you want to work. Try also to build a network of people in your area who can introduce you to others where you want to work or to those in your area who have responsibility for operations in the area where you want to work.

☑ Milestones

The following milestones recap what you need to do to complete this chapter. Include those items you are unable to complete in your summary-level open-items list.

❑ 1. Begin to gather the names of people to include in your initial contact list. Indicate your relationship with them, and consider grouping them by relationship: friends and acquaintances. Focus only on names at first.

❑ 2. If you're making a job change, practice your 30-second pitch about what you're seeking until you feel comfortable that you can say it without hesitation.

❑ 3. If you're pursuing or exploring a career change, practice what you'll tell people about what you'd like to do and what information you're trying to obtain to help you make a decision. Be as brief as possible.

❑ 4. If you're changing jobs, prepare a list of topics that you can use to get your existing circle of contacts up to speed about what you've accomplished and what you're targeting in your job search.

❑ 5. If you're pursuing or exploring a possible career change, prepare a list of questions that you want to ask others. Don't try to determine whom you'll ask at this stage; just focus on the type of information you want to know.

❑ 6. Prepare a list of possible networking organizations and contact each to determine the profile of attendees, cost to join, frequency of meetings (and cost of meetings, if any), average number of attendees per meeting, and opportunities for your involvement. Determine which organizations should be your focus.

❑ 7. Contact local hotels to determine which organizations hold monthly meetings at their facility. Obtain contact details for organizations that interest you.

❑ 8. Search the Internet for trade shows, contact your local chamber of commerce and other organizations, and ask acquaintances if they know of networking opportunities.

❑ 9. Contact outplacement firms that have an office in your area and ask if they know any networking groups that are open to the public. Ask if you can attend their networking events.

❑10. Contact recruiters in your area and ask if they know any formal or informal networking groups that meet on a regular basis for executives in transition. These groups often ask recruiters to be speakers at their events.

❑11. Ask recruiters where they network.

Communicating

I know they heard what I said, but I'm not sure they understood what I meant.

Chapter Overview

During a job search, you never know when others don't understand your message as you intended it. You may have the most powerful resume and have your message down pat, but, if you don't communicate effectively, you'll never get to first base and you won't get a second chance because people will be hesitant to tell you what you need to know to improve. This chapter will:

» Improve your verbal communication so the message you want to convey is the message they hear.

» Convey what you want in letters that won't be ignored by the reader.

» Recognize what others are telling you when they aren't saying it.

The main sections in this chapter include:

» The different ways you communicate.

» Verbal communication.

» Written communication.

» Addressing a redundancy.

» Milestones.

You've spent a lot of time perfecting your resume and exploring where and how to network. Now you need to make sure your verbal and written communication projects a confident, take-charge message that others will respect and react to positively.

The Different Ways You Communicate

Whether you're communicating verbally or in writing, you do it in three different ways:

1. Image.

2. Language.

3. Values.

Image

When you meet someone, even before you exchange words, you size him up and form an impression—good or bad—based on his attire, appearance, and demeanor.

Employers and recruiters do the same. They'll start to size you up the moment they see you. Without words, instinct tells the employer or recruiter whether they're going to like you. Recruiters often say they can size up a candidate within four minutes of meeting them.

Even with a positive first impression, employers and recruiters still might screen you out later in the interview, but a negative first impression will inevitably eliminate you from the running, and they aren't likely to share the real reason with you.

Illustration by Steven Lait.

Language

When you speak, your words, mannerisms, and physical appearance create a powerful first impression. If you come across as obsequious, self-important, overpowering, or egotistical, you may think you're having a conversation, but the other person is probably thinking more about your style and demeanor than what you're saying.

> *I know that you believe you understood what you think I said, but I am not sure you realize that what you heard is not what I meant.*

> —Attributed to Robert McCloskey, U.S. Dept. of State

If you put others in an uncomfortable or inferior position by using jargon, technical terms, or making reference to all the important people you know, the other person won't perceive you positively and isn't likely to become one of your network contacts.

Values

Your image and the language you use reflect your core values. How you carry and express yourself are continual statements to those around you about your character, integrity, and self-perception of your worth.

When you're talking to another person, she sees and hears what you say through her personal values filter. She'll assess you based on *her* values. Likewise, when she's talking, you hear her words through your personal values filter and assess them based on *your* values.

Verbal Communication

If you aren't noticing how the other person is paying attention to you, you may be unaware that you're having a wasted conversation. The four key ways to tell if you're successfully communicating verbally with another person are described here:

Characteristics of a Good Listener

Characteristics	Signs that indicate they're listening
1. Attentiveness He's paying attention and connecting with you.	• He's looking at you and not gazing around the room. • He's making some audible sounds ("uh huh," "yes," "right," "I see what you mean") indicating he's paying attention.
2. Interest He's interested in what you're saying.	• He's commenting intelligently about the subject. • He's asking good questions about the topic of conversation. • He expresses interest.
3. Understanding He understands what you're saying.	• He's asking questions that indicate he understands. • He's not talking about unrelated topics. • He gives some indication that he's familiar with the subject and understands the technical language you're using.
4. Memory He remembers you positively.	• The conversation ends at a logical place, not resulting from a distraction or interruption. • He expresses pleasure in meeting you or shows some appreciation. • He shows an interest in meeting with you again.

When you've finished and part, briefly think about the conversation and whether you conveyed what you wanted and how receptive he was to you. Think about what you might do differently with the next person. Repeat this review with each person you meet until you're comfortable with what you said and how they reacted.

Listening is a key part of communicating. Even when you're talking, you need to be listening. If you're doing any of the following, *you* aren't being an active listener:

⟫ Finishing his sentences for him.

⟫ Talking "over" him.

⟫ Talking, but not listening or thinking, before talking again.

⟫ Concentrating on what you want to say next and missing what the other person is saying.

If you can identify with any of this, get a copy of *Listening: The Forgotten Skill: A Self-Teaching Guide* by Madelyn Burley-Allen (John Wiley & Sons, Inc., 1995). The book is an easy read, and the exercises will help you improve your listening skills.

Some people think they're good listeners without recognizing that they actually aren't. If you suspect you might have a problem in this area, consider having someone accompany you to observe your interaction with others or have them videotape you from the sidelines.

When you play it back, watch it with someone else. Observe your mannerisms, not just how you're conversing. Are you standing too close? Are you speaking too loudly for the situation? It's often difficult to recognize these things yourself, particularly when you aren't aware of them. You may be surprised by how someone else thinks you come across. Arrange to get feedback on your networking and communicating style during the early stages of your networking. You don't want to find out you're doing something wrong after you've already turned off half your network!

Chapter 8 covered how to start a conversation in the **Initiate** phase; how to obtain help, support, and information in the **Obtain** phase; and how to get referrals in the **Use** phase. The types of questions you're asking while networking are usually easy ones, because you're in the building and research phases, when a job offer is not your primary objective.

Although you might have had a few bad starts or situations where you weren't adequately prepared, you probably learned from them and quickly recovered. The people you meet during the early stages of your networking are usually forgiving. When you get to the Use phase, however, you're at the top of your **IOU** networking triangle. You don't want to make your mistakes when contacting your target person; you may have only one chance.

When you make direct contact with potential employers either verbally or in writing, you must have your act together. You'll be contacting potential employers through a referral from your network or, if you were unable to find anyone in your network who was able to give you a referral, you'll be contacting them directly.

Let's start by looking at some of the basic do's and don'ts when calling companies. I've assumed most employers will be companies, but the concepts would be similar if they aren't (for example, partnerships, foundations, non-profits, and government organizations).

What You *Want* to Do When Calling Companies	What You *Don't* Want to Do When Calling Companies
• Be clear about what you want and with whom you want to speak. If not, you'll soon find yourself talking with the HR department.	• Don't sound important or impatient. She is much more important to you than you are to her.
• Prepare your questions ahead of time and have them in front of you when you call.	• Don't ramble and waste time trying to "chat her up." It will be transparent, and she'll see you as trying to use her for your own selfish means.
• Treat everyone with equal respect regardless of who answers the telephone.	
• If you're calling to get the contact details for your target person, be prepared to ask your questions if, surprisingly, he takes the call.	• Don't ask obvious questions you could have answered easily by doing a minimal amount of research or by looking at the company's Website.
• Be polite, be patient, and maintain a sense of humor.	• Don't ask questions designed to show how smart you are.
• Be genuine and gain the respect of the gatekeeper, your inside link to your target person. Don't treat the gatekeeper as an adversary; you want to get gatekeepers to *want* to help you.	• Don't be formal. Act natural and let your personality show.
	• Don't be an interrogator. You'll put others on the defensive, and they'll most surely attempt to get rid of you.
	• Don't stretch or misrepresent the relationship of someone who referred you to the person you're talking to or the person you want to reach.
• Keep your message short and focused. If the person you reach is confused or unclear about what you want, you won't get her time, or you'll get HR.	
	• Don't be a "name dropper." It's a turn-off.
• Do what you say you'll do. If you tell her you'll call at a certain date and time, call.	• Don't call from a cell phone while traveling. It may not bother you, but it will distract or possibly irritate the person you're calling.

Preparing in advance is crucial, because you never know what you'll encounter or whom you'll wind up talking to when you call companies.

On the next few pages, I show seven typical situations you'll likely encounter and include suggestions on how you might approach each. Tailor your approach to fit your style and the situation. Practice the conversations, but don't use them as a script.

When you call, be prepared to overcome the obstacles (gatekeepers): receptionists, administrative assistants, voice mail, and—the ultimate obstacle—the HR department. If you don't have an entrée to the target person, these obstacles may become huge hurdles that you'll need to overcome.

Assistants are usually very good at being gatekeepers because they have lots of experience with others who are trying to get the attention of the target person, such as salespeople and others looking for a job. Assistants are also quite willing to give you inside help if they like you. Getting the assistant for your target person to like you and help you should be one of your objectives. Here are some suggestions on how you can respond to situations that you'll probably encounter when making telephone calls to companies.

Situation 1: Initial call.
You call the company directly to talk to your target person, John Smith.

POSSIBLE APPROACH:
Call as if you already know John Smith or he knows you. When they answer, say, "John Smith, please." Use a confident approach. In your last job, when you had to call someone that you knew at another company, what words did you use and how did you sound? Use a similar approach.

Situation 2:   Why are you calling?
The gatekeeper asks, "Does Mr. Smith know you?" or "Does Mr. Smith know why you are calling?" or "Can I ask what this is regarding?"

POSSIBLE APPROACH:
State your reasons for calling. For example:
▶ "I'm researching working in the X industry, and I understand Mr. Smith is experienced in the field. I'd like to ask him a few questions." (If she refers to John Smith as Mr., continue to use the formal Mr. Smith because that's how the other person is referring to him. If you use the informal John, she might think you're being presumptuous because you don't already know him.)

183

➧ "I understand Mr. Smith has responsibility for [area of responsibility] and I wondered if he could spare a few moments to answer a few questions about...."

➧ "Mr. Jones at [name] company suggested I call Mr. Smith to see if he could answer a few questions about [the object of your call]."

Avoid going into too much detail about your questions at this stage. You're not calling to ask your questions, only to see if Mr. Smith would be willing to talk to you—and if so, you'd like to schedule a conversation with him. If you get to talk with Mr. Smith, give him some idea about what you want to discuss with him and ask if you could schedule a meeting where you can ask him your questions.

Situation 3: Are you looking for a job?
They ask you point-blank. Hey, it happens!

POSSIBLE APPROACH:

➧ "I'm in the process of making a career change, and I need to ask some questions of someone in [the position you are targeting or the position of someone who would know about it], such as Mr. Smith, before doing so. I'm not calling for a job."

➧ "I'm doing research into [your target] positions (or industry), and I need to talk to someone like Mr. Smith who I understand has experience in the [field or function]."

➧ "I'm in the process of making a career change and I think I may be interested in your industry, but I'm not really sure I understand it as well as I need to. I was hoping Mr. Smith/you might be able to answer some of my questions to help me better understand if this is something I might like to pursue."

➧ "I'm in transition (or between jobs or exploring a career change) at the moment, but I'm not calling for a job. I need [describe the information, help, answers, etc., that you need.]"

Don't belabor this subject. Keep it as brief as possible. If gatekeepers sense you're honestly looking for help, they'll usually put you through to your target person or an assistant and let him decide whether to help you.

Situation 4: The gatekeeper won't let you talk to Mr. Smith.
POSSIBLE APPROACH:

Try to establish a connection with the gatekeeper.

➧ Confirm with her that Mr. Smith has responsibility for whatever it is you want to know, and that he's the person who could answer your questions.

▶ If you handle this professionally, the gatekeeper will often put you on hold and then ask your target person if he would be willing to talk to you. If Mr. Smith is willing but too busy now, ask the gatekeeper if Mr. Smith (or the gatekeeper) could suggest a better time.

▶ This may also be an opportunity to share one of your questions with the gatekeeper, which will serve to validate your call as having a legitimate purpose and that Mr. Smith is the right person.

▶ Use all the charm you can muster to develop a personal relationship with the gatekeeper. Remember: You are in the **Initiate** phase right now. You want the gatekeeper to know you're a nice person and you would sincerely appreciate her help.

Situation 5: You reach Mr. Smith's voice mail.
POSSIBLE APPROACH:

▶ Leave a short message similar to what you say in Situation 3.

▶ Call back at different times and leave pleasant, sincere messages regarding why you're calling. Make it short and businesslike. Leave your telephone number with the times you're generally available. Leaving your telephone number is a courtesy. Don't expect him to call back.

▶ If you consistently get voice mail, call the gatekeeper again and ask when you're more likely to get through to Mr. Smith directly, rather than his voice mail. There may be times or days that are best to reach him.

How many times do you call Mr. Smith before deciding this approach isn't working? That's a difficult question to answer, because it depends on the situation. I've known people who said they reached their target person on the 10th call, and the target person even apologized for not getting back to the caller sooner. The target person agreed to meet. Vary your message, keep it short, and make sure it's clear you're looking for help. If you sound sincere, you're more likely to hear from your target person.

TIP When you call to leave a message, don't rush through your message. Make it brief and take your time to make sure you speak clearly. When you leave your telephone number, repeat it slowly so the person you called can make sure she wrote it down correctly. Keep your message short and on-target, as some recording systems have time limits..

Situation 6: **You decide to send a letter because you haven't been able to talk to Mr. Smith.**

Possible approach:

» Ask the gatekeeper if there are any specific points she thinks you ought to cover if you were to write Mr. Smith.

» Ask, "If I sent a letter to Mr. Smith, would you see that he gets it?" The gatekeeper, whom you have now connected with by using your professional approach (and because you haven't tried to circumvent her authority), will probably make sure Mr. Smith is aware you're sending a letter and might even have some positive comments about you.

» Write a letter asking for a meeting, and send it *without* a resume. Explain the purpose of your call—what you're trying to do (such as making a career change from industry X to Y, and so forth)—and you would like to interview him to get his viewpoints on the field, the industry, or an approach that might help you to decide the best course of action.

» Do not hint, suggest, or imply that you might be interested in working for his company. Mention that you will call on a specific date to see if you can arrange a meeting. *Without fail, you must call him on that date.* If you're not able to talk to Mr. Smith when you call, ask the assistant/gatekeeper if she knows the status of your request and ask if she would please let your target person know you called.

If you think sending an e-mail instead of a letter would be easier, ask the gatekeeper if an e-mail would be more appropriate.

Bear in mind, though, the mere click of a mouse will swiftly delete e-mails and anti-spam software may delete your e-mail before the reader even sees it.

Personally, I'm more inclined to read letters, so I suggest you not send an e-mail. A professional letter says you cared enough to take the time to print a letter and go to the post office to mail it. Similarly, birthday cards I receive by e-mail don't give me the warm and fuzzy feeling that the person cared enough about me to send a *real* card. You're trying to get someone's attention to help you. I strongly suggest that you make the effort and show that you're prepared to go out of your way in order to get his help. Many years ago, John Housemen did a Smith Barney TV commercial where he said, "We make money the old-fashioned way. We earn it." You, too, may need to show that you're working hard enough to earn someone's help.

Situation 7: You talk to Mr. Smith but are unable to get a
meeting.

PossibLE APPROACH:

➧ Send Mr. Smith a letter thanking him for his time and the information he
shared with you.

➧ Remind him in your letter about your planned career objectives and the
purpose of your meeting. (He might have second thoughts and call, agreeing to meet.)

➧ Reiterate (assuming you made this request when you talked to him) that you
would appreciate if he could suggest someone else you might talk to who
could give another perspective on your (whatever it was you wanted from
Mr. Smith).

Written Communication

When others look at your letter or resume, they'll make an instant judgment about you. If your format has small print, narrow margins, long paragraphs, and is busy-looking, you'll make a negative first impression before they
read a word.

If your letter or envelope contains misspellings, or you address your letter
to the "hiring manager," or refer to a Ms. as Mr., it's possible that no one will
bother to open your envelope or read the letter.

You'll find an overabundance of books devoted to writing letters for people
in transition at your local bookstore. I'll attempt to simplify what your approach
should be by giving basic examples for the ones you're likely to write most often.
You can then tailor your letter to fit your situation.

Purpose of a Cover Letter

In Chapter 6, I compared your resume to a sales brochure. It highlights
what you're looking for, the skills and experience you bring to the table, and
what you've achieved, and then summarizes your career history.

Your cover letter, on the other hand, is what the reader sees first, so it must
bridge the gap between what the reader is expecting or wants to know, and what
your resume says. Remember the menu analogy in Chapter 6 where you, as the
restaurant owner, are trying to direct the reader's attention
to what you want them to know. You don't want to tailor
your resume every time you send it out or you'll defeat the
purpose of your cover letter and you'll have difficulty remembering which version of your resume you sent to whom.

T	Never send your
I	resume to
P	someone without
	a cover letter.

If you're sending your resume in response to a request after you've had a significant discussion with someone, the cover letter may only need to be a transmittal letter.

Because you'll address your letter to a specific person, your letter should tell that person what you think she wants or needs to know. If you send your letter without an expressed, clear purpose, the reader won't read it and may even discard it along with any attachments, such as your resume.

Here are some situations where the purpose of your cover letter will be different:

- ⟫ You're transmitting your resume in response to a request.

- ⟫ You're responding to an advertisement or posting on the Internet, and you want to draw their attention to your skills and experience that match what the advertisement indicates they want.

- ⟫ You're sending your resume to a recruiter on a speculative basis.

- ⟫ You're sending a letter to a company on a speculative basis because no one in your network was able to serve as a referral.

- ⟫ You're sending a letter to a company proposing a new position that you think the company needs, but doesn't now have.

- ⟫ You're making a career change and, therefore, need to connect the dots by highlighting how your skills and experience translate to another industry or company.

- ⟫ You're sending your resume to a company at the request of one of your contacts who has made an introduction for you.

> **T I P** A letter that is short, clear, to the point, and relevant to what's of interest to the recipient stands a much better chance of being read and viewed positively than a letter highlighting your many skills and experience that aren't relevant to the reader.

Basic Letter Format

Use plain white paper for your resume and contrasting white or off-white bond paper for your letters. Envelopes should match your letter paper. Use paper with a smooth surface, especially if you're using a laser printer. If the paper has a watermark, be sure the watermark is face-up when you print the letter.

> **T I P** When you fold your letter and send it through the mail, toner occasionally smudges depending on the paper you use. To check this, mail a letter with your resume to yourself from another location to see how they come through.

The following figure shows how to structure a business letter. The numbers in circles on the letter relate to comments following the example.

①
Jack Welch
123 Liberty Lane
The Hamptons, NY 10001
T: 212-123-4567 ◆ E: jack@aol.com
②

January 1, 2009

③

Mr. George Allen   ④
Chairman of the Board
Templeton Equity Investments
1 Market St.
San Francisco, CA 94618
⑤

Dear George, ⑥
⑦
I've just about finished what I set out to do here at GE.

Please contact me if you have an opportunity where you think I might be able to add value.

Yours truly,
⑧

Jack

① Leave a 1-inch margin around your page. Use a 12-point serif font such as Times New Roman or CG Times. Keep it simple. Content is king. Fancy fonts are a distraction.

② Leave a space of two lines between your contact information and the date. Use a smaller font for your name and contact details.

③ Increase or decrease the space between the date and the address fields to balance your letter on the page.

④ Use the addressee's full name, title, company, and address.

⑤ Leave one line between the addressee block and your salutation (two lines in the UK).

189

⑥ Most of your letters should use the formal Mr., Ms., or Dr. If you think the recipient would expect you to use their first name, use "Dear [first name]," such as when you already know the person or you're at a very senior level. When trying to decide, envision how you would expect to see the letter if the recipient of your letter were writing you.

⑦ Leave one line between the greeting and the first paragraph. Your opening paragraph should be an introduction limited to two to three lines maximum. The remaining paragraphs shouldn't exceed four or five lines each.

⑧ Sign your name similarly to how you address the recipient. For example, if you addressed your letter to Dear George, you would sign Jack. If you addressed your letter to Mr. Allen, you would sign Jack Welch.

When writing, use the language of the industry or the profession you're trying to address. If you're writing to an accountant, use accounting terms. If you're writing to an engineer, use engineering terms.

Letter-Writing Basics

▶ Limit your letter to one page.

▶ Avoid the use of jargon and clichés.

▶ Avoid large words and esoteric or complex statements. Don't try to impress the reader.

▶ Be careful with abbreviations. Even people within the IT industry don't know what all the acronyms mean.

▶ Avoid hackneyed statements or phrases that don't add substance or value to your message, such as the most common: "I am enclosing my resume for your perusal." or "Enclosed herewith please find...." Make each word in your letter count.

▶ Other points to remember:

  - Always ask someone else to read your letter to make sure your overall message comes through clearly and succinctly. If you make revisions, ask someone else to read it to make sure the letter still says what you mean.

  - Use a spell-check on *every version* of your letter.

  - Be brief, and address what's relevant to the reader. Don't repeat what's in your resume. It's okay, however, to expand on something in your resume, highlight it, or connect the dots between your industry and theirs.

  - Don't think you must always send your resume with your letter. The objective of your letter is to create an interest in you as a resource that provides solutions. There might be a situation where you only need to send a letter. In this case, your letter could extend to no more than one additional page. If the reader has an interest, he'll request more information.

---

8 Basic Letters You Are Most Likely to Write

Here are the eight basic letters you'll need most often:

1. Letters transmitting resumes.

2. Letters responding to an advertisement.

3. Letters to recruiters sent speculatively.

4. Letters to companies sent speculatively.

5. Letters sent to a company contact referred through your network.

6. Letters sent to an employee in a target company referring to an article he wrote.

7. Letters to companies when you know a *retained* recruiter is involved.

8. Letters to send when you've successfully found employment.

1. Letters Transmitting Resumes

A transmittal letter arises when someone you've talked with asks you to send your resume to him, or to someone else. If the recipient is already expecting your resume, you may not need to reiterate your career objectives or highlight your skills and experience. A typical transmittal letter follows on page 192.

If you met with a new contact whom you didn't know before and, after the meeting, she asked you to send your resume to her, you should include one or two paragraphs reminding her what position you're seeking and an achievement story that demonstrates your skills and experience. You might also want to add a paragraph that reiterates or addresses a topic you discussed when you met.

2. Letters Responding to an Advertisement

Responding to a print advertisement or an Internet posting often makes you feel like you're taking a positive step toward getting a position that sounds right for you, and you're anxious to hear back. The disillusionment comes after several weeks pass and you don't hear a thing.

To add to the frustration, there's usually no way to contact whoever placed the ad to check on the status of your resume submission. Chapter 7 talked about the small likelihood of a senior person finding a job from an advertisement.

If you see an advertisement for a job that you think is appropriate for you and decide to send your resume, make sure there's sufficient information about the position and the industry for you to identify in your letter why you're qualified. If the position or industry is defined only broadly, such as just "manufacturing," or is undefined, it probably isn't a real job. A new contingency recruiter is probably attempting to add resumes to his database, and responding won't be an effective use of your time.

Arnold N. Other
123 S. West St.
Seattle, WA 98101
206-123-4567 • another@hitechco.com

June 30, 2009

Mr. Bill Lachluster
9988 W. End St.
Chicago, IL 60606

Dear Bill,

It was nice seeing you again yesterday. I agree it's been more years than we both would have liked, but I'm glad to know our friendship has stood the test of time.

As you requested, I'm enclosing my resume. Please bear in mind that I'm conducting research right now to determine if my planned career change as **VP Marketing** in the pharmaceutical industry to the healthcare non-profit sector would be a good career move for me and, if so, how to pursue the change.

I would appreciate you keeping my resume confidential, as it will change when I've finished my research.

As we agreed, I'll contact you in three weeks to give you an update on my research.

Yours truly,

Arnie

Enclosure (resume)

Assuming the advertisement adequately describes the position and otherwise looks like a genuine opportunity, your response should address each of the skills and experience the advertisement indicates the company wants. Cover only the stated requirements of the job. Don't stray into other areas that aren't specific to the advertisement. (I'll address requests for salary history in Chapter 11.)

Your letters should use the following format in four paragraphs:

1. Reference the source of the advertisement (publication and date or Website URL).

2. Identify the skills and experience they say they want that you have.

3. Summarize an achievement story that demonstrates those skills and experience.

4. Indicate any preferences or limitations for contacting you, such as an absence, or include a concluding statement.

An example of a letter responding to an advertisement is shown on page 194.

When recruiters place advertisements, they usually receive hundreds of responses, sometimes more than a thousand. To manage reviewing such large numbers, they typically prepare a 5" × 8" form identifying the assignment, position title, and three to five major attributes their client wants. See page 195 for an example of how a recruiting firm might prepare and use such a form.

Although each recruiting firm will have its own system and forms, the review of your resume works something like this:

1. A reviewer, typically an administrative or research person working with the recruiter, quickly reviews the resumes (generally ignoring the cover letters) to see if each person's resume reflects some pre-determined number of the requirements. If not, the resume is set aside. If it does, the reviewer attaches the form and enters the person's name.

2. The reviewer checks off the applicable attributes that the candidate meets and enters the information requested in the blanks.

3. The reviewer looks at the required attributes that he checked and, again based on pre-determined criteria, enters a number in the upper right Code box. For example, if they have all the qualifications, they would be coded 1, if they have four of five, they might be coded a 1 or 2, and so on (on a scale of one to five with one being the ones that are closest to meeting all the requirements).

4. The reviewer sorts the resumes by code, with the 1's on top followed by the 2's, and so on. The reviewer passes the documents to the engagement recruiter.

Misty Fortune
21 Crestfallen Road
Boyle Heights, CA 90010
Tel: (213) 123 4567
misfortune@email.com

January 15, 2009

The Wall Street Journal
Box CS1234
545 E. West St.
Dallas, TX 75240-1234

Dear Sir or Madam,

I'm responding to your advertisement in *The Wall Street Journal* on January 10, 2009 for the position of Chief Financial Officer with European market experience for a consumer electronics company.

Having worked in the consumer electronics manufacturing industry for the past six years, I'm very familiar with the issues involved in a rapidly expanding consumer electronics business with European operations. In my role as CFO for Watts Consumer Electronics, I have had direct responsibility for all accounting and financial reporting functions, including being the primary interface with our external auditors. I oversaw the IT department, took a lead role in developing HR policies and procedures, and simplified international transfer pricing policies.

Reporting to the President, I participated in all strategic discussions involving our U.S. and European operations. In my most recent role with this $500 million company, I had four direct reports and 35 indirects. I am looking for an expanded opportunity to help a company that is anticipating a rapid growth in the European market.

I would appreciate the opportunity to learn more details about this position as I believe I have the skills and experience this company requires.

Sincerely yours,

Misty Fortune

Enclosure (resume)

5. The recruiter looks at all the 1's and 2's first, and if she finds enough "good" candidates, she looks no further. If she doesn't have enough candidates coded 1 or 2, she might look at the 3's and, possibly, 4's.

6. If the recruiter finds a reasonable sample to consider, she (or a researcher) calls or e-mails each candidate to set up a telephone pre-screening interview.

7. If the recruiter does not find a reasonable sample to consider, she'll go back to her client and discuss whether the client is willing to modify their requirements and in what ways.

If you see an advertisement and think, "I could do that!" and send your resume, the recruiter who's handling the assignment will probably never see it unless you have enough of their required attributes.

Some recruiting firms might have someone review all the responses and decide whether to keep them in their database for future consideration. But if they don't think they could reasonably expect a client to ask them to recruit someone at your position and with your industry experience or if your resume is not well prepared, they'll dispose of your resume and cover letter.

Top Talent Executive Search, LLP
Candidate Selection Criteria

Name __Jason Smith__   Code 2

Client name   __FedCo Retail Depot__

Assignment reference no. __SR-12021__

Position being recruited __Chief Operations Officer-OTC__

Client's industry __FMCG- Fast Moving Commercial Goods__

Recruiter name __Suzy Recruiter__

Required attributes:

☑ Ten years functional experience in sales __9__

☑ Three or more years in a senior sales management or executive role with regional or national responsibility __5__

☑ Eight years experience in the pharmaceutical industry for branded or OTC products __12__

☑ Undergraduate degree in the sciences __BS Biology__

☐ MBA from a major top quality university

Preferred attributes:

☑ Lives on East Coast

☐ Membership in AMA

☐ _____

Reviewer __Agnes Researcher__

Responding to a fax number

If you're responding to a fax number instead of sending a letter with your resume, include three pages containing your cover letter and two-page resume.

Responding by e-mail

If you're responding by e-mail, send *one* document file that includes three pages: your cover letter, using a transmittal format, and your two-page resume. If you e-mail your cover letter and resume as separate files, they may not even open the file containing the cover letter. Even if they do open it, it may still not find its way to your resume.

I recommend that, when responding by e-mail, you send your letter and resume in Microsoft Word format, because that's what most businesses now use, or use .rtf (rich text format), which retains most formatting, such as bolds and indents. Keep your letter and resume simple, without special fonts, symbols, or extensive formatting, such as tables. Different software programs or even different versions of the same software might not translate your documents the same way you prepared them. Your attention-grabbing ➤ or ✓ may look like §, ?, or □.

Don't send a text-only version unless they specifically request it. Text versions are hard to read because you can't highlight what you want to emphasize.

3. Letters to Recruiters Sent Speculatively

If you send your letter and resume to a recruiter as part of a job search mailing campaign and not in response to a specific request by them relating to an assignment they're *currently* working on, recruiters will classify it as a "speculative resume." You might also hear some refer to these types of resumes as sent "over the transom." (For those too young to remember, transoms were narrow windows above doors that were usually left open for ventilation even after business hours. You could then literally throw your envelope "over the transom" and safely into the office.)

Before you prepare your letter and send your resume to recruiters speculatively, check out their Website or call. Whereas many recruiters keep resumes and maintain them in a database, many small boutique search firms do not.

Larger recruiting firms divide their business into industry or functional segments, and consultants often specialize in only one particular industry or function. If the information isn't apparent from their Website, you can try to call them to find out who specializes in your field or function so you can address your letter to him specifically.

Many of the larger firms prefer that you use a resume-submittal facility on their Website. It may be as simple as entering your name, contact details, some basic information about your function and industry experience, and then posting your resume.

Alternatively, they may require you to complete a questionnaire, which creates a profile patterned like a resume, and then allow you to upload your resume. Some may not even accept cover letters or resumes.

If you're able to send your resume, include a one-page cover letter structured as follows:

❖ **Tell them what you want.** Start with the basics: position, industry, and location—for example, "I'm searching for a Head of Production (VP/ Director level) position in the plastics extrusion industry in a $1 billion-plus company, preferably in the Northeast."

❖ **Include one achievement story.** Expand on an achievement that illustrates your skills and experience in your industry. Keep it short and focused.

❖ **Indicate your salary requirements.** Recruiters need to know salary information so they can assess whether you fit one of their clients' opportunities. They'll want to know this information early on. Specify a prospective compensation range and not your previous actual salary. If you're uncomfortable including this information, it's acceptable to omit it and talk about it later in an interview.

❖ **State why you're available.** This will be one of their first questions, so save the recruiter time by stating it up front: "My most recent employer (realigned my division, closed a manufacturing facility, eliminated a business line, and so forth)."

❖ **Acknowledge that you understand how they work.** Include something along these lines: "I understand you handle assignments in the [blank] industry and that your firm is driven by corporate clients and not candidates. I would appreciate hearing from you if you're currently involved in an assignment that matches my skills and experience. You may retain my resume on your system for future assignments that might match my career objective. However, I would appreciate your contacting me before you forward my details to a client for any potential opportunity." (Don't be surprised if you get a form letter in response that indicates they only work for companies but will keep your information. You really weren't expecting them to read your letter, were you?)

If you call recruiters, don't call more than about three times. If they're currently handling an assignment needing someone with your skills and experience, and you've sent a resume which shows you're qualified for the position, I can assure you they'll call you immediately.

If they aren't handling an assignment needing someone with your skills and experience, they won't have the motivation or time to take your call or call you back. Don't take it personally. Clients are paying the bills, and they expect the recruiter to focus on finding candidates for them.

A Shared Experience

Recruiters' days often stretch into evening and weekend interviews when they have multiple assignments at the same time. They often don't have time to talk to people who aeren't connected with one of their current assignments.

Following on page 199 is an example of a cover letter to a recruiter whom you've been *unsuccessful* at contacting.

4. Letters to Companies Sent Speculatively

Ideally, you'll have already identified your target companies and the target person in each one. You will have then contacted your network to see who knows the target company or target person. If you're able to find this connection, you'll be able to write a letter making the connection. I've known executives who've said, "I'll just circumvent the networking bit and send letters directly to the CEO. Surely, they'll know whether there's an opportunity for me."

Alternatively, you might feel you don't have a good network, and, instead of working to build one, you'll just send letters to employers instead. After you've sent more than 1,000 letters (as recommended by one book targeting executives that claims it's all about numbers) with nary a positive response, you'll recognize that building a network is not an option—it's a must!

Unfortunately, there will be instances when your network won't be able to help you connect with your target person, and you'll have to approach them on your own, without a referral. If you've followed the suggestions in this book, the speculative letters you'll need to send will be few.

When you construct your letter, you'll have to know the following:

⊳⊳ Does the job you want currently exist? Or does the need for the function exist, and you must convince them to create the position?

⊳⊳ Do you have an introduction, or are you writing speculatively?

Louis Knox
1 Park Place
New York, NY 10014
212-123-4567
lknox@nyinternet.com

February 23, 2009

Ms. Sharon Peyton
Midtown Executive Search
987 W. East St., Ste. 9000
New York, NY 10002

Dear Sharon,

I've not been able to reach you by telephone, and since I understand you handle assignments for senior operational executives, I wanted to send you my resume.

I'm looking for a CEO position in a $1 billion-plus pharmaceutical company based in the Northeast U.S. that is looking to expand its product line. My salary expectations are in the range of $1 million to $1.5 million.

I successfully led MegaPill for over 10 years, taking it from a $300 million dollar OTC and generic drug manufacturer to a $1 billion ethical biopharmaceutical company where I negotiated its sale to MegaBioPhar plc for a threefold increase in value to the shareholders of MegaPill.

I understand you work for clients only, and I would appreciate your not disclosing my resume to clients or potential clients without discussing the opportunity with me beforehand.

Yours sincerely,

Louis

Enclosure (resume)

» Are you writing to the person who would be making the hiring decision, or have you not been able to identify that person?

» If you have a referral, is she a close friend of the person you're writing to, or only an acquaintance?

» If you have a referral, do you know whether your target person respects her opinion?

I'll cover some suggested letter formats, with the hope that the ones I do cover will give you ideas about communicating in situations I don't cover. You'll have to consider the following objectives in each of your letters to companies. If you shortchange any of them, you'll have wasted an opportunity. Carefully consider these five objectives:

1. Identify the recipient of your letter.
2. Get past the gatekeeper.
3. Find the hook.
4. Describe what you bring to the table (that you believe they need).
5. Ask the question.

Your letter will have to accomplish each of these objectives in sequence. If it doesn't, your letter won't make it to the next objective. Let's look at each of these in detail.

Objective 1: Identify the recipient of your letter.

Address your letter to the target person—the one with the authority to employ you. If you've been unsuccessful determining that from your network or calls to the company, here are some examples of whom you might target:

◆ If you're aiming at the CEO or president level, address your letter to a member of the board, ideally to someone on the nominating committee.

◆ If you're aiming for a C-level/VP executive position, such as CFO or Vice President of Marketing, address your letter to the CEO, President, or Executive Vice President. Whereas members of the board may pressure the CEO to employ someone at that level, they don't usually get involved in C-level appointments below CEO.

◆ If you're aiming for a director or manager position, you'll have to do some digging to find the appropriate level. Your network is usually the best source for this, followed by gatekeepers. Aim for the person one level above the person to whom you would report. If your target is the person to whom you would report, he might see you as a threat to his job. If your target is one level above your potential boss, he might see you as a candidate to replace your potential boss.

◆ When you've decided the addressee of your letter, you can then decide how to craft the message. The ultimate objective of your letter is for the intended recipient to read and consider what you say in your letter.

Objective 2: Get past the gatekeeper.

Most gatekeepers are responsible for screening out unwanted telephone calls and correspondence. Telephone the company before you send your letter and ask to speak to your target person. You'll likely get his gatekeeper. When you do, confirm:

⋙ That the person still has the same responsibilities.

⋙ The target's job title (also confirm whether it's Mr., Ms., or Dr., if in doubt).

⋙ The spelling of first and last names. (For example, Judith may not appreciate being referred to as Judy, Robert may not use Bob, and Bill may be Bill, not a nickname for William.)

If the person you're targeting has left the company, try to find out details of his replacement, such as when she started and where she worked before. You might be able to use this information in your transmittal letter as well as to investigate potential openings at her former employer. New executives often make personnel changes within a few months of their starting, so this is a good time to let her know what you can bring to the table.

Receptionists may have information on a new executive. If they won't provide it, ask to talk to someone in the department where the person works, such as her assistant. Tell that person you're sending a letter to (use her name) and that you'd like to verify the spelling, etc. In a large company, avoid getting into a discussion about the purpose of your letter, because the gatekeeper probably will tell you to send your letter to the HR department.

If you have a referral, use that person's name to authenticate the reason for your call. Don't attempt to mislead the gatekeeper, because you'll need her help and support later, and, if you antagonize her, she'll surely let your target person know when the gatekeeper sees your letter.

If you don't have a referral and she wants to know what you're calling about, review the "Verbal Communication" section of this chapter.

Objective 3: Find the hook.

Personalize your letter by including something of interest to the reader—the hook—that will make him notice you and read more. The hook can be anything from something about the person to something important about the function, the company, or the industry.

You'll greatly enhance the likelihood that your target person will read your letter if you find a way to pique his interest in what you have to say. If you want to grab his attention, the best way to do it is with a hook.

Your hook can be as simple as starting your letter with the following:

» "I read that you...."

» "Mr. Smith suggested I write to you regarding your planned...." (but make sure the addressee knows Mr. Smith).

» "I understand that you're...."

» "As a fellow member of the...."

A more substantial hook is something that would interest the reader about some knowledge you have concerning what the company is doing, planning to do, or from your experience, should consider doing. Or it could relate to the function or the industry in general.

You can often find this type of information from your contacts during the **Obtain** phase. If you draw a blank and can't find anything, complete Exercise 9.1.

Exercise 9.1: Find the Hook

1. Using a notepad, put the name of the company at the top of a sheet of paper.

2. Under the company name, write a short paragraph describing what they make or sell and how they get their products to market or deliver their services.

3. Draw a line down the center of the page under the paragraph. Identify and list on the left side what you think are the business or operating issues associated with what they do. These could be, for example, research, testing, manufacturing, quality control, distribution, sales, support, service, systems analysis, accounting, cost control, work scheduling, or management information systems.

4. On the right side of the paper, write down your skills in each area, including specific knowledge gained in previous jobs, your accomplishments in those areas, expertise gained in those areas, or something that you can bring to the table in one or more areas.

You should now have an area that you can use as your hook. For example, you can start your letter with:

"I know the difficulties in maintaining high standards of service for fleet vehicles when they need to be on the road constantly."

Make sure this is a *very short* statement that highlights an issue. (Don't call it a problem, because companies don't think they have problems.)

> "While VP, Fleet Maintenance at Rent-A-Wreck Ltd., I reduced the downtime of our fleet by 3%. This translated into an annual savings of $675 per vehicle per year and, with more than 200 vehicles, we saved over $135,000 in the last year alone."

Present yourself as a solutions-oriented person.

They may not have a "problem" with their fleet maintenance turnaround or quality of service. The point is that you addressed an issue that a company using fleet vehicles must be evaluating already or, if not, they certainly should be. The fact that you have accomplished something in that area tells them that you're a resource, a progressive, thinking person who's concerned about saving the employer money.

Objective 4: Describe what you bring to the table (that you think they need)

Keep their interest up. Tell them what you can *do for them* that would make them *want* to see you. Tell them how your experience can help them accomplish something. For example:

> "My experience in developing a cost-reduction program for the Megalopolis Company saved them in excess of $300,000 over two years. I believe I could provide you with valuable assistance in your efforts to reduce the operating loss in the Stifled Division, which you recently announced."

If your skills aren't "dead on," indicate how they translate to their company's products or services. ***Don't EVER assume they'll understand.*** Companies and recruiters often stereotype or typecast people. ***You MUST bridge the gap and connect the dots for them.***

Show that you're flexible and can adapt to new circumstances or situations. Communicate that you're progressive and welcome change. Indicate that you can assist, support, and help—not take over, manage, run, or infer that you can "do it your way."

If you sense they want someone to reorganize and make drastic changes, and your style prefers building infrastructure and harmonious operations, don't waste your time or theirs. Your preferred style will come out in an interview. If you're a change person and they need one, your letter must stress how you've successfully made changes elsewhere. If you prefer building infrastructure and smooth operations, your letter needs to stress how you have achieved that for others.

Objective 5: Ask the question.

When you've hooked them into reading your letter, close by telling them what you want. Don't ask them to call you, because they won't. If you want an interview, say so. If you're going to call them, say so. Then tell them when, and make sure you call when you say you'll call. I've received many of these letters with resumes. I'd set them aside and then dispose of them if they didn't call when they said they would.

5. Letters Sent to a Company Contact Referred Through Your Network

One of your network contacts has given you the name of someone he knows in one of your target companies. After several telephone calls and leaving messages on their voice mail, you haven't been successful at talking to your target person. You decide to send a letter. The target person's assistant has confirmed the contact details in an earlier conversation and has told you a letter would be the preferred contact method if you were unsuccessful at talking to him.

The following page shows an example of the type of letter for this situation.

6. Letters Sent to an Employee in a Target Company Referring to an Article He Wrote

Your research turned up an article written by or about someone relevant to you within one of your target companies. You know the name of your target person, but haven't been able to find anyone in your network who knows him and could introduce you. Your letter can use this article as your hook to get his attention. You'll want to demonstrate how your skills and achievements can help him get to a higher level. Use an achievement story to demonstrate what you've done before and can do again.

An example of how you can construct your letter is shown on page 206.

7. Letters to Companies When You Know a *Retained* Recruiter Is Involved

You know the company is recruiting for someone with your skills and experience, and you know they've already engaged a *retained* recruiter to find that person. Do you write your letter to the employer or the recruiter?

If you know that a recruiter is handling the assignment and you haven't had any previous contact with him, send your letter to the recruiter with a copy to the company. You can tailor your letter to each differently, but be sure to include a copy of the letter that you sent to the other party.

If the employer likes what you have to say, they'll make sure the recruiter considers you along with other candidates.

If you write to the employer only, they'll pass your letter and resume to the recruiter, because they have a contract that covers recruiting for that position. If

Bart Ender
52 Country Club Circle
New Haven, CT 06511
Tel: 203-123-4567 • Email: bartender@togomail.com

April 30, 2009

Mr. Hal Lucinate
Chief Operating Officer
Metal Products Company
123 High Street
Hopeless, CA 90069

Dear Mr. Lucinate:

Jesse James, Chief Executive Officer at Lackoff Controls, suggested that I write to you.

I recently left Ace Metals where I was VP Production for over six years. I took on a poorly performing production facility with low morale and high product spoilage. I restructured the production process and retrained personnel. I also engaged professional trainers, set specific objectives, and monitored their effectiveness.

Within nine months, we increased production by 10%, reduced absenteeism by over 30% and reduced spoilage by 6%. Over the next five years, we consistently increased production by 10% annually and reduced costs from absenteeism and spoilage by more than 6% annually.

Jesse suggested there might be some mutual benefit if we could meet and, as I always take Jesse's advice, I will contact you early next week to see when that might be most convenient.

Yours sincerely,

Bart Ender

Enclosure (resume)

Ali Money
52 Pikes Place
Seattle, WA 98101
Tel: 206.123.4567 • Email: alimoney@spendmore.com

July 30, 2009

Mr. C.L. Everly
Vice President Sales and Marketing
National Products Company
123 High Street
Seattle, WA 90069

Dear Mr. Everly,

I read with interest your article in *Sales Executive* about EQ as an indicator of future successful sales leadership.

As Midwest Sales Manager at Global Manufacturing Co., I initiated training programs for sales staff that had low EQ. I developed programs that addressed the specific points that our tests had highlighted and set up a mentor program that resulted in a 30% sales improvement for this group.

Based on this success, Global implemented the training and mentoring program nationally. In August, Mega Global acquired Global, and the new Global VP of Sales asked me to relocate to the corporate office in River Bottom, Arkansas, and implement the training programs globally.

Not wanting to relocate, I would very much like to meet you to discuss possible opportunities in this area. I will call you early next week to see if we can meet.

Yours sincerely,

Ali Money

Enclosure (resume)

the recruiter receives your resume from the employer, he'll try to determine if you sent your letter directly to the company despite knowing he was handling the assignment. If he thinks you did know, he'll question your professionalism and ethics. You can probably guess how positive he'll be toward you.

If you've had some conversation with the recruiter about the position and he told you he felt you weren't close enough to be considered, don't attempt an end run and write directly to the company. The company would still have to forward your resume to the recruiter. Not only would the recruiter be unwilling to help you in the future, but the employer wouldn't view you positively either.

8. Letters to Send When You've Successfully Found Employment

Success! All the work you've done finally results in you accepting your ideal job. Because you've remembered the acronym IOU, you know you now need to let everyone know that you have successfully found employment.

Include all those in your network, even those you don't think helped you. You don't know whether they put great thought into it but decided, reluctantly, that they couldn't be of much help. It's safer not to judge who helped the most and who, you think, didn't help you at all. Consequently, you should include everyone in your network in your list.

Include all the recruiters and the people who interviewed you and rejected you for other positions. Now is your opportunity to demonstrate your professionalism by including them in your list. Now that you are employed, the recruiters might even want to talk to you because they know you might now be looking to engage a recruiter at your new company to make changes in staff.

Although a thank-you card might be seen as more personal and an e-mail will take much less time, take this opportunity to do some promotion of you and your new employer by sending a letter. Create two versions: one you can send to your contacts and one to recruiters and the employees in companies who had interviewed you and turned you down.

Your letter needs to cover the following four points:

1st paragraph: Indicate your new position, when you started, and the name of the company.

2nd paragraph: Describe the company, including its size, markets, products or services, and so on. This is a chance to promote your new employer.

3rd paragraph: Explain how this new position furthers your career, what strengths you have that you'll use. Remember that most of these people will be aware of your career search objectives, so connect the dots from what you told them you wanted to what you will now be doing.

4th paragraph: For those in your network, thank them for their help and support. For recruiters and interviewers in companies, thank them for their interest and consideration. Conclude with a statement encouraging them to contact you if they think you might be able to help them in the future.

Following is an example of how you might prepare your thank-you letter.

Oliver Pleese
123 Towne Ave., New Haven, CT 06511
203-700-1000 - opleese@gosh.com

February 1, 2009

Mr. Donald Trump
185 Lexington Ave., 13th Floor
New York, NY 10010

Dear Don,

I am excited to tell you that I have accepted the position of Vice President Worldwide Sales for bio-health services and products with Global Overseas Services Holdings, Inc. (GOSH). I started in my new role on January 15, 2009.

GOSH is a $3 billion bio-health company committed to improving the health and welfare of society through high-quality laboratory diagnostics, clinical and scientific research, and education for health professionals and the public. They were recently featured in Fortune and Forbes as one of the most innovative life sciences companies that are making significant improvements in accurate evaluations of the efficacy of new and innovative treatments.

I accepted this position because it enables me to build on my strengths at developing customer rapport and building long-term relationships. The change to this industry also enables me to broaden my experience by working one-on-one with customers who are expecting a high degree of professional service in addition to purchasing our products.

Thank you for your help and support during my job search. I don't think I would have found this unique opportunity without your involvement. If I can ever be of help to you, please do not hesitate to contact me. I will be there for you as you were for me.

Sincerely,

Oliver

Consider enclosing a brochure about your new company so your contacts can become more knowledgeable about where you are now employed.

In your letters to recruiters and the employees at companies where you interviewed, consider changing the last paragraph to something such as the following:

> "Thank you for the opportunity to have known you during my job search. I appreciated your consideration. I hope you would contact me if you think I might be able to return the favor by helping you. I look forward to hearing from you soon."

Don't let the disappointment of being turned down at another employer keep you from sending them a thank-you letter. They will be pleasantly surprised and, if you do need to approach them at some time in the future, they will be much more receptive to you.

Addressing a Redundancy

Communicating a job loss that resulted from a redundancy (layoff), termination, forced resignation, or a "mutual agreement" needs careful consideration, complete objectivity, an absence of emotion, and plenty of practice.

I know because I've been there *and* I've been on the other side of the table listening to others attempt to explain why they lost their jobs. This is a subject that you'll have to perfect and practice over and over until you get it right.

If, consciously or subconsciously, you have the least bit of irritation, angst, or anger, trained interviewers will detect it immediately in your voice, your choice of words, and your facial expression.

This subject is so loaded with emotion that many people fail to communicate it effectively. You might ask, "Well, how can I put a positive spin on being laid off after putting in 20 years of dedicated work with long hours?" Your past is dead; you can't control or change what already happened. *Let it go!* That chapter of your book is closed, and you're writing a new chapter. Focus on the new chapter and where it will lead you.

We all know the best time to start looking for another job is when you're still working. It's certainly easier to say, "I've decided to move my career forward by looking for a new opportunity where I can...."

If you're looking for a new job because of a redundancy, it's something that has been forced on you, not something you've chosen. Consequently, if you use the same language concerning a redundancy as you would for a job or career change that you initiated, you're being less than truthful.

Discuss redundancy in your cover letter only if you think you need to clarify it up front. Potential employers and recruiters will soon learn the truth at the time of your first interview, anyway. If you give the impression in your letter that you're looking for a career change and it comes out that you're actually unemployed, you're likely to have a short interview.

When you send your letter and resume in response to an advertisement, ignore the issue of redundancy, because you are responding to a request for candidates with certain skills and experience. Let the dates on your resume cover the question of when you left or are

TIP Although you may be bitter about your redundancy, recruiters and potential employers need to see your positive attitude. Try, for example:

▶ "For every door that closes, another opens, and I'm now looking for a new and challenging opportunity."

▶ "That chapter has closed, and I'm now focused on the next chapter in my life and the opportunities that will present to me."

leaving your last employer. You can deal with the redundancy issue in an interview when it will inevitably come up.

When you're sending a letter to a potential employer or on the recommendation of someone who's acting as your go-between or referral, consider addressing your redundancy, because the recipient will assume you're contacting him because you're unemployed.

There are no hard and fast rules on this subject, so you'll need to use your judgment. Try to answer the question by putting yourself in the recipient's shoes. If you were the recipient of the letter you plan to write, would you want to know why the person is unemployed? If so, then you should cover it in your letter.

Here are a few examples of how to address a redundancy in your letter:

◆ "Following the sale of ABC Ltd. to Megacorp Ltd. in March 2009, I, along with another 60 employees, or about 30% of its workforce, were made redundant last month. I now have an opportunity to broaden my experience in the retail home furnishings market and continue my career progression in motivating sales teams."

◆ "Following the merger of ABC, Inc. with XYZ Inc., it became clear that there was going to be a wide divergence in management's philosophy toward customer service in the new company. I shared my views with senior management, and we have reached an amicable agreement for my leaving at the end of the next quarter. While I am contractually obligated until then, management has agreed that they will allow me to cancel my contract earlier, at my request."

◆ "Due to declining revenues in the Albatross Manufacturing segment of White Elephants, Inc., it became clear last year that a radical restructuring of the business was needed if we were to survive. The parent company decided not to provide the financial resources we needed to modernize Albatross's production operations, and, in late 2008, we commenced closing some product lines and merging others with White Elephants'. I and three other senior executives were asked to manage the rundown and final merging of the retained business activities into the parent. Having successfully completed that at less cost than initially forecast, the parent was unable to provide another challenging opportunity for me. Consequently, I am using this opportunity to...." (Note: The details in this paragraph illustrate examples of issues you might want to use in developing a much shorter paragraph that works for your situation.)

Each of these examples explains the issue of redundancy objectively and succinctly, without emotion or commenting on the appropriateness or fairness of the event. Explaining your layoff unemotionally will cause the reader to think of you as positive and objective. If, however, you go into detail about how unfair it was or how you disagreed with the decision, the reader will view you as negative and subjective.

☑ Milestones

The following milestones recap what you need to do to complete this chapter. Include those items you are unable to complete in your summary-level open-items list.

❑ 1. Before making telephone calls, prepare draft scripts for what you plan to ask and how you would answer various questions that you can anticipate others will ask. Use the drafts as a working list you can edit and add to when you begin calling. Don't write out complete sentences, but rather use bullet points to highlight what you want to cover.

❑ 2. Prepare standardized letters to send to recruiters, to respond to advertisements, and to send to companies. Create a template for how you want to open and close the letter. If you're clear about what you plan to say, complete the body, keeping your letter to one page. When you prepare each letter, you can start with your template and revise it as necessary.

❑ 3. Complete Exercise 9.1: Find the Hook. Identify some hooks you can use, and practice writing a short paragraph about them that fits into your template. Look at your achievement stories for inspiration. These will also help you prepare statements you can use in your networking.

❑ 4. Test your letters by having your mentor, a trusted colleague, or career coach review them and give you feedback on what message the letters convey to them. What the reader perceives is more important than what you think you're saying in your letter.

❑ 5. Practice how you will respond to a question about a redundancy, if that is your situation. Ask another person to listen to you for any signs of emotional discomfort.

10 Interviewing

*I'd have come across better if I'd only known
how to prepare.*

Chapter Overview

Have you ever attended an interview and felt uncomfortable not knowing what was going to happen, what questions would be asked, how decisions would be made, and what you could have done to better prepare yourself? If you answered yes to these questions, you're among more than 90 percent of interviewees.

In this chapter, I'll share my views from the perspective of a recruiter, employer, and career coach. Taken together, these views will help you:

» Prepare to answer the questions interviewers will ask.

» Prepare to make sure you pass the unspoken evaluation.

» Exude confidence during an interview.

» Convince employers and recruiters that you're the best person for the job.

The main sections in this chapter include:

» Creating the best image.

» Pre-interview preparation.

» The interview.

» What interviewers want to know about you.

» Post-interview.

» Milestones.

This chapter takes you through the interviewing process. Although you may think many of the guidelines are obvious and needn't be mentioned, far too many candidates didn't know these simple tips at our interviews.

During my seven years leading a boutique international executive search firm in the UK, I participated in an abundance of interviews with our recruiters and, at my urging, most of our corporate clients.

212

If an interviewee didn't come across positively on *all* of our evaluation criteria, as well as our clients' criteria, he didn't make it to the shortlist and didn't get the job, even if he had the best skills and experience. The sad part is most never knew the real reason they weren't selected!

Creating the Best Image

A Shared Experience

When I owned my search firm in the UK, one of my assignments for an American manufacturing company's British facility was to find a Finance Director (equivalent to a CFO in the United States) who was knowledgeable in U.S. accounting and financial statement presentation.

One candidate, a Brit working for a Fortune 500 American company on the Continent (Europe), had the right amount of experience and knowledge of U.S. accounting. During our phone interview, he seemed a strong contender who came very close to matching all of our client's requirements. After my initial phone screening, I invited him in for a face-to-face interview.

I remember him walking down the hall to meet me: His shirttail was sticking out, his tie was loose, and his shirt was open at the collar. His pants were wrinkled, and he wore casual shoes similar to what I might have worn on weekends. Okay, he did just get off an airplane, but still....

I couldn't get that initial image out of my head and, while the interview was pleasant, it wasn't very long. No, he didn't make the shortlist because I knew I couldn't risk his attending a client interview looking the same way.

We gave him one of our recruiters' standard rejection reasons: "Other candidates were a better match for our client's requirements."

Chapter 9 identified three ways you communicate: through image, language, and values. If there's ever a time when all three are examined under a microscope, it's during an interview. *Everything* about you adds up to the impression you give: how you look, how you act, and what you say.

The first impression you make is pivotal. Even before you speak, your attire, personal grooming, and organization greatly influence the direction and duration of your interview. Recruiters often say they can tell within the first four minutes whether a candidate will get serious consideration.

Many times that decision is based solely on the person's appearance and demeanor, not on their skills, knowledge, and experience. I'll review the things my recruiters and I noticed that created issues for us in the following four areas:

1. Appearance.

2. Personal grooming.

3. Personal organization.

4. Travel arrangements.

You may think they are unimportant, but they create impressions that are hard to overcome.

Appearance

Clothes are the first thing people notice about you. Know your audience, and dress for the occasion. Executives and managers should dress for a professional environment, meaning men should wear a coat and tie, and women should wear a dress or suit. Men, forget the suspenders and bow ties unless it is common in the industry.

If a recruiter has already interviewed you and you're going to interview with the potential employer, ask the recruiter about appropriate attire. If you don't feel comfortable asking, being over-dressed is better than being

Illustration by Steven Lait.

underdressed. If you're underdressed, you'll feel at a disadvantage.

Recruiters and employers notice the following:

» **Clothes**—wrinkled, spotted, ill-fitting, or uncoordinated.

» **Jewelry**—excessive, noisy, ostentatious, or inappropriate.

» **Shoes**—scuffed, worn heels, holes in soles, broken laces, or brown shoes with a blue or black suit.

» **Socks** (this is mainly for men) —threadbare, holes, color doesn't match outfit, or won't stay up when you cross your legs, exposing your bare legs. (The image of the executive I interviewed who sat picking the lint off his socks is still clear in my mind.)

» **Briefcase, handbag** —worn out.

Personal Grooming

Interviewers may not be looking for them, but will notice the following about your personal grooming:

◆ **Bad breath**—alcohol, garlic, onions, fish.

◆ **Visible body piercing or tattoos**—think about the norms for your chosen industry.

◆ **Cigarette smell**—lingers on your breath, in your hair, and on your clothes long after you put the cigarette out.

◆ **Aftershave, perfume**—excessive amounts or overpowering smells.

◆ **Fingernails**—unkempt, garish color, excessive length for men or women.

◆ **Hair**—past due for a haircut, uncombed or not brushed, or a distracting hairstyle or color.

◆ **Facial hair on men**—often perceived as hiding something, having eccentricities, or indicating aloofness. When looking for a new job, it's best to be clean-shaven. You can always grow the hair back after you get the job.

Personal Organization

◆ **Use a diary** (hard copy or Personal Digital Assistant). *You're* the administrative support person responsible for your schedule. Write *everything* in your diary. Do it right away, and don't rely on memory.

◆ **Carry a notebook.** When you interview, have the notebook containing your notes about the company and your list of questions. Record the name and title of every person with whom you speak, confirming the spelling of their names, and include a brief summary of the conversation (after the meeting).

◆ **Check your briefcase.** If you take your briefcase, you'll probably open it during the interview, so make sure it's neat and orderly ahead of time.

◆ **Bring extra resumes.** Carry three or four clean copies of your resume.

◆ **Plan ahead for presentations.** If they ask you to make a presentation, it would probably occur at a second interview. Inquire in advance if there'll be a projector for your laptop or an overhead projector. Bring hard copies of your presentation in color.

If you plan to use PowerPoint, print three slides to a page so your audience can take notes. If the technology doesn't work (a common problem), your handout will save the day and show that you think and plan ahead.

◆» Go to the company's Website, copy the logo, and paste it into your opening slide. Companies like to see that you took the time to use their logo.

- ❖ Keep your slide presentation to key points, and speak to those points.

- ❖ Content is king. Keep it simple.

- ❖ Look at the people in the meeting, not at your slides.

- ❖ Speak directly to each person to make a connection.

◆ **Eat in advance.** Always eat something before the interview. It will give you a boost of energy, help your concentration, and keep your stomach from rumbling.

◆ **Check your appearance.** When you arrive, go to the restroom and check your appearance from head to toe.

◆ **Observe your surroundings.** As you walk into or through the office, absorb the corporate atmosphere. Keep your eyes and ears open for details about the company, its people, the office environment, and the building. Your visit will help you decide whether *you* want to work for *them.* Make notations in your notebook about the environment to help you remember what you noticed. If people aren't talking to others or don't look up, it could be a sign of a pressure environment.

◆ **Prepare to wait.** Put a business or professional magazine or newspaper in your briefcase that you can read while waiting. You want them to see that you think ahead. Don't take any non-business publications. Review the contents and skim or read the lead article or a topical one. Your interviewer may ask if you saw the article in such and such magazine about something relating to their company or the industry. You may also be able to use something topical as a starter for "small talk" at the beginning to help break the ice.

Travel Arrangements

You may think the following are inconsequential, but they're the most frequent causes of interviews getting off to a shaky start:

◆ **Parking**—Call and ask for the company's interview location, directions, and parking instructions. Make sure you have plenty of change in case you have to pay for metered parking.

◆ **Directions**—Check, copy, or download a map that shows exactly how to get there. If you know someone who works in the general neighborhood, ask about the usual traffic flow for the time of day of your interview. Consider making a dry run to the location so you know what to expect. You don't want to arrive and find one-way streets or construction that impedes your arriving on time.

◆ **Be on time**—*On time means around 15 minutes before your scheduled appointment.* This lets the interviewer know you're there, and gives you AND them time to use the restroom and prepare. If you can't be there within this time frame before your scheduled time, call to let them know where you are and when you anticipate arriving.

◆ **Lateness**—If you think you're going to be late, call the interviewer or her administrative support person as early as you can, explain the circumstances, and tell her when you expect to arrive. The interviewer may have meetings or interviews scheduled back-to-back. If it's a problem, immediately try to reschedule your interview. If you simply arrive late without notifying her, you show insensitivity and lack of respect for the interviewer's time.

When you're comfortable with knowing the physical considerations, you can start looking at how to prepare yourself mentally.

Pre-Interview Preparation

You are (or will certainly feel you are) at an immediate disadvantage if you must begin your interview with an apology. The need to apologize puts you under needless stress.

It's perfectly normal to feel nervous, even after the most thorough preparation. Interviews are stressful. But the better prepared you are, the less nervous and stressed you'll feel. *Some* stress is good. Feelings of anticipation and a desire to do well will help you perform better.

The interviewer may also be anxious. Interviewers have only a few minutes to make decisions with enormous adverse repercussions for their employer and, possibly, for their own job if they get it wrong.

Interviewers will initially be trying to find reasons to screen you out. They're not career coaches trying to help you find a job! Not all interviewers are experienced at interviewing or even good at it. Consider this, and adjust your style so that you're not competing to control the interview or appear to be trying to dominate it.

Interviewers will know early on whether you've done your homework. If it appears that you have, they'll mentally shift attitudes. The interview will be less of an interrogation and a screening-out, and more of an attempt to find reasons to hire you.

You need to come across not as a job seeker but as a resource they need. To accomplish this effectively, the following will help:

◆ **Be knowledgeable about the company.** Do your research. Know what their Website says and what was in their latest SEC filing and press release. Read recent news articles affecting the company and the industry. (The library is an excellent resource for this.)

◆ **Find out something about the interviewer.** Sometimes you can obtain information if you speak directly to her when you arrange the interview. Other sources of information may come from your network, the interviewer's administrative support person, a receptionist, the company's Website, a name search using a proprietary database you can access remotely from a library database, or an Internet search.

◆ **Prepare for probable questions.** Review the types of questions you think he'll ask so you're ready for them in advance. Know how you want to respond, but don't try to memorize the actual words.

◆ **Understand your most recent employer's business.** Understand how your job fits into the larger perspective of your most recent employer. Know its products, markets, niche, and so forth. When asked questions about your most recent employer, interviewers may probe your overall understanding of the business. *A word of caution:* Don't disclose confidential or proprietary information. If you do, the interviewer will assume you would do the same with their proprietary information. Companies sometimes interview candidates from a competitor for the sole purpose of gathering proprietary information.

◆ **Prepare to ask questions.** Prepare a list of questions for the interviewer. You want to ask questions about the business and the position: What are the expectations of you in the role? What specific results do they expect you to deliver and when? Why did the last person in the position leave? Include questions about the culture, such as turnover in the company or department. What are the company's "hot buttons"? What operational changes are being considered that might affect [the business or the job]? Phrase your questions so that the interviewer can't answer with a yes or no. Use "how," "why," and "what" types of questions.

If you have sensitive questions that might not be appropriate during an initial interview, such as a recent lawsuit, hold off asking them until you think the company is seriously considering you, and you both know each other a little better.

218

The Interview

How well you do in an interview most often depends on how well you prepare. However, you may encounter some things that will be out of your control. The employer may cancel the interview at the last minute, decide during the hiring process not to fill a position, decide to promote someone from within, or rethink his needs and decide to restructure the company, eliminating the position.

You might make some erroneous assumptions about the interviewer's preparation for the interview and find that she may *not*:

- ◈ Be a skilled interviewer.
- ◈ Be knowledgeable about the specifics of the job.
- ◈ Have read your resume.
- ◈ Understand how your experience relates to the job.

Listen carefully to the questions the interviewer asks so you can evaluate which of these assumptions is true and adjust your message to the realities. For example, if you sense that the interviewer hasn't read your resume, make sure you mention one or more of your achievements, so that your memorable story will set you apart from others.

Though the interviewer typically takes charge, don't be shy about asking pertinent questions if you feel the interviewer isn't prepared or asking relevant questions. This is *your* interview as much as it is hers. If you don't convey enough positive information about yourself and obtain enough information about the company, the interviewer won't have enough information to consider you seriously, and you won't have enough information about them to know whether you want to work there.

Following are suggestions regarding the mechanics, procedures, and rules about interviews in general.

When You First Meet the Interviewer

- ◆ Make eye contact as you shake hands, and smile.
- ◆ Sit after the interviewer sits or when invited to sit.
- ◆ Scan the interviewer's office. Look for things that tell you something about her. Look for photos of children or places visited, citations or awards on the wall, pictures, statues, or books that you also may have read.

Open the Communication Channels

◆ Establish rapport as quickly as possible. Comment briefly (positively, if possible!) on the usual things (the weather, the journey, the view from the office). Don't make insincere or patronizing comments. Remind the interviewer who introduced you, if it was someone in your network.

◆ Let the interviewer set the tone. Don't try to take control.

◆ Be yourself. Act natural. Exude good humor, energy, enthusiasm, and openness. You need to appear as your true self.

◆ Don't become too chatty. You're there for an interview. Keep the subject focused on the reason why you're there.

Body Language

◆ Your body language is unspoken but observed, and makes a powerful and influential impression. Interviewers may be trained in NLP (Neuro-Linquistic Programming) and will look for nonverbal messages that reveal clues to the *real* you.

◆ Interviewers look for signs indicating when you're nervous, feeling under pressure, or hiding something, such as clenching your jaw, clasping your hands together tightly, blushing, facial sweating, throbbing at the temples, crossing your arms, or nervously bouncing your leg up and down as if keeping beat to a fast musical score.

◆ During the interview, observe the interviewer and assess whether her nonverbal signals are consistent with what she says. Does she appear open- or closed-minded? Inquiring or interrogating? Truly interested or just going through the motions?

General Rules for Answering Questions

A good interviewer controls timing and content but doesn't dominate. Make sure, as well, that the interviewer doesn't feel threatened or dominated; aim for 50/50 to 60/40 your speaking/listening. Recruiters typically have you speak more than 50 percent of the time.

Techniques to remember in your interview:

◆ Listen to the question, think about how to answer, and then respond.

◆ When asked multiple questions, answer each part separately.

◆ Focus your answers on this particular job.

◆ Give short, succinct answers—*two minutes maximum*. Expand on them only if asked.

❖ When asked open-ended questions, tailor your response to how it relates to the job or use examples from your past.

❖ If the question is unclear or you're unsure how to respond, ask for clarification.

❖ If the interviewer uses a word you're unfamiliar with, ask her to explain it. Don't try to bluff based on what you think it means.

❖ Tell the truth. Just relate the facts. Don't justify, and don't stretch it.

❖ Keep cool even under intentional provocation. Interviewers sometimes do this to test your mettle.

❖ Focus on the employer's needs. They seek to employ you for the skills, knowledge, and/or experience *they think they need.* Don't go off on tangents.

❖ Maintain a positive attitude. Talk positively about your current or former employer, associates, bosses, and so forth, regardless of personal feelings. *You never know who knows whom.*

❖ Don't be overly sensitive. Interviewers often look for something to criticize just to see how you react. Be prepared to accept criticism where it's due, and treat it as constructive. Don't be afraid to admit your mistakes. No manager learns without making mistakes. If you say you haven't made any, you're either not a manager or not telling the truth.

❖ Look for opportunities to quantify your answer using percentages or other numbers as these help the interviewer to put it into perspective.

❖ Most interview questions will be behavioral or situational, where they ask you to describe an incident from your past.

Use the **STAR** method to respond to these types of questions. **STAR** stands for:

Situation: What was the situation you were in or what position did you hold? This frames your response or sets the stage for your answer.

Tasks: What was the task or what were the tasks that needed to be accomplished?

Action: What did you do and how did you do it (that enabled you to achieve or accomplish the tasks)?

Results: What were the results, achievements, solutions, etc., that directly followed because of your involvement? This completes the story.

Here's a **STAR** example:

You are asked to describe a situation where you were in charge of training and you had to balance the needs of directly providing training and managing a small training team.

Your response could be:

(Situation) "As the newly promoted manager of sales training for the LoSales division at Truncheon Corp., I had responsibility for three sales trainers who had been my peers and who had been with the company longer than I."

(Tasks) "The HR Director asked me to develop new training programs and revitalize the effectiveness of current programs. I knew, however, that my new responsibilities could take me away from the training part of the job I loved, and I didn't want that to happen."

(Action) "I gathered my trainers together and explained my mission and asked for their help in revising our programs and looking into new programs that would allow me to stay involved in providing training. We brainstormed different options and finally settled on each person selecting the specific subject that interested them the most and agreeing to become the subject matter expert in that area. I took on the training program 'Team Management Skills for Newly Promoted Managers.'"

(Results) "Within six months, the overall quality of the group training improved and the sales staff began to use the trainers as individual coaches in addition to their roles as group trainers. After one year, sales per person increased 20% and sales staff turnover was down by more than 50%."

This story is intended to convey examples and is more detailed than you should use. Keeping your story concise will help the interviewer to repeat it to others from memory.

An interviewer may ask forced-choice questions, such as, "Are you people-oriented or task-oriented?" If so, they're looking more at how you answer than the answer itself. There's no one right answer to these types of questions. Think carefully and give an honest but balanced response.

Inappropriate or Illegal Questions

If the interviewer asks you an inappropriate or illegal question, be professional and maintain your composure and positive attitude. Illegal questions may be unintentional—an innocent mistake by an unskilled interviewer. Perhaps there's a valid reason for asking the question, but the interviewer phrased it poorly. Sometimes the questioner knows the question is inappropriate, but is testing your reaction.

When you know a question is illegal, inquire what information the person is looking for so you can answer the question more specifically. For example, if she asks you if you're married or if you have young children, what she might really be trying to determine is what restrictions you might have on overtime or travel that might affect your ability to perform the job.

You can respond by saying you think she's asking you to describe any limitations you may have regarding travel, overtime, or relocation. If you react negatively to an illegal question and respond with a challenge, such as, "That's an illegal question," your interviewer will probably apologize, but your chance of getting a job with that company may be remote. Even when you encounter a clearly illegal question, use your finesse to answer with a reasoned response, addressing the substance of the question.

"Tell me about yourself" is often cited as one of the first questions interviewers ask. We occasionally asked that question, but only at the very end of our interviews, because we didn't believe we learned anything useful from the answers. But many interviewers still ask it.

This is a leading question, enabling the interviewer to gather information about your personal life so they can "better understand you as a person." Their intent may only be to "better understand" you and not pry into your personal life. You're there for an interview for a job so keep your response focused on your career, qualifications, and education.

Explain how you chose your major, why you took your first job, what positions you held, what challenges you had, some memorable learning experiences, why you left companies, and what brings you to this opportunity. Include things in your personal life that have had a positive impact on your career or have helped form your beliefs, such as a personal challenge or interest, such as scaling a mountain, involvement in a community initiative, teaching language skills, or reading to children in an educational environment, and so forth.

General Rules for Asking Questions

Ask questions when you're sincerely interested in the answer. Don't ask perfunctory questions that don't serve a purpose. It's okay to ask relevant questions even if you think you already know the answer. You need to confirm your assessments and judgments.

Prepare your questions in advance. Use open-ended questions such as the following:

◆ "Could you tell me about the budget? What is it based on? Who prepares it? Who compares actual to budget? Who reports the differences and to whom?"

◆ "You mentioned the possibility of promotion. Could you tell me how you assess criteria for this and how often you make appraisals?"

◆ "Can you tell me why the position is open?"

◆ "Why did the person who formerly held this job leave?"

◆ "What qualities did you see in the previous job holder that made you hire him?"

◆ "Are any internal candidates currently being considered for this job?" (If so, ask how the company, group, department, and so forth would react to someone new coming in.)

◆ "How will the department react to and accept a new manager from outside the company?"

◆ "What is the morale in the department right now?"

◆ "What do you see as the biggest challenges for the person taking this job?"

◆ "Have there been any employee legal actions against the company from this department?" Ask this if you suspect a problem (for example, sexual harassment).

◆ "What do you think is the most important action the incoming person should take first?"

◆ "On what factors would I be evaluated during the first 90 days (or other time period)?"

◆ "What would you expect me to accomplish within the first 90 days (or other time period)?"

◆ "Do you anticipate any reorganization or change in business focus that might impact this department or this position within the next year?"

On the day of your interview, you may think you'll be interviewed by only one person. After that initial interview, however, they may have others interview you as well. The questions the secondary interviewers ask may be predetermined, but usually they are decided on by the interviewer at the time of the interview. This is your opportunity to ask each interviewer the same questions to see if you get consistent answers.

If you are interviewed by the person for whom you would work and are then interviewed by their peers or subordinates, ask them to describe the person who would be your boss and what it's like to work for her.

Write summarized answers on your list and if someone tells you something inconsistent with what others say, note that for follow-up in your closing interview.

Make sure to collect a business card from everyone who interviews you. If the person doesn't have one, confirm the correct spelling of his name and job title. Don't leave the premises without getting this information, as it will be difficult to get it later.

Closing the Interview

Don't leave with a vague "we'll be in touch." If the interviewer doesn't take the initiative in telling you what happens next, it's up to you to find out. Ask where the company is in the process, how many people have they already interviewed, how many more will they be seeing, what additional interviews may be required of you, and what type of tests, if any, will the company be using (psychological, EQ, and so on).

If there are open issues regarding travel expenses, ask the interviewer how to handle them. When you leave the interview, don't forget you're still *on stage.* Even if you don't think it went as well as you'd hoped, be cheerful and polite to everybody. You don't know who gets to weigh in on your hiring. Your assumption that you performed poorly may be incorrect. The interviewer may believe that you came across very well under intense and perhaps difficult questioning.

The interviewer may escort you back to the reception area or to the next person who will interview you. Don't be lulled into thinking the interview is finished. This is a time when skilled interviewers assess how comfortable they feel with you. Innocuous-sounding questions at this time may have more meaning than you realize.

Panel Interviews

If you will be involved in a panel interview, anticipate that they can seem like pressure cookers. Keep in mind that the interviewers' questions can often be more structured requiring a more formal interaction when responding even when you are responding to a question asked by someone with whom you think you have a more informal relationship.

If introductions are not made at the start, ask the names and positions of *all* persons in attendance in a circular fashion, so you can address them by name when they ask you questions. This is where your notepad will be crucial.

Take time to respond to questions. Think about each question and paraphrase it back to the group before you respond. This will demonstrate that you think before you respond, and will ensure that everyone understands your answer in the context of how you paraphrased the question. If you paraphrased incorrectly, someone will likely clarify the question.

When you respond, look at the person who asked the question and say her name when you answer. If you get multiple-part questions from the same person, jot down key words as she asks the questions. If several people are asking you questions at the same time, they may be testing your stamina under pressure to see how you react to multiple simultaneous demands. *Smile* and go with the flow. Use your notepad to jot down the key words and then answer them in the sequence asked. If you don't have a notepad handy, you can easily become overwhelmed.

Pressure Interviews

Pressure interviews occur when the position requires a strong change-management style, or when contentious negotiations, such as with unions, will be a key responsibility. You can deal effectively with pressure interviews by remaining calm, showing that you're prepared, and handling questions in an organized way—by making frequent use of your notepad.

Review your most important interview questions ahead of time. This will pay enormous dividends in pressure interviews, because few candidates prepare for interviews. If the position requires difficult negotiations, plan for a pressure interview knowing that an interviewer will probe into your past, looking for weaknesses, situations where you failed to prepare, and negotiating failures.

Be ready to describe how you overcame them and adapted to changing circumstances. No one became skilled at dealing with difficult situations or people without making mistakes along the way and learning from them. Don't hide those mistakes. Talk about them, and demonstrate that you've already gone through the learning phase.

What Interviewers Want to Know About You

There are only three basic things interviewers want to know about you:

1. **Can you do the job?** Do you have the skills and experience to do what we want?

2. **How well will you fit into our culture?** Will your attitude and style be in concert with ours?

3. **Are you telling the truth?** Is what I am hearing the real you?

When I stress these three points, people often remind me of Southwest Airline's philosophy: Hire for attitude, and train for skills. (Refer back to the beginning of Chapter 3 for a reminder about this issue.)

If you're an executive candidate who will be expected to lead and manage, but don't have the right skills and experience, your attitude probably won't be relevant. It's also true that, if you have the right skills and experience but the wrong attitude, you're probably out of the running.

Of course, interviewers will never ask you the questions directly, but instead will ask you to describe situations in your past that will help them answer their three questions. Keep the following points in mind when you respond.

Do You Have the Skills and Experience We Want?

Employers want the skills and experience *they think* they need. It doesn't matter if independent observers, the recruiter, or even you think they really need something different.

Employers often don't reconsider their needs when recruiting a replacement leader or manager and, as a result, don't reassess whether the business or the position has changed, resulting in their now needing someone different.

You must focus on what *they say they want,* not on your perception of what *you think they need.*

Is Your Experience Analogous to Our Company and Industry?

The first person to interview you at an employer may be someone in HR whose only job has been with that employer. Consequently, they may not understand, be open to understanding, or even be capable of understanding, how your experience relates to their employer, even if you believe your experience is in the same industry.

For example, an interviewer for a specialty boutique retailer may think your experience at a national retail chain is not comparable to his business, even if you were selling similar products to his. Remember: The initial interviewer's role is often to try to find reasons to screen you out, similar to the initial screening process for resumes described in Chapter 6.

If you think you're being stereotyped, include examples in your follow-up thank-you letter reiterating the similarities, and immediately get in touch with your contact who helped you connect with the company to discuss the events of the interview. Ask if there is some way she can assist to help you bridge the perceived gap in the mind of the interviewer.

How Do We Know You Really Have the Skills and Experience You Say You Have?

They'll be looking for situations from your past that confirm you have the skills and experience you say you have. Be ready to tell achievement stories that demonstrate your claims. They may not remember all your skills and experience, but they'll remember your stories and use them to tell others about you.

How Committed Will You Be?

They're looking for evidence of commitment in the past. They don't want someone who looks at this position as just another job. They're looking for passion and evidence of enthusiasm in your work and for their industry.

If an employer doesn't detect any passion in you for his business, he may screen you out, sensing that you're not searching for the right job for you but, rather, just another job.

Will You Be a Stable Employee?

Have you jumped ship every couple of years, other than for short-term projects common in engineering and IT? In today's environment, breaks in employment are more common than in the past. Even so, they'll probe the nature of your job changes as they try to find out if you can demonstrate personal stability. They won't want to recruit for this job again in the near future.

Will You Fit in With Others in Our Organization?

They'll probably ask (directly or indirectly) about your attitude and relationship with superiors, peers, and subordinates. Here, they're probing your emotional intelligence. (Refer back to Chapter 3.)

Can We Believe What You're Telling Us?

Ah, the really difficult area starts now. This is something interviewers are asking themselves throughout an interview. When they probe certain areas in granular detail or seem to ask similar questions in different parts of the interview, it isn't necessarily because they're bad interviewers asking unimportant questions or repeating themselves. They might be assessing your honesty and forthrightness.

They may use other methods to assess your attitude, truthfulness, and "fit," such as psychological tests like the Disc, the Bar-on EQ-i, SHL's OPQ, or one of many others marketed to employers as *the* pre-employment test. Or they may send you to an assessment center where you'll take a number of personality tests and have behavioral interviews by psychologists.

They'll also want to speak to previous employers, check your references, and, possibly, engage a company to conduct a background investigation. I can't overemphasize the importance of coming across as being *authentic*. If there is the least contradiction between how you think about yourself and what they think about you, they'll feel uncomfortable and will probably decide against you. You probably won't know the real reason why they selected another candidate.

Be prepared to justify everything you say. Interviewers often discover the most telling answers from responses to the following questions or statements:

- ❖ Could you be more specific?
- ❖ For instance...?
- ❖ Could you give an example?
- ❖ Tell me a time when you....
- ❖ Describe a situation when you....
- ❖ Why?
- ❖ What exactly do you mean?
- ❖ I don't understand. (They probably do, but want you to explain in more detail, want to see if you modify your answer, or they want to see how well you can translate something technical in non-technical terms so other non-technical people understand.)
- ❖ What did you learn from that?

A Shared Experience

In my search practice, we usually tried to ask behavioral questions about events the candidate should have experienced (such as, "Tell us about a situation where you had to choose between meeting a deadline or a certain quality standard, and you knew you couldn't meet both.").

If you responded you hadn't experienced that situation, we would act surprised. We'd then ask: "What would you do if you had to deal with that problem?" After you gave a balanced answer, we'd ask for an example. Amazingly, we almost always drew a response that related to an actual experience.

Next, we had to assess whether you had forgotten the actual situation (possible, but unlikely), or you intentionally tried to avoid answering because of a problem you preferred not to talk about, or the final answer you gave about your "real" experience was not the real experience.

If we heard more than one example like this, we concluded we couldn't reasonably assess what was the true story or who you really were without additional and expensive psychological testing. You can probably guess what our decision would likely be. Next candidate, please!

It doesn't take an interviewer long to determine whether you've been through outplacement or you've been over-coached on how to respond to interviewers' questions. I've had to stop interviews when I felt the answers were too "perfect." I'd ask the candidate if he or she was using an outplacement firm or a career coach and, if so, I'd tell them that I was discontinuing the interview, and he was no longer a candidate.

I'd then explain the three objectives of an interview and that the answers he was giving made me suspect I wasn't getting the truth or a true picture of the real person. I explained that I felt I was getting a packaged presentation and, consequently, wasn't able to make a good determination of him. Based on this, I couldn't recommend him to my client.

If you haven't been involved in successful interviews recently, get some practice interviewing in front of an observer who can be frank with you about how you come across before you attend the real thing.

Preparing for Interviews

This form, available online because of space restrictions in this book, lists those questions interviewers commonly ask. Print the list, review it, and make notes or enter keywords that will remind you how you would answer each question.

If the question is appropriate, assume the interviewer will ask you for an example. Don't write out long answers; use only phrases or keywords.

Color code or use a number from 1 to 3 to prioritize the questions you think you will have more difficulty answering. Take this list with you when you attend an interview and review the high-priority ones immediately before the interview so you'll be ready to answer confidently and succinctly.

If the interviewer asks you other questions during the interview that you had to struggle to answer, note them after your interview and add them to your list of interview questions so you'll be prepared for your next interview.

I've heard people tell me that every question the interviewer asked them were ones on the list they were prepared to answer. They felt confident in the interview, aced it, and got the job. The interviewer later told them after they were hired that they chose them largely on the strength of how well they performed in the interview. They stood head-and-shoulders above all other candidates.

I know I've said it before, but I'll say it again just in case the message hasn't sunk in yet:

PREPARATION IS KEY TO A SUCCESSFUL INTERVIEW.

Post-Interview

Assess your performance soon after each interview—within half an hour if possible. An assessment is your personal quality check to improve your performance. If they invite you back for another interview, these notes will be useful in your preparation.

Post-Interview Notes

This worksheet illustrates the information you might want to note after an interview.

Post-Interview Notes

Company_____Date_____	
Place of interview_____ Time_____	
Interviewer_____Job title_____	

Interviewer	1. Describe the interviewer—characteristics, etc., so you remember him.
	2. What was your impression of the interviewer?
	3. What did the interviewer do or ask that caught you off-guard?
	4. What suggestions did the interviewer give you?
	5. What impressions do you think the interviewer has of you?
You	6. What questions were the most difficult to answer?
	7. Which questions did you not answer well?
	8. What issues were raised but not answered or left open?
	9. Is there anything you think you did wrong that you could do differently next time?
	10. What goals did you have for this meeting that you didn't meet?
Company	11. How would you describe the physical location?
	12. What were your impressions of the people you met?
	13. How would you describe the culture of this organization?
	14. Is this a place where you would like to work?
Job	15. What skills and experience would you use in this job that you like to use?
	16. What do you see in this job that is a negative? How important is that?
	17. What values of yours are met by this company and this job?
	18. What values of yours are NOT met by this company and this job?
	19. Why do you want this job? (They may ask this question in a subsequent interview.)
To Do	20. Who needs to do what next?
	21. When do you expect to hear back about the next step?

At a second interview, you may get questions in areas where you hedged answers or gave unfocused or unclear responses in the first interview. If you noted those areas in a post-interview appraisal, you'll be able to prepare thoughtful answers for the second round.

Send a one-page letter to the employer's primary interviewer the same day if possible, but no later than the following day, thanking him for the meeting. Send separate letters to other interviewers if you have something specific to add or clarify that came up in your interview with them. Express continued interest in the job and comment on any particular point you feel needs to be emphasized more or that you didn't mention or get across during the interview. Use thank-you cards if you only want to send personalized, handwritten notes.

☑ Milestones

The following milestones recap what you need to do to complete this chapter. Include those items you are unable to complete in your summary-level open-items list.

❑ 1. Review the points in "Creating the Best Image."

❑ 2. Review the points in "Pre-Interview Preparation," and make a list of items you can use as a checklist before you attend an interview.

❑ 3. Review the points in "The Interview" so you're familiar with things you want to observe and consider when you go for an interview.

❑ 4. Review "What Interviewers Want to Know About You," and download Worksheet 10.1: Preparing for Interviews. Write *key words* that will jog your memory of what you'd say in response to the questions.

❑ 5. Prioritize your interview questions into at least three groups, reflecting the importance you attach to the questions or the difficulty you anticipate in answering them.

❑ 6. Practice interviewing, and have another person observe your response to questions you consider most important or difficult.

❑ 7. Prepare a list of questions you might want to ask during an interview. For example, confirm that your values and preferences for the work environment and the people you want to work for match their corporate culture.

❑ 8. Using the guidelines in "Post-Interview," prepare your own Post-Interview Form or use Worksheet 10.2: Post-Interview Notes.

Negotiating Your Salary

You can't negotiate your salary without knowing your options.

Chapter Overview

Most of the advice you'll hear at seminars and workshops, and read about in books on negotiating your salary focus on the best scenarios under ideal circumstances. Being out of work or making a job change on your own are not ideal circumstances. Your ability to effectively negotiate your salary hinges on many things, not least of which is your current employment situation.

In this chapter, I'll describe the options that are available to you based on my experience in various scenarios I observed in my search practice and in working with executives. You'll learn:

- » How to find your ideal salary and your bottom line.
- » What factors outside of your control you need to consider when negotiating.
- » Negotiating techniques in various situations you'll likely encounter.
- » How to recognize the signs when an offer is getting close.
- » What to say when the salary issue comes up in conversation.

The main sections in this chapter include:

- » General rules and guidelines.
- » Finding your preferred salary.
- » What benefits are most important to you?
- » Strategies for talking about salary.
- » Timing of the offer.
- » Milestones.

General Rules and Guidelines

Your ability to negotiate your salary will depend on several factors—some positive and some negative—that may not totally be in your control, such as:

- The state of the economy.
- The vibrancy of the industry.
- The profitability of the company or profit margins in the industry.
- The type and size of the company.
- Whether and how long you've been unemployed.
- The uniqueness of your skills and experience.
- Your track record, achievements, and experience.
- Whether you currently have a job and a headhunter contacted you about a new opportunity, you initiated a job search because you want to leave your current employer, or you've been unemployed for several months.
- Whether you worked in a declining industry and now want to move to a more robust one.

If the position you seek already exists, most companies will have an established salary and benefits for it. Unless you can bring something to the table the predecessor didn't have or wasn't able to do, there may be few options to justify an increase. Some high-profile companies or industries have reputations for paying low salaries, particularly when there's an abundance of qualified candidates who want to work for them.

If the economy is in a downturn or recession, an abundance of candidates combined with a stagnating business environment will increase competition for jobs and depress salaries.

Companies are often willing to offer higher salaries to people from companies with reputations for high-quality management, such as McKinsey & Co., GE, P&G, Microsoft, and so forth. You may have to take a salary cut if others consider your prior industry experience "old-line."

Competitors or smaller companies are often willing to attach a premium to employees of a company where there is a high regard for some aspect of its business process.

Graduating from a prestigious university, such as Harvard, Stanford, MIT, and so on, usually enhances pay.

Considering these factors, you should assume your salary will be negotiable and prepare yourself. If it turns out it isn't, you'll know soon enough. If you're considering an opportunity because a recruiter contacted you during their search, you have many more options than someone who is looking for a new job. The suggestions in this chapter, therefore, are directed more at those who are in transition or who are initiating the job search on their own.

The general rule is not to disclose to employers your most recent salary or how much you want until you've been offered the job. Sometimes you won't have an option. Salaries for management positions, especially in large companies, may be structured across the board and effectively non-negotiable. Salaries for executive (C-level) positions usually can be negotiated.

If a recruiter asks you about your salary early in the interview process, be up front with her, because she needs to assess whether you're in a range her client will consider and accept. The recruiter will know what salary range the client is willing to pay, depending on the skills and experience of the candidate.

Recruiters sometimes go to bat for outstanding candidates if they think their client's salary range is too low. Similarly, recruiters will be up front with you if they think your salary expectations are too high for the industry or what they think their client is willing to pay.

Companies often criticize recruiters for trying to boost the salary of candidates because their fee is based on the final salary offered and accepted. My experience as a recruiter and in conversations with others in the field is that recruiters often find themselves in the middle as a neutral arbitrator trying to find an acceptable balance between what the candidate says he wants and what the marketplace says the company should be paying.

If the employer asks you for your salary during the early stages of an interview, you need to have done your homework in the following sections so you can respond appropriately.

Finding Your Preferred Salary

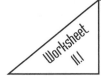

Calculating Your Salary Requirements

To begin, you need to know what salary you *need* and what salary you *want*. You can compute these two amounts by preparing a schedule similar to the worksheet on page 236.

Note: You can determine an approximate effective tax rate by looking at your last year's federal and state tax returns. Add the total tax you paid to both and divide it by your adjusted gross income as shown on your federal tax return.

When you've completed the worksheet, you will know the salary you need to cover basic living costs, as well as the salary you want to support your lifestyle. Any salary less than your **Break-Even Salary** won't cover necessities. You'll have to make it up from other income sources. Any salary less than your **Preferred Salary** won't cover all your lifestyle choices. If you list your Lifestyle Expenses in priority, you can quickly estimate which ones you'll have to give up or cut back on.

Calculating Your Salary Requirements

No.	Description	Periodic amount	No. of periods	Total for year
1	Required Expenses (round to 100s):			
2	Mortgage/Rent			
3	Insurance – House			
4	Insurance – Vehicle			
5	Insurance – Life			
6	Groceries			
7	Clothing			
8	Utilities			
9	Vehicle payments			
10	Vehicle operating costs			
11	Cable			
12	Property taxes (monthly average)			
13	Household expenses			
14	Gifts/Donations			
15				
16				
17				
18				
19				
20	Total Required Expenses			
21	Add income taxes (your effective tax rate)			
22	**Break-Even Salary**			
23	Lifestyle Expenses (round to 100s):			
24	Vacations			
25	Entertainment			
26	Eating out			
27				
28				
29				
30	Total Lifestyle Expenses			
31	Add taxes on Lifestyle Exp (your effective tax rate)			
32	**Disposable Salary**			
33	**Preferred Salary** (total of break-even and disposable salaries)			

236

When you know your salary options, you can then look at which benefits are most important to you so you can assess whether the company's total package is in your range of expectations.

What Benefits Are Most Important to You?

Exercise 11.1: Prioritizing Benefits

Review the following list and rate items from 1 (most important) to least important. When finished, circle your top five.

___ 401(k)	___ Expense account
___ Bonus or profit-sharing	___ Health plan for family
___ Cafeteria on-site	___ Life insurance
___ Childcare facilities	___ Pension plan
___ Company car or car/mileage allowance	___ Savings plan
	___ Stock option plan
___ Country club or health club membership	___ Training/Education reimbursement

You now have a foundation of knowledge about salary and benefits that you can use to evaluate offers. Add to this the work you've already completed in Worksheet 1.1: Identifying Your Values, Exercise 1.1: Known Likes and Dislikes, Exercise 1.2: Goals Summary, Worksheet 4.1: Personal Living Preferences, Worksheet 4.2: Workplace Preferences, and Worksheet 4.3: People Preferences. You are now armed with considerable knowledge about what is important to you and are better prepared to evaluate potential opportunities.

Strategies for Talking About Salary

Be cautious with disclosing too much, too soon, about your most recent salary. If you see yourself as a job beggar, you'll be too eager to get the job and reluctant to negotiate. If you see yourself as a valuable resource, you'll keep your options open until you know whether *you* really want the job, and how badly *they* want *you*.

Avoid revealing your previous salary because it can stereotype you and the amount can be misleading. Salary doesn't include bonuses, commissions, allowances, other cash considerations, and fringe benefits. Besides, your salary in your last job may not have any relevance to the job for which you're interviewing.

If an employer or recruiter asks directly, you can't ignore the question. You can often deal with this by talking about your salary in terms of compensation or remuneration *ranges* over time, not absolute amounts at a point in time.

Here are suggestions about how to address salary in different situations.

An Advertised Job States Responses Will Not Be Considered Without a Salary History

Advertisements in newspapers are expensive. Anyone who spends a large amount of money to place an ad for a real job wants to find someone with the skills and experience they need in their organization.

In ads for management positions, the statement "responses without a salary history will not be considered" generally means that either no job exists and the company or recruiter is doing a salary survey to find current market rates, or a job does exist, but they don't know what to pay or they want to pay a rock-bottom salary.

If you possess the skills and experience the company wants, they'll *want* to talk to you whether you include salary or not.

> **A Shared Experience**
>
> My search firm in the UK placed advertisements in national newspapers for senior opportunities when it was difficult to find candidates using traditional search techniques. We sometimes asked respondents to include their salary history. In these instances, what we hoped to find was current market information on the salaries of the people who were interested in the position because we were unable to find enough accurate information on current salary structures. It usually accomplished what we wanted.
>
> Responses without the requested salary information were processed the same as those with the requested information. Admittedly, for those who didn't provide the information, that was one of the first questions we asked them when we called for an initial interview.

Your approach should be different depending on whether your cover letter and resume will be going to a recruiter or an employer.

Responses to Recruiters

If your cover letter is to a recruiter, include a statement about your total compensation expectations within a range, because a recruiter needs to know how close of a fit you will be to his client's compensation structure.

Recruiters want to facilitate a match so they can collect their full fee. Consequently, they often find themselves in the role of running interference for candidates if there's a significant mismatch between a candidate's salary expectation and their client's salary structure. They often talk to candidates before interviewing them to discuss these types of mismatches.

Responses to Employers (Or You Don't Know if They're Employers or Recruiters)

If your cover letter and resume will be going to an employer, or you don't know whether they are a recruiter or employer, don't include any information about salary in your response.

If the position is at an executive, director, or manager level, "Responses without salary history will not be considered" may be a correct statement by those companies that want to know what you made in your last job so they can use that information to their advantage, not yours. Companies with this attitude are usually more interested in finding the least-costly candidate, rather than the most-qualified candidate.

Review your values and determine whether you really want to work for a company with that attitude. If you choose to respond to the salary issue, use a prospective statement such as: "My compensation (or remuneration) expectations are in the range of $150,000 to $175,000." By using a prospective approach, the employer or recruiter knows the range of your expectations and can decide if it's reasonable. If it's in their range and they still want to know your salary history, they'll call you for that information; if they invite you in for an interview, they'll ask that question early on.

In your cover letter don't hamper your ability to negotiate your compensation by including some "flexibility" statements like mentioning you're more interested in a new opportunity and are flexible, because they'll conclude you'll accept an amount well below the salary range you noted in your cover letter.

You're Asked for Your Last Salary During a Telephone Interview

During the conversation, they ask something along the lines of:

- ❖》 "What's your current salary, Mr. Smith?"
- ❖》 "What was your salary at XYZ Co., Mr. Smith?"
- ❖》 "… and what salary are you looking for, Mr. Smith?"

How do you respond?

If a recruiter with whom you have a prior relationship calls and assures you he won't convey the information to a potential employer, you may need to disclose your total compensation to him. If you don't have that prior relationship or don't yet feel comfortable with the recruiter who's calling, be cautious about responding. Here are some ways to address salary in verbal discussions with others:

◆ "I'm very interested in the opportunity, but you should know that (my total package in recent years was) (I'm looking for a package) in the range of $175,000 to $200,000."

◆ "I'm very interested in making a shift to the [blank] industry where I have an opportunity to [blank] with a growing company, and my (compensation) (remuneration) expectations range from $175,000 to $200,000."

◆ "My income from ABC Megabust, Inc. ranged from $200,000 to $250,000 in recent years. I'd be interested, though, in using my business development skills and the contacts I developed over the past 20 years in the [blank] industry to help a smaller growing company expand its markets." (The significant range here could infer a discretionary bonus. If you're making a change from a large company where salaries are often higher to a smaller company that can't pay that much, you may need to indicate you're flexible, even if that puts some of your salary negotiation at risk.)

◆ "My previous salary isn't relevant to this job because I took my last job (as a way to transfer my skills to a different industry) (to learn a new industry or job) (on a short duration because it enabled me to move to a new location, learn a different skill, finish education, etc.)."

◆ "(I am bound by an agreement) (I have a gentleman's agreement) with my previous employer not to disclose my compensation for competitive reasons. I'm looking at opportunities in the range of $200,000 to $250,000." (If you use this approach, make this agreement with your previous employer beforehand, so you'll be telling the truth. The interviewer will probably check this out.)

◆ "My last employer, Bigdot.gon, failed to attract additional venture capital funding. We restructured the business and took significant salary reductions in an attempt to continue to operate until the economy recovered. Unfortunately, we were unsuccessful. I don't think my salary at Bigdot.gon would be relevant. (You might at this point mention the salary range you're expecting.)

Try to turn the questioning away from salary by stating, "My compensation at GungHo.com was based on a combination of salary, bonuses and stock options, coupled with equity participation, so it's not comparable to this opportunity."

See how they respond. They may continue the interview and leave salary alone for the moment (your best option). If, instead, they ask what you want, express your interest in the opportunity, and see if they'll provide a salary range. For example, say, "I'm very interested in this job with Newco. Can you give me some indication of the salary range?"

If you're still not successful at turning off the salary inquiry and the question is pressed, you might try this: "I am looking for something in the range of

$XXX,XXX to $YYY,YYY." (This is why you need to do your homework and know your **Break-Even Salary** and your **Preferred Salary!**)

Make sure your salary expectations and those of the company are at least in the same range. Beyond that, you don't want to get into serious salary negotiations until they've expressed a desire to employ you.

If they try to negotiate salary up front, indicate that before you can do that, you really need to complete the interview process. You can say that both you and the company need to make sure you want each other first. There needs to be a clearer understanding of what *they* need and what benefits *you* can provide. When that process is completed, you'll both be in a better position to assess your worth to them.

At times, you may be in a situation where the salary is predetermined, and that's that! This is more common at lower levels than at executive levels. Regardless, you need to play the salary card close to the vest and not commit to a salary too early in the process. If you do, you won't be a very happy employee if, after you're hired, you realize you could have negotiated more.

Timing of the Offer

Signs That Indicate They're Seriously Considering You

If the employer hasn't raised the salary issue or if you've successfully put them off, the following signs will tell you that the topic is imminent:

- ※ They ask you back for a second or third interview.
- ※ They ask you out to lunch.
- ※ They give you an informal tour.
- ※ They arrange for the interviewer's boss, department head, or the CEO to interview you.
- ※ They tell you confidential information about their plans or business strategy.
- ※ They ask you to dinner, perhaps with your spouse or partner.
- ※ They become more conversational and talk about non-business matters, such as current events, politics, and education, to elicit your views and reaction. (Here they're trying to get a feel about whether you'll fit in with the company culture.)
- ※ When you visit the company again, people take notice of you or you get the feeling that you are (or have been) a topic of conversation.

When You Receive an Offer

At some point during the interview and negotiation process, if you're the desired candidate, the company will make an offer of employment. If the offer is verbal, explain that you can't accept a verbal offer of employment. You need to see it in writing. If the company is unwilling to put the offer in writing, a valid offer probably doesn't exist.

If they say they need to get your approval of the salary before they prepare an offer letter, explain that you can't assess the reasonableness of the salary until you can evaluate the entirety of the offer in writing. If they ask if you'll accept a certain salary, all you have to do is decide if you'd consider it. If you would *consider* it, tell them so, and ask them to put it in writing.

When you receive the written offer *signed* by an appropriate officer or person in the company, you'll need to decide whether to accept, negotiate, or reject the offer. If you've done your homework, you'll be able to evaluate where the package fits in relation to your **Break-Even Salary** and **Preferred Salary**.

Even if you think you're *likely* to accept, ask for some time to think about it, and discuss it with others before deciding. Ask when they need your decision, and commit to respond by that date.

If they insist you need to give them a yes or no immediately, explain that it's an important decision for you and them. You don't want to make a decision that turns out wrong for you or them and, consequently, you need time to evaluate it and discuss it with others. If they won't give you at least 24 hours, my advice would be to pass on the offer. Something is amiss if they don't want you to think about it or talk to others.

If you want to negotiate the offer, start by assessing where you think they were coming from and what was involved in their decision to offer the position to you. For example, you might ask:

- "Why did the previous person in this position leave?"

- "How long have you been looking for someone to fill this position?"

- "How many others have you interviewed and considered before offering the position to me?"

- "Have you made this offer to anyone who declined it?" (You can follow this question with "Why did they decline?" and "When did this happen?")

- "How many candidates were on your shortlist?"

- "When would my first salary review take place?"

- "What did you see in me that made you decide to offer me the position?"

At this stage, you need to be confident that you're a valuable resource and not a job beggar. If you're currently employed and you've been headhunted (found by a recruiter during a search), you're in a strong bargaining position. If you've been unemployed for several months, you'll be in a weak bargaining position.

Knowing what questions to ask and how to phrase them will be a delicate maneuver on your part. If you come across as aggressive and challenging, they may withdraw the offer. You'll only feel confident if you're prepared. If you want to negotiate the offer at this stage, here are some suggestions on how to approach the subject:

- » Ask for more money. Suggest a higher amount or explain that you were thinking more in the range of $X to $Y. Wait for a reply. Let them think about how to respond.

- » Ask about enhancing or expanding a specific benefit.

- » If the offer is at the low end of a range, emphasize some special skill or experience you have which you believe makes you worth more.

- » Suggest a performance incentive. Ask if they would consider a bonus if you meet a specific objective in the first year.

- » Ask that a car or other allowance be included in your salary instead of as a separate allowance. (This will start you on a higher base salary, so when they calculate future salary increases, the percentage will be on the higher starting base.)

Because each situation is unique, you'll need to tailor these suggestions to your situation. Most large employers have salary ranges within which hiring persons can make an offer. Typically, they'll start at the low end of the range, assuming that, if you negotiate, they can show some flexibility. If they don't have that flexibility, they'll tell you.

If you want to negotiate above their salary range, the person making the offer may have to go to a higher level to get approval. If he says the offer is firm, you'll have to decide if it's reasonable.

Your success at negotiating depends on convincing the employer that you're the needed resource and you're a confident, take-charge, solutions-oriented person. The employer's willingness to reconsider an offer depends on how badly you're wanted and if they believe you're clearly the outstanding candidate for the job—and they don't want to risk losing you over a few dollars.

If you decide to reject the offer, thank them for their consideration and explain why you're unable to accept the offer. They may be willing to go back and revise the offer, if it's out of line with industry norms.

If a recruiter presented you to the company, contact the lead consultant as soon as you have your offer in writing. Explain your concerns and get her viewpoint. She may be willing to convince the employer that their offer needs reconsideration.

> Recruiters often have to step in at the offer stage and educate employers about the status of salaries in the current market. Employers are often not up to speed on current salaries and benefits.

Milestones

The following milestones recap what you need to do to complete this chapter. Include those items you are unable to complete in your summary-level open-items list.

❑ 1. Review "General Rules and Guidelines" and become familiar with how the factors listed are likely to influence your ability to negotiate your salary.

❑ 2. Complete Worksheet 11.1: Calculating Your Salary Requirements (either the Word or the Excel Worksheet version) to determine your Break-Even Salary and Preferred Salary. Prioritize your Lifestyle Expenses so you can quickly determine what you will have to forgo if an employer offers you a salary less than your Preferred Salary.

❑ 3. Review the prioritization of your preferred benefits in Exercise 11.1: Prioritizing Benefits.

❑ 4. Review the suggested strategies and terminology for how you plan to answer the questions posed.

Keeping Yourself Focused and on Track

Creating Your Strategic Plan

*A job or career search without a plan is like a
journey without an end.*

Chapter Overview

Chapters 1 through 11 give you the information and insight you need to
know and do before making a job or career change. You're now ready to use
your skills and knowledge to create your strategic plan in pursuit of your career
aspirations.

But wait! What do you do first? How do you keep track of everything you
need to do in some sort of a logical order? How do you put all the information
you just learned into some sort of a plan—a strategic plan?

> *Tell me and I'll forget;*
> *show me and I may remember;*
> *involve me and I'll understand.*

> —Chinese proverb

If I approached this book only by communicating the lessons, techniques,
and experience I gained, you'd probably finish it, put it on the bookshelf, and
perhaps remember and implement some of it. However, I actively involved
you in the process, to not only learn how to implement what I suggested, but
to also get that "a-ha" and be able to tailor the information to your particular
circumstances.

Although there's no one way to conduct a job or career search that works
for everyone, this chapter will help you put together a coherent plan so you can
move forward quickly toward your goal: a new job or career. This chapter includes the following sections:

» Organize your environment.

» Develop your strategic plan.

» Special situations: diversity, gender, age.

When you've completed this chapter, you'll be able to prepare a personalized action plan that you can implement immediately.

Organize Your Environment

If you don't organize your environment and set policies for your home office, you'll waste time on unproductive details, miss important telephone calls, or come across poorly when you most need to start on the right foot. You may have had administrative support in your last job, but you are now your own administrative support.

The following suggestions will help you organize the administrative side of your search.

Working Environment

◆ View your home workplace as you would any other office environment, minus the hassle of a commute.

◆ If you don't have a home office, set space aside so you have a regular workplace that's relatively free of distractions and with convenient access to a telephone, a PC with Internet access, and a printer.

◆ Get supplies (paper clips, stapler, plain white paper, and so forth) so they're handy when you need them.

◆ Purchase bright white smooth quality paper for your resume and contrasting off-white bond paper and envelopes for letters.

◆ Create a template for your letterhead so you don't have to re-create it each time you prepare a letter. Make it look different from the font you use in the body of your letter. (See examples in Chapter 9.)

Quiet Business Focus

◆ Situate your workplace away from distractions and noises.

◆ You may be working from home, but you're at work. You need to set boundaries as to when you'll be available to your family.

◆ You can't conduct research efficiently in a noisy environment.

◆ If you try to carry on a conversation with a contact or an interviewer while dogs bark, kids clamor for your attention, or babies cry in the background, you'll lose a contact or a job opportunity.

Set Rules

◆ Determine between what hours you'll conduct research, make telephone calls, and manage correspondence.

◆ Set times for making telephone calls, researching on the Internet, and networking. Get into a routine that others, including family, will remember.

◆ Allocate time for the family and make sure they know when you will be available.

Administrative Resources

◆ You'll be your own administrative support, so you need to know how to prepare and edit your resume and type your letters and envelopes.

◆ Learn word-processing software.

◆ Learn the search methodology of various search engines, such as Google.

◆ Research the Internet to see what's available and how to find what you need to know.

◆ Get a dictionary and a thesaurus and USE THEM!

Telephone Etiquette

◆ Make sure your family members are clear on who is permitted to answer the telephone and what they should say when you aren't there.

◆ Give your younger children examples of what to say and how to take accurate messages. (This may be a tough one for teenagers!) A well-behaved child who knows what to do and takes information down correctly makes a positive impact on callers. As a recruiter, I was always impressed when a pre-teen answered the telephone and knew what to say and do.

◆ Don't put people on hold to take another call. They'll think you think that the other caller is more important than they are.

◆ Use your local telephone company's voice-mail system and record a professional message. Set it so incoming calls automatically go to your voice mail if you're on the phone. If you or a family member uses the phone a lot and someone returns your call, you don't want him to get a busy signal.

Illustration by Steven Lait.

◆ Do not attempt to take calls on your cell phone while you are traveling, even if it is hands-free. The other person may not appreciate having to only hear part of the conversation because of a poor connection, diminished voice quality, or a dropped call.

E-Mail Etiquette

◆ Use an e-mail address that closely approximates your name, such as cwellenstein@, carlwellenstein@, or carlw@. Don't use nicknames or other monikers, such as armybrat3@, blondysuzy@, gizmoguy@, or sszzyyxx@. Using your name as part of your e-mail address allows the recipient to know who's sending the e-mail without having to open it.

◆ Do *not* use a spam blocker that requires the sender to respond to your ISP's filter questionnaire, such as by requiring the sender to enter data that matches stylized letters and numbers in a box (commonly used by Earthlink). E-mails acknowledging receipt of your letter or resume cannot handle such a request. We're all dealing with unwanted e-mail but, if you want others to help you, don't ask them to take their extra time just so you can minimize the spam you receive.

◆ Review your e-mails before you send them. Grammar and spelling errors in e-mail are just as important to correct as if they were in a letter. Avoid using abbreviations, like thx for taking my call, glad to c u, and don't end with :-), and don't use emoticons. many senders of e-mail think capitalization and punctuation are optional. who ever thought that was ok is wrong its difficult and confusing to read.

◆ Make e-mail easy for recipients by including their messages when you reply. Set your e-mail program to include the sender's message on all replies.

◆ Keep your message brief and to the point. People at work can't take the time to read lengthy e-mail.

◆ Be careful with the content of your e-mail. Many companies scan incoming e-mail for words like resume and job search, and they may automatically delete any attachments.

Research and Reference Material

◆ Learn what reference material is available at your local library.

◆ Select some companies in your industry or field of interest; see what you can find out about them on the Internet and compare that with what you find at the library.

◆ Get a library card that enables you to access library research data from your home PC.

Prepare a Budget

❖ Using the example in Worksheet 11.1: Calculating Your Salary Requirements, prepare a monthly budget reflecting the line items covering the next 12 months.

❖ Update this budget with actual numbers for the first few months to make sure your estimate reasonably reflects your actual expenditures. Adjust your remaining budget, if necessary.

❖ Determine NOW when you will have a shortfall, and consider how you plan to cover your expenses.

Overcome Procrastination

When you work from home in isolation, you tend to let your thoughts divert you from your new job—which is to find your next job! Particularly in a difficult economy where you feel you're getting nowhere, you begin to spend less time on your job search and more on distractions.

Minimize procrastination by organizing your workplace, and planning daily and weekly tasks—and sticking to them. The following section will help you do that.

Develop Your Strategic Plan

Your personal strategic plan, like a business plan, is a dynamic document. It will change as circumstances warrant and as you progress in your job search or career change. If you're searching for a new job, your plan probably won't change much. If you're making a career change, however, you should expect your plan to evolve as you go through the **Obtain** phase and you gather more information about your career objective.

Throughout this book, I've attempted to show you *what* you need to do, explain *why* you need to do it, and then give you guidelines on *how* to do it. Your strategic plan will build on the material, exercises, and worksheets you've completed and enable you to implement your search in a logical, organized, and productive manner.

Your plan will consist of the following three simple and dynamic documents:

1. The first will be a **Task Plan** that lists specific objectives that will keep you focused on **what** you need to do.

2. The second will be a daily **To-Do List** that will help you **manage** your time and describe **how** you will accomplish a specific objective.

3. The third will be a **Contact Sheet** that will help you to **keep track** of all your contacts, your conversations with them, and what activities are to happen next with them.

Here is how they work interactively.

1. Task Plan

Your Task Plan is a list of all the key things you need to accomplish over the next several weeks. The information you enter should be generalized, such as "Complete resume." You don't need much detail here.

Prepare a **Task Plan** or **Open Items List** using a format similar to the following figure. (Because you will be updating this form often, I suggest you prepare it in Microsoft Word as a table so you can insert and delete rows and sort it by column.)

Task Plan

No.	Objective	Resp.	ECD

The headers should include:

No.   (Number). A priority group number rather than a sequential row number. For example, you might identify all the tasks you need to complete first as 1s. Those that need to be done next would be 2s and so on.

Objective. A description of what you want to accomplish. For example, you might have "Complete resume" or "Review resume with John Bloggs."

Resp.   (Responsibility). Identifies who is responsible for completing each task. Usually it's you, but it could be someone you've asked to review your resume and give you comments or someone who is to get back to you after they talk to a referral.

ECD   (Estimated Completion Date). The date you expect that task to be completed. This could be a completion date or a required follow-up date.

Start by reviewing the **Milestones** section for each chapter and listing all the open items on your task plan. Enter who is responsible for completing it and a tentative ECD. Do NOT enter a priority number yet.

Next, add personal- and business-related (job or career search) tasks that will require your time and insert a tentative ECD. Don't include daily recurring tasks, such as going to the gym, and don't forecast too far into the future (for example, three months) because you'll be updating the list often.

Now, review your Task Plan and enter a priority number in the left column. I'd suggest limiting your priorities to no more than 5. If they are farther down the list than that, they probably don't need to be on it until they get closer to needing to be done. Sort your list by priority number and/or by date so you know what needs to be accomplished first and by when.

2. To-Do List

Review your **Task Plan** for the next week and prepare a **To-Do List** for each day listing what you plan to do every day to accomplish the general tasks on your Task Plan for that week. If you do it for a week at a time, you can anticipate schedule conflicts and be able to see your plan taking shape going forward.

◆ Using a PDA or a small notepad titled To Do (with the day and date), list your objectives each day for the next week (using a separate sheet for each day if using a notepad) that will lead you to completing the key tasks on your prioritized **Task Plan**. Include the personal things, such as going to the gym or the post office, so you can keep track of all your goals for that day. Refer to your **To-Do List** daily (keeping it on top of your desk if on a notepad) as a constant reminder and check off the ones you complete.

◆ Indicate the priority by day for each task or group them by 1s, 2s, 3s, and so forth. Don't fall into the trap of listing the easiest ones as your highest priorities. Choose those that are most important for that day as the highest priority.

◆ Try to keep track of how much time you spent on each objective for each day of the first week. It will help you to make more realistic time commitments in the future. You'll probably begin by having too many tasks each day and not allocating enough time for each.

◆ Pick the times of day that you'll make telephone calls, research on the Internet, and so on, and adjust your schedule over the first few weeks so you're able to stick to those times. Don't make all your telephone calls or prepare letters in one day because you won't be able to follow up with them effectively if you have too many commitments. When you do follow-up, try to make all your calls together so you don't tie up your telephone throughout the day.

❖ At the end of each day, revise the next day's **To-Do List.**

❖ At the end of each week, update your **Task Plan,** and prepare tentative To-Do Lists for each day of the following week.

3. Contact Sheet

You now need a way to keep all the information about your contacts in one place where you can also keep track of your conversations with them and have a way of making sure you follow up with them on a timely basis.

If you already use a contact-management system, such as Microsoft Business Contact Manager, ACT, or GoldMine, and are experienced with it, consider using it. If not, don't spend time now buying and learning a new software program. Instead, use Worksheet 12.1: Contact Sheet (available online in its entirety, along with instructions).

Contact Sheet

Name	Source
Job title	Referral date
Company	Work tel.
Address	Home tel.
	Cell/Mobile
	Date resume sent
E-mail:	

On the top part of your **Contact Sheet,** enter the contact information that you've been accumulating for each person in your network. Start with summarized information about that person, including conversations, referrals, leads, and so forth. Enter a follow-up date on the last line of text, and file the **Contact Sheets** alphabetically in a three-ring binder. Enter the follow-up date in your personal diary, such as a Day-Timer, a PDA, or one of the software programs described previously.

When you have further conversations with a contact, start a new line with the date and enter a summary of the discussion, followed by any actions you or he are to take, and the next contact date.

Create scripts (examples of what you want to say) and keep them handy when you call. Determine your objectives before you make the call, using keywords. Don't write out sentences. If you don't make a list before you call, you'll remember after you hang up all the things you forgot to ask!

Conducting a job or a career search is probably new to you, and you'll be doing many things you aren't comfortable or confident about. If you don't have a clear strategic plan for the near term and look at it on a daily basis, you can easily become overwhelmed and find that you'll be distracted into doing things that don't help you achieve your ultimate goal of getting a new job or career.

Your **Contact Sheets** will prove extremely helpful to you after several weeks of conversations with many people as it will help to highlight and remind you about those who know each other and could become your Power Contacts. (See "Expand Your Network" in Chapter 8 on page 163.)

Getting Started

Here are 10 reminders to help you get started:

1. Review your open items from each chapter and list all open items in your **Task Plan**.

2. Decide your priorities and put them on your daily **To-Do Lists** for the next week.

3. When you've completed your resume and reviewed it with your mentor and/or others, practice what you plan to tell others what you want.

4. Prepare your **Contact Sheets** and telephone everyone. Use e-mail only if you've been unsuccessful in talking to them. Start with your personal contacts who know you best, and you know you can count on them to help.

5. Contact others you know less well. You'll probably have to spend more time with these contacts to get them up to speed so they will *want* to help you.

6. Tell each person what help you need from her. Make sure she knows what you've done recently and where you're looking to go next. For example, are you looking for names of companies in an industry that you can explore, or names of people in companies you could talk to about your job search or a possible career change? Arrange to meet those you haven't seen for a while or who may need that extra personal touch.

7. Follow up your conversations with an e-mail that reiterates what you've done and where you're going. You want to get your message out to as many people as you know as quickly as possible.

8. If you think things are not moving as quickly as they should and your network is not getting back to you as soon as you'd like, keep in mind that your priority is not theirs. Be persistent but don't be a pest.

9. Focus on expanding your network and making sure they are clear about your objectives and your expectations of the help you need from them.

10. It's not the number of business cards you collect or the number of people in your network that's important. It's the quality of the people and their willingness and ability to help you with your research and move your search forward.

Special Situations: Diversity, Gender, Age

There's much concern about discrimination in recruitment. From my years in executive search, I wasn't aware of any of our search consultants ever showing bias against candidates based purely on race, gender, or national origin, and, to my knowledge, none of our clients ever asked us to exclude candidates or not offer them candidates based solely on these characteristics.

You'll notice I didn't include age in the previous examples. Although we did encounter an occasional instance of overt age discrimination, we typically encountered it more covertly. I'll explain the reasons for discrimination in each of these three areas and suggest how you can deal with them.

Diversity

I'll define diversity as race, religion, and country of origin. It's important to remember that companies employ people who have the skills and experience they need and can fit in and adapt to the company's "culture."

If you don't fit the profile of the existing employees at a potential employer, you're probably going to experience discrimination, unless that employer is making a determined effort to broaden the diversity within their organization. If you consider your diversity a disadvantage, you'll probably find that to be true. It can become a self-fulfilling prophecy.

Instead, look for reasons why a company should consider you for your diversity, and focus on what you bring to the table that someone without that diversity can't.

For example, if you're Hispanic, you're probably multi-lingual, and, not only do you speak Spanish, but you bring a comprehensive understanding of Hispanic culture. A non-Hispanic may have learned the language in school, but doesn't understand the subtleties and nuances that a native speaker might. Your strength is that you're able to be sensitive to different regional dialects, and other Hispanics are more likely to have more confidence in you and prefer to deal with you. You'll need to look inward and identify what makes you different, and why that should give you an advantage over other candidates.

On the other hand, you might not find any advantage to your diversity. For example, if you're black or Native American and can't find an advantage because of your race, there may not really be any. Forget about your diversity, and focus on the skills and experience you have that an employer needs.

We never encountered discrimination against blacks, and none of my clients ever expressed a desire to discriminate based on race. I'm sure there are situations where there is covert discrimination. If that happens, it's probably not a company you would want to work at anyway.

I've seen discrimination against diversity candidates, but it tends to relate to their inability to speak English clearly. I suspect that, if Arnold Schwarzenegger weren't a movie star and governor of California, he would encounter employment discrimination just based on his accent.

Here are some suggestions if you're in this category:

⟫ Focus on the skills and experience you have that an employer needs; diversity from your perspective isn't an important issue to an employer.

❥ Identify if your diversity gives you an advantage over others without that diversity. If so, diversity from your perspective should be an important issue to an employer.

❥ If you're targeting larger companies, they will probably be more open and receptive to candidates of diversity because governmental initiatives require them to be more open to candidates of diversity.

❥ If you're targeting smaller companies, focus on the uniqueness of what you can do for them that someone who doesn't have that diversity can't do as well. Consider the first two points in this list.

❥ If you think a strong foreign accent is holding you back, rather than focusing on that diversity, work with someone who can help you overcome that issue.

Gender

Gender issues typically relate to women. In my experience, I never encountered discrimination either overtly or covertly against women. I have been involved in situations where the client thought a man or a woman would be better for a particular situation based on the position profile.

For example, one client needed a merchandising executive for a company that was going to focus on upscale outdoor entertaining. The client felt the ideal candidate would probably come from a women's fashion retail environment, a belief we shared. Naturally, we focused our search on women.

There are some unfortunate issues, however, that do affect women in their job search. If you're a woman, you probably already know this, and you may not find this subject covered in other career books.

Issue 1

Men who are determined, aggressive, and risk-takers are often admired and promoted to higher levels of management, whereas women with the same characteristics generally are not. If they are, they're often criticized for doing what a man would be praised for doing. Trying to get others to change their attitude is a waste of time.

If you bear these characteristics and have been criticized for them, try to find a more subtle way of accomplishing the same thing. Women are often considered to have higher levels of EQ (see Chapter 3) than men, and should be able to recognize the impact they're having on others more easily than men. It may not be fair that women need to be more subtle than men, but in some situations, they just do. It's reality.

257

Issue 2

Men get more distinguished as they get older, whereas women...well, they just get older—that's the perception by many. How does this affect your job search? Because the first assessment of you will be visual (see Chapter 9 and Chapter 10), there will be a much stronger need for you as a woman to keep up your appearance. Again, it may not be fair, but it's reality.

If you're in your 40s and you see a woman who appears much older than that when you look in a mirror, you need to pay careful attention to your appearance. This doesn't mean you need to rush out for a facelift or Botox treatments. It means you need to make sure you present a professional appearance. Look for younger-looking styles of clothing and choose colors that don't accentuate your age.

Issue 3

Being overweight affects both men and women. Unfortunately, from my experience, it negatively affects women more than it does men during a job search.

A Shared Experience

Remember the example of the merchandising executive? One of the candidates we chose to interview had all the skills and experience our client wanted. When she arrived for our first interview, we couldn't help noticing she was more than 100 pounds overweight. She was very pleasant and came across as a dedicated and inspiring merchandising executive.

Unfortunately, we felt our client wouldn't think she'd present a professional appearance to the retail staff or customers. Over my recruiters' vocal objections, I decided we had an ethical obligation to tell her the real reason why we couldn't put her forward to our client.

When I did so, she acknowledged she thought that might be a problem. She said she had had several other interviews for other positions, but no one told her that. She admitted she never seemed to make it to the shortlist.

She thanked me for being honest and vowed she would do what she needed to do. No, it wasn't to sue me, but to work on an aggressive weight-loss program and change her attire!

I'm not trying to initiate a debate on the unfairness of hiring decisions for women versus men. I want to point out that they do exist, and you need to consider these issues seriously, even though virtually no one will tell you to your face—and certainly not in writing—the real reason you didn't make it to the shortlist or get the job.

Age

Age discrimination is alive and flourishing! Despite laws attempting to eradicate this, age discrimination is ingrained in the employment process. Sometimes it's covert; other times it's flagrantly overt.

I remember one VP of HR, who was in his early 40s, tell me, "Don't bring me any candidates in their 40s. They're too old." He explained they had too many "older" employees who were close to retirement. If they didn't start recruiting younger people, they were concerned they wouldn't be able to adapt to new technology as quickly as they needed to survive for the long term. Although I didn't think it fair, it certainly made strategic sense for the organization!

A Shared Experience

When I left public accounting at 49, I had difficulty finding employment and soon realized it was partly because of my age. I vowed when I started my search firm, I would not discriminate based on age and would even go out of my way to seed our shortlists with older, well-qualified candidates that we would present to clients.

I immediately got involved in the search process and actively participated in selecting candidates to interview. I soon became disillusioned with the candidates we interviewed who were in their 50s. After asking more probing interview questions, I discovered a high percentage of them were really looking for a position where the demands wouldn't be too great and they could coast into retirement.

I soon became calloused, and, when I did decide to interview a candidate who seemed "a bit older," our questioning was much more rigorous.

Unfortunately, our clients weren't so understanding. When they encountered candidates who seemed older, they set aside their resumes while they looked at the other candidates first, or their review was more critical and they found more objections as to why they wouldn't be able to consider them.

If you're in your late 40s or older, prepare your strategic plan with the following in mind, regardless of whether you're male or female:

◆ Contacting recruiters will be less effective for you, unless you have the name recognition and track record of a Jack Welch. Recruiters are looking for younger candidates because that's who their clients want to employ. Exceptions to this would be when a company needs someone older to do something a younger person wouldn't have the experience to do. An example would be in a turnaround situation where a seasoned person with the experience and industry contacts could be critical to the company's success.

◆ You'll need to make a *compelling* case as to why an employer would want to choose an older person for more money over a younger person for less money.

◆ Your resume should reflect the activities you're involved in outside of work, which demonstrate you're not a couch potato.

◆ Your skills and experience need to show you are techno-savvy. Many executives tell me they don't know how to use e-mail. At work, their support person prints their incoming e-mail and sends replies for them. When they're in transition, they often use their spouse's e-mail address and have her handle e-mail. This clearly sends the wrong message to prospective employers: that you're not up to speed technically and not able to adapt to or embrace change. If we suspected you weren't adept in this area, we would probe your use of the Internet. If it sounded as if you didn't know how to use it proficiently, you weren't likely to land on a shortlist.

◆ You'll need to place more reliance on building your network and using it for referrals. A recommendation from someone whom the potential employer already knows can often overcome the age issue.

◆ Consider targeting smaller companies if you have a large-company background. You bring a wealth of experience that someone can gain only from a larger, more sophisticated company. Smaller companies may need that experience and won't be able to find it in younger candidates who would be less motivated to move to a smaller company.

You'll need to overcome an initial perception that you won't be able to make the transition from a big company atmosphere, where you had a lot of support, to a smaller company, where that won't be the case. Your responsibilities in a smaller company are typically much broader. Your strategic plan would need to address what you will say that will overcome that perception by potential employers.

Conclusion

Where to Turn for Additional Help

This book provides comprehensive information for a job search or career change. My intent was to cover all the salient points in sufficient detail so you can implement your plan knowing what you need to do, why you need to do it a certain way, and how to do it.

No book can cover every situation for every job and career. If I did that, no one would buy all the volumes needed to cover everything, and reading them would be a career in itself. Besides, I don't have all the answers. Many times, I need to send my clients on research expeditions to find answers that make sense to them. Answers are often found where you don't expect them, and it may take some digging to find information you can rely on.

Some of my clients wind up in jobs neither of us even knew existed, and they occasionally find situations where I've been able to help them successfully create their dream job. There's no magic to it. I trust the process I've described in this book because it just seems to work—consistently.

I was constrained by the length and dimensions of this book and, consequently, couldn't include all the reference material or forms in a user-friendly size. If you go to the **Career Center** on my Website, *www.ExecGlobalNet.com,* you will find information on:

- » Profiles of the different Personality Types (Reference 1.1: Myers–Briggs Type Characteristics).

- » Recommended books covering specific career-related issues (Reference 1.2: Career-Related Reading List).

- » Where and how to find what you need to know (Reference 4.1: Where to Get Additional Information).

You'll also find full-size copies of most of the worksheets shown in this book that you can download for your personal use. Putting them on my Website also enables me to keep them current, something I can't do with a printed book.

After you've finished reading this book and completed all the worksheets, you still might have some unresolved questions or issues that relate to your situation. Here are some suggestions.

Contact Me!

E-mail me at *cwellenstein@ExecGlobalNet.com* to see if I can help. If I can't, I'll try to point you in the right direction. I wrote this book for you! I'll make sure I consider your questions when I release a revised edition.

Engage Me

If you have questions about some aspect of your career or your situation and would like to talk about it, you can purchase a one and one-half hour Career Overview session where we can talk. If you think you might need more help or assistance over a longer period, I can accommodate a limited number of coaching clients. E-mail your request to me at *cwellenstein@ExecGlobalNet.com.*

Engage a Local Career Coach

There are many excellent career coaches throughout the United States and in most Westernized countries around the world. I encourage you to find one you can meet. Here are some suggestions on how to find one:

- » Ask people in your network if they know a career coach. Some may refer to themselves as career counselors.

- » Search the Internet for coaches in your location.

- » Search the International Coach Federation Website (*www.coachfederation.org*) for career coaches.

- » Search the Website of the Association of Career Professionals— International (*www.acpinternational.org*). I'm a member of this organization and often refer people to other ACP International member coaches around the world.

- » Search the Professional Coaches and Mentors Association Website (*www.pcmaonline.com*). I've served on the board of this organization and know many good coaches. They're predominately in California, but many travel extensively and/or work virtually with clients around the world.

You've done your research and found some career coaches. Now how do you choose who to select? Career counselors and career coaches may be very different or very similar. It's not a well-defined industry. Consequently, there aren't any academic degrees or uniform qualifications, certificates or tests that qualify or certify someone to be a career counselor or coach.

Most career counselors work in universities, colleges, and high schools, and most will have training and certificates in counseling. They're more appropriate for working at the student level, where the individual has negligible work history and the counselor needs to do more testing to be able to draw out reasonable recommendations.

Career coaching, on the other hand, is a wide open market. No universally accepted career-coaching qualifications or certifications exist. I know people who claim to be career coaches, and do a lot of testing and work with people to help discover their true passion, but they don't have a clue how to help an executive or manager find a job.

I've seen bad resumes prepared for executives by career coaches and resume writers who think they know what recruiters and employers want to see. The good news is that you're most likely to find your next job through someone you know or meet during your networking. Your resume may not play an important role if a potential employer bases his decision on the recommendation of someone he knows and trusts.

My recommendations for what to look for in a career coach include the following, assuming you have several years of work experience and are at a senior staff, manager, or executive level. A good career coach:

◆ Is **familiar** with and understands business, the positions in business, and functional career paths from her personal work experience, not from what they understand it to be as told to them by others.

◆ **Understands** and is conversant in a range of different industries, like manufacturing, retail, professional services, etc.

◆ Is **NOT the expert** on what you should be doing. Only you can do that.

◆ Will have some success stories to share with you.

> **A Shared Experience**
> A client who was a senior logistics manager at a media and electronics conglomerate loved what he did but couldn't develop any passion for the industry. Recognizing he might be suffering from burnout, we discovered that his passion was sailing and whatever new job he found he wanted to spend more time doing that.
>
> He didn't know where his research would take him, and neither did we. We knew if we helped him figure out what to ask and where to point

> him, he'd be able to get information that made sense to him. We knew enough about logistics to know that his skills translated across different industries, so we didn't waste his time sending him off on dead ends.
>
> Well, to keep a much longer story short, he found a distributorship whose new young owners also wanted to mesh their love for sailing with building a business. They were great at sales but what they lacked was any logistics experience. Our client was taken on. Without a lot of other details, he spent his time sailing boats made by their customers, showing off new products by their suppliers, who, by the way, paid his expenses to take people out sailing to show off their products.
>
> Granted, he didn't make the money he made with the conglomerate, but he wasn't complaining, and neither was his family!

- ❖ **Can clearly explain to you how she will work** with you and what process she will put you through. If it sounds confusing or proprietary, it may only be smoke and mirrors.

- ❖ **Will have some professional training and experience in coaching.** Professional (not academic) career coaching educational programs were started by career coaches who saw a business opportunity in selling training programs to those who want to call themselves career coaches. Some of these programs are worthwhile for conveying the experiences of seasoned career coaches; others are only opinions of those who started their own training program.

I attended the Job and Career Transition Coach (JCTC) program facilitated by Richard L. Knowdell and felt that it covered all the areas I believed were important to a career-transition coach. Dick does an admirable job keeping his program practical, relevant, and up to date, incorporating the experiences of other coaches.

Other coaching programs, both academic and professional, teach techniques that are critical to a coach's ability to work with a client without personal bias or trying to impart personal beliefs.

I suggest you ask prospective coaches about their professional training as well as their personal experience and make your own assessment as to the adequacy of their background and training. If a coach suggests his training enables him to tell you what career you *should* pursue, be wary. That's not what coaching is about.

Coaching skills are important, and you should inquire about a coach's professional training. Perhaps even more important will be his business experience—whether he has experienced his own job and/or a career change, and whether he understands how recruiters, employers, and the job market actually work.

It's my belief that the most effective career coach for mid-level-and-above job and career changers will be one who has learned what's important in the field, not in a classroom or training environment, where theories are the primary ideas communicated.

This book and my opinions do not come from a career coach training program where an instructor conveyed her theories about how to find a job or make a career change. They came from my own job and career changes. I experienced firsthand how recruiters and employers make decisions. I couldn't have gained this insight from a program that taught career coaching.

If a career coach suggests he *thinks* a such-and-such approach would work, he's not expressing knowledge, only a theory. Look for career coaches who know from personal experience what works and what doesn't, not from what they heard from another career coach about something she found "helpful."

A Final Thought

If you have questions about any of the content in this book, want clarification of any point, or have found an error that needs to be corrected, I want to hear from you.

I've tried to use personal examples to illustrate and support my "process." I don't have all the answers and haven't experienced every possible situation. I'm learning new things all the time and will include them in future revisions. If you would like to share your own experience with others in future revisions, I encourage you to write and tell me about it. If there's one thing I've learned—and keep learning over and over again—it's this:

THERE IS NO ONE WAY THAT WORKS FOR EVERYONE.

Thank you for reading my book and I hope it helps you find the career of your destiny.

Carl J. Wellenstein
ExecGlobalNet, Inc.
P.O. Box 1194
Downey, CA 90240
Tel.: (562) 923–0615
E-mail: cwellenstein@ExecGlobalNet.com
www.ExecGlobalNet.com

Index

About the Author

CARL WELLENSTEIN helps executives, managers, experienced staff, and professionals find careers they are passionate about and guides them from where they are now to where they want to be. He has professional certificates as a job and career transitions coach (JCTC) and in coaching and mentoring.

Carl started his professional career in 1971 as an auditor and CPA with Arthur Young & Co. (now Ernst & Young) in Los Angeles. He had a wide range of clients and spent five years building a professional practice as a country partner in Saudi Arabia. After returning to the United States and subsequently leaving Arthur Young, he decided to change his focus from numbers to people.

In 1992, he moved to the UK and launched an executive search firm, Bartwell International (UK) Ltd. Focusing on international search assignments over seven years, he chose senior executives as his recruiters and created and refined a team-based process that clients came to appreciate and acknowledge as providing superior results.

Carl is the founder and president of ExecGlobalNet, Inc. (*www.execglobalnet.com*). He is a frequent speaker and writer on career issues for people making mid-life job and career changes. Adapting his team-based recruitment process for employers, he also helps employers develop and implement a best-practice employment process that improves their ability to employ the right people to meet their needs. He is married, has two children, and resides in Southern California.